THE FREELANCE BOOK

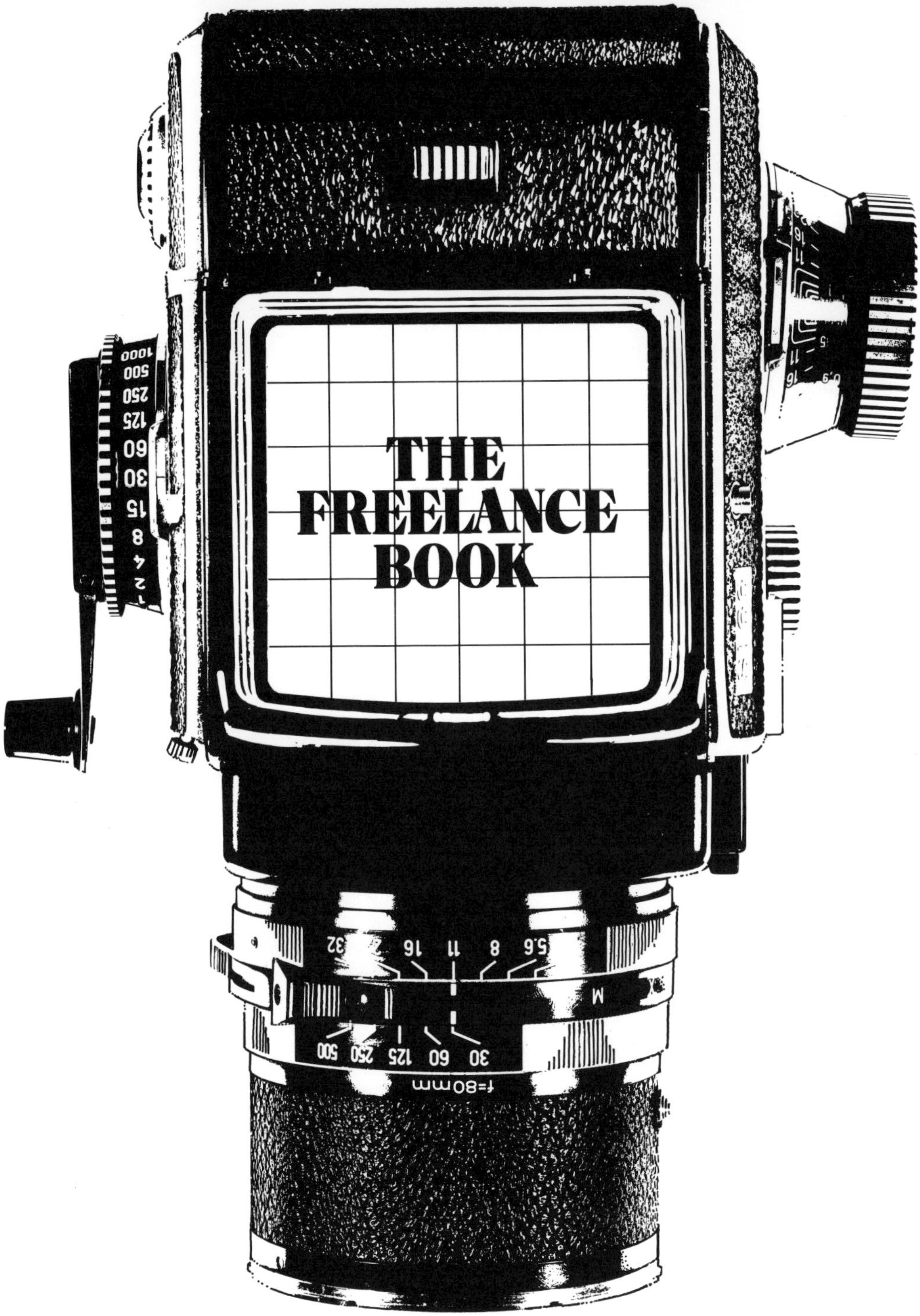

THE FREELANCE BOOK

Edited by

John Tracy & Stewart Gibson

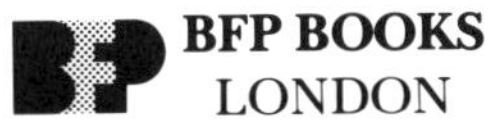

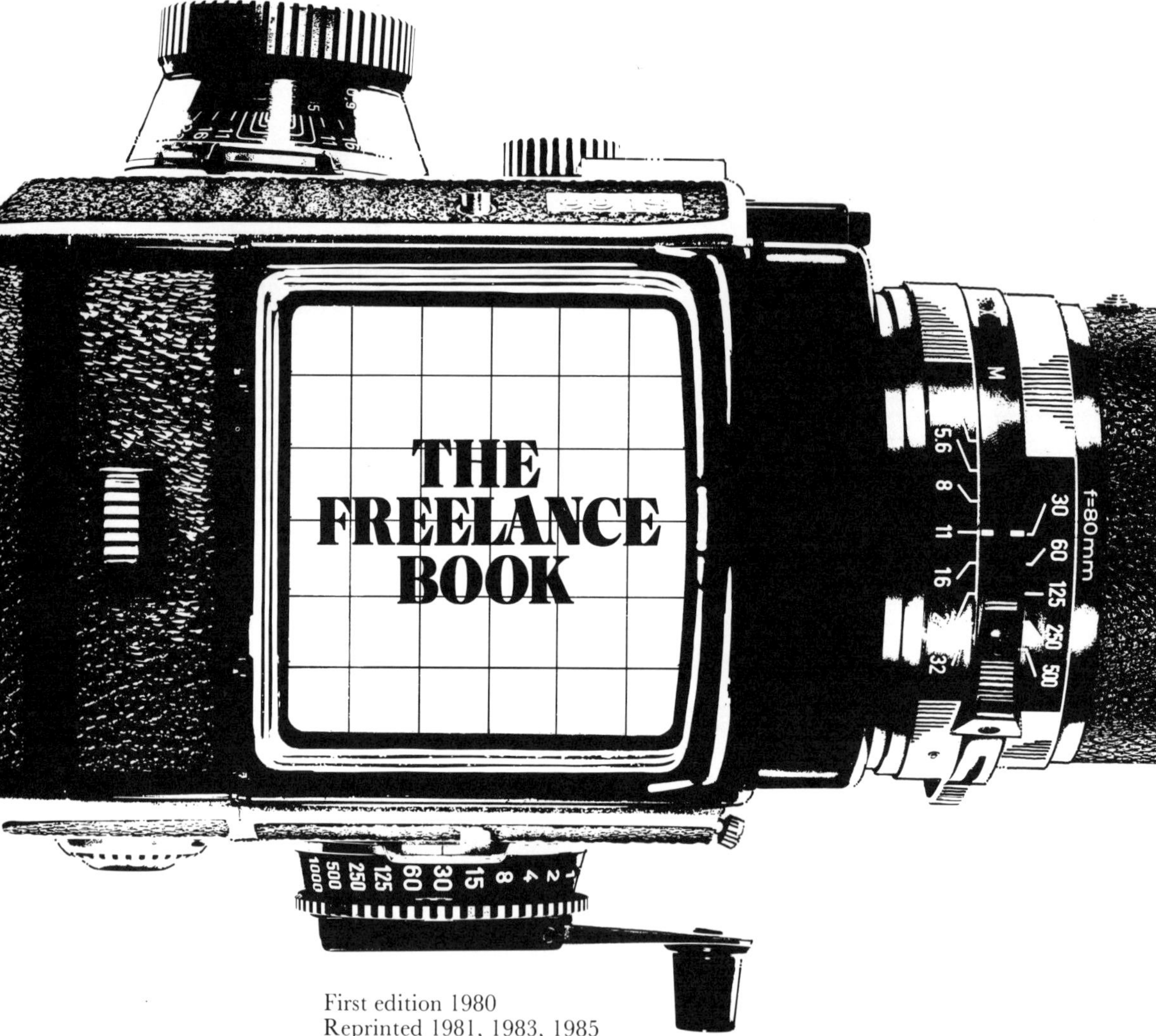

First edition 1980
Reprinted 1981, 1983, 1985

ISBN 0 907297 00 5

Published by BFP Books, a division of the Bureau of Freelance
Photographers, Focus House, 497 Green Lanes, London N13 4BP, and
printed in Great Britain by A. Wheaton & Co Ltd., Exeter.

CONTENTS

ABOUT THE CONTRIBUTORS

John Tracy, head of the Bureau of Freelance Photographers, sold his first picture at the age of 14 – to *Photo News Weekly* for 10s.6d. Upon leaving school he went to work for a Fleet Street press agency where he learned all aspects of the business of producing pictures for publication. He has also had considerable experience in advertising and commercial photography, and for some time ran a company which serviced major advertising agencies in London. In 1965 he founded the Bureau of Freelance Photographers, as he felt there was a growing need for an organisation which would provide the freelance photographer with information on markets and trends. The BFP has since grown into a highly influential and authoritative body and has a current membership of some 10,000.

Although only a part-time freelance, **Tony Boxall** has sold pictures to numerous publications throughout the world. In addition, he regularly enters photographic competitions and has won over 300 prizes ranging from modest cash awards to prizes of photographic equipment and holidays abroad. In 1969 he was awarded the coveted title of Photographer of the Year by *Photography* magazine in a competition that attracted more than 20,000 entries. He is a Fellow of the Royal Photographic Society.

Among the publications that have used his pictures are *Weekend, Woman, Woman's Own, Titbits, Cosmopolitan, She, Evening News, Evening Standard* and the *Daily Mirror*. He has learned what many consider to be the real art of freelancing: producing pictures of the type that will sell again and again. One famous Boxall picture has clocked up well over £1,000 in reproduction fees.

John Wade is the editor of *Photography* magazine. That makes him both a writer and a photographer. His interest in cameras began when he was fourteen and he remained a keen amateur for years before making it his living.

After some ten years in local journalism, working for newspapers in the south-east of England, he decided to try his hand at freelancing. That was when photography began to play an important part in his career, as he used his own pictures to illustrate articles. During that time, he wrote and illustrated anything that would sell, for markets that ranged from women's magazines to *Reader's Digest* and from local newspapers to Radio Four.

He also wrote a twelve-part series for *Photography*, a fact that stood him in good stead for the appointment of deputy editor when the position fell vacant. Six months in that job led to the editorship in 1977.

He wrote and illustrated *A Short History of the Camera*, published in 1979 by Argus Books, and his latest book, simply called *Portraiture*, will be published by Newnes-Butterworth early in 1981.

Lorna Minton studied photography full-time at the Regent Street Polytechnic. During holidays she supplemented this training by assisting in a portrait and 'general practice' studio.

After completing her training and gaining the Intermediate IIP and City & Guilds Certificates, she took up a photographic position with the British Tourist Authority. Later wishing to broaden her experience, she joined a Chelsea studio where she was involved in producing photographs for advertising campaigns.

This was followed by a job on the editorial staff of the *Photographic Retailer*, a position which enabled her to combine her photography with her interest in writing, which has subsequently stood her in good stead as a freelance.

Nowadays, she happily combines freelancing with looking after a husband, house and three children. Her photographs have appeared in numerous books and magazines including *Nursery World*, *Where*, *Australian Photography*, *Child Education*, *Mother & Baby* and *Sailplane & Gliding*. She has also sold pictures to greetings card publishers as well as undertaking a wide variety of assignments ranging from air-to-air photography to photographing iced cakes.

Raymond Lea is a part-time freelance and a prolific contributor to the photographic press, his pictures and articles having appeared in *Amateur Photographer*, *Photo Technique*, *Practical Photography*, *SLR Camera*, *Minolta Photoworld* and *Praktica Photography*. Additionally, his pictures have appeared in such publications as *This England*, *Country Life*, *The Field*, *The Lady* and *The Countryman* as well as in numerous county magazines.

His particular speciality is the many types of unusual artefacts and curios to be found in Britain, and this led to a book on the subject, *Country Curiosities*, which he both wrote and illustrated.

His pictures have also appeared in various Focal Press photo books as well as in books devoted to animals and the English countryside.

He dislikes any kind of 'formal' photography and steers clear of studio portraiture, weddings or functions.

Dennis Mansell started his career as a photographer with a local newspaper, during which time he freelanced in his off-duty hours supplying pictures to Fleet Street newspapers and other outlets. As a 'stringer' with Associated Press, his pictures appeared in numerous overseas publications, and were used in many exhibitions including the Dutch World Press Photo Exhibition.

During this time, he received many invitations to move to Fleet Street, but decided to turn them down in favour of full-time freelancing. As well as undertaking a wide range of commercial and industrial assignments, he has concentrated on building up a file of stock pictures, including a large number of travel subjects, which he sells through an agent to markets world-wide. He provided all the illustrations for James Wentworth Day's *Book of Essex* which was published in 1979.

Although having had no formal photographic training, **Ralph Medland** has achieved considerable success as a freelance – particularly in the glamour field. He learnt photography, he says, through books and lots and lots of practice and perseverence. He reckons he could have short-cut this process by working as an assistant to a professional photographer – something he always wanted to do early in his career and which he would still recommend as just about the quickest way of learning the ropes.

Nevertheless, the lack of such training doesn't appear to have affected Ralph Medland's success as a glamour photographer, for his pictures have appeared in the *Daily Star, The Sun* and the *Daily Mirror* as well as in glamour calendars and numerous overseas publications.

He is also a frequent contributor to the photographic press, his articles and pictures having appeared in *Amateur Photographer, Photography, Practical Photography* and *SLR Camera*.

Ray Forsberg had been an established angling author and freelance photographer for twenty years. He has written and illustrated a number of books on angling, and co-authored the *Observer's Book of Sea Fishing*.

His articles and pictures have appeared in numerous publications on angling and related subjects including *Angling, Angler's Mail, Fisherman, Fisherman's Weekly, Coarse Fisherman* and *Sea Angler*. He has entered and won a number of photographic competitions, and his work has also appeared in *Amateur Photographer*.

Willie Pereira was born in Nairobi, and started his career in the photographic department of the Kenyan Police where he worked as a darkroom and studio assistant during the Mau Mau emergency. Later, he joined a press agency, his pictures appearing in such publications as the *East African Standard* and *Drum*. This was followed by a spell with a company specialising in aerial photography.

Eventually, he came to Britain to study journalism at the Regent Street Polytechnic in London. Following this he became a reporter with the *Oxford Mail & Times*, a position he held for 15 years before deciding to take up full-time freelancing.

As well as contributing to numerous house journals around the country, his photographs have appeared in publications as diverse as *Darts World* and *Titbits*. He has also written and illustrated local guide-books, and has sold pictures to tour operators for use in their brochures.

Roger Ashford gave up a career as a teacher to become a full-time writer and photographer. He specialises in producing feature material on a wide range of topics for an equally wide range of publications. He also undertakes commercial photographic assignments.

Among the magazines which have published his work are *Antique Collector, Country Life, Jackie, The Lady, Art & Antiques Weekly, Choice* and *Amateur Photographer*.

He has also written for educational publishers and has undertaken photographic assignments for the local radio station, Radio Orwell.

He is at present engaged in writing and illustrating his first book in association with another photographer.

Ted Schwarz is a well-known American freelance photographer and writer whose work has appeared in numerous publications around the world. He has written and illustrated a number of books on professional photography, including *The Business Side of Photography,* and is a contributor to the *Eastman Kodak Encyclopedia of Practical Photography.*

He started his photographic career running a general practice studio, and eventually branched into commercial work and then into the editorial field. Nowadays he works exclusively for magazines and book publishing companies. His pictures have appeared in all types of publications from the German *Stern* and the British *Titbits* to the US *Physician's Management.*

He is also a prolific writer and in addition to his photographic books, he has authored biographical and historical works as well as books on child development and drug addiction.

As well as being a Senior Tutor with The BFP School of Photography, **Brian Durrant** is the BFP's resident technical expert. He has a wide experience of photography, not just as a freelance, but also in the industrial field. He was for some time Chief Group Photographer of an international engineering company, in which capacity he was responsible for a wide range of industrial and commercial photography.

His special interest in photographic equipment and apparatus stemmed from his years as manager of a large camera store in his home town of Chelmsford.

Dave Saunders spent two years as production editor of *Amateur Photographer* before deciding to turn freelance. Nowadays he takes photographs and writes articles for a wide variety of publications. His work has appeared in such publications as the *Daily Telegraph Magazine, Executive Travel & Leisure, You & Your Camera, Adventure Sports, Sound International, Teaching Geography* and *Now* magazine.

ABOUT THE BFP

Since the Bureau of Freelance Photographers was founded in 1965, it has established itself as the major body for the freelance photographer. It has a worldwide membership of some 10,000, comprising not only full-time freelances, but also amateur and semi-professional photographers. The Bureau is primarily a service organisation, and membership is open to anyone with an interest in freelance photography.

Probably the most important service provided by the Bureau is the *Market Newsletter*, an up-to-date guide to market requirements. Widely regarded as the most authoritative publication of its kind, this well-researched monthly keeps BFP members in touch with the market for freelance pictures. It gives full information on the type of pictures currently being sought by a wide range of publications and other outlets. The *Newsletter* is considered essential reading for the freelance and aspiring freelance who needs to keep in touch not only with market opportunities, but also trends and developments.

Other services provided to members for the modest annual subscription include:

● A periodic *Market Survey Special* covering specific markets such as The Greetings Card & Calendar Market, The Glamour Market, Farming Publications, etc.

● Advisory Service. Advice on all aspects of freelancing is available to members. In addition, members who prefer to sell their work through an agency can obtain individual advice on the matter.

● Fee Recovery Service. The Bureau tries to protect its members' interests in every way it can. In particular, it has been able to assist individual members in recovering unpaid reproduction fees.

● Exclusive Items. The Bureau offers various items exclusively to members. These include Contributor's Submission Forms – designed to accompany submissions to editors – and Model Release Forms.

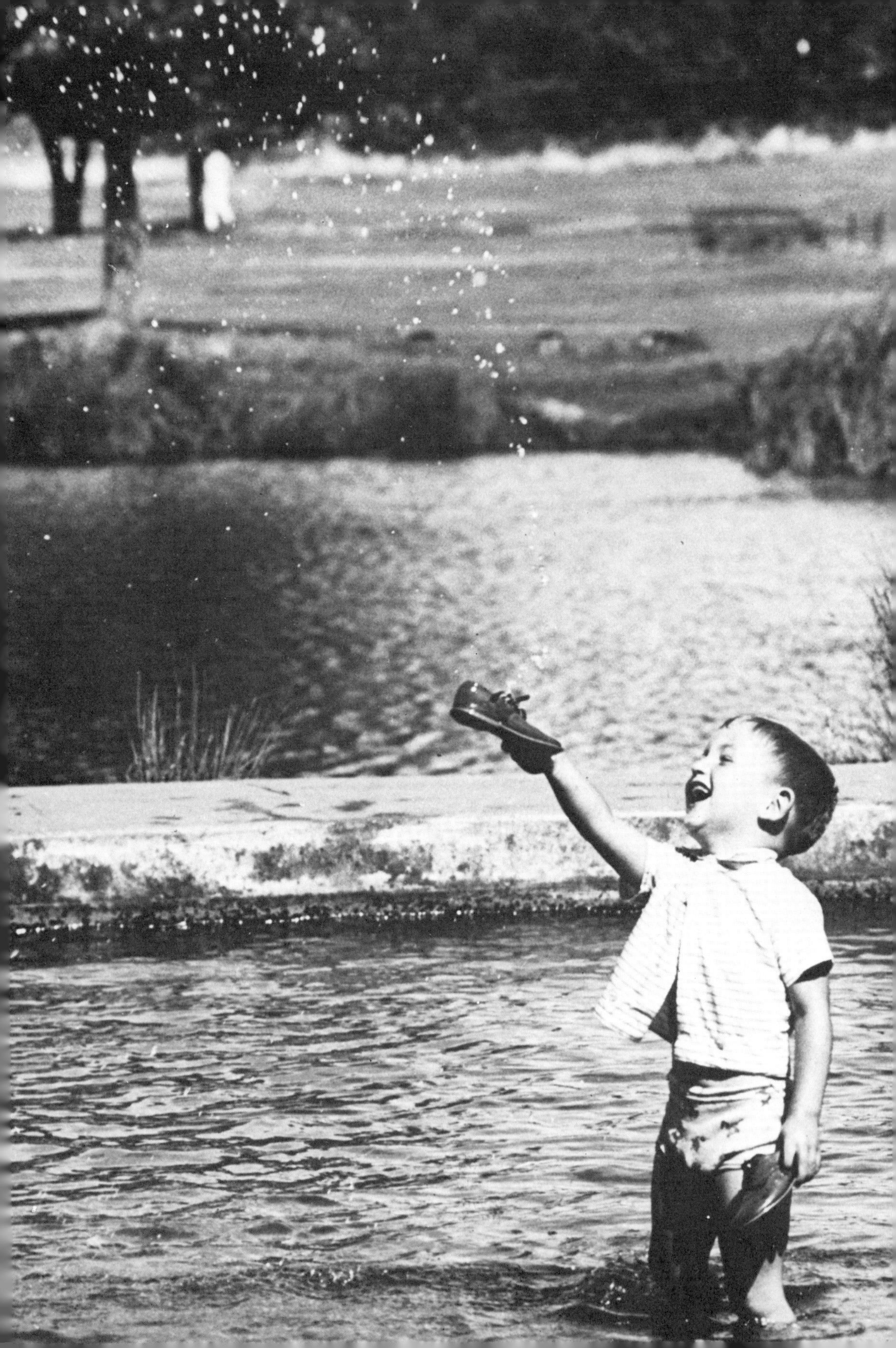

1

MAKING A START

by John Tracy An introduction to freelancing by the Head of the Bureau of Freelance Photographers. Your first steps on the road to money-making photography.

'That's a good photograph – I bet you could sell it to a magazine or newspaper.' A familiar remark? Or how about this one: 'How on earth did that photograph get into print? I can take better pictures than that!'

Thoughts like these have led many an amateur photographer to try his hand at freelancing – or selling pictures for publication. And fortunately for the aspiring freelance, there is a vast market for photographs. You have only to consider the fact that there are some 5,000 magazines and periodicals published in Britain alone to appreciate the size of the potential market. After all, most publications use photographs – so it follows that most of them present a possible market for freelance pictures.

And it's not only magazines that offer an outlet for freelance work; greetings card and calendar publishers, book publishers, tour operators and advertising agencies all present a potential market for the photographer who can produce the right type of material.

But, I hear you ask, what chance does the amateur photographer stand of selling his work? Isn't he up against the professional freelance as well as the staff photographer?

Well, it is certainly true that the big circulation national magazines have their own staff photographers as well as using material from professional freelances. But the big nationals are only a small sector of the market. True, they represent the more glamorous and better-paying sector, but the fact is there are thousands of specialist publications which are only too willing to consider freelance work. And it is true to say that, regardless of the size of the magazine, an editor isn't concerned about who took a particular picture. If he likes it, and it suits his requirements, he'll use it – even if it was sent in by an amateur photographer who had never previously submitted a picture in his life!

This famous photograph – by Tony Boxall – combines the three ingredients which invariably make for a successful freelance picture. Firstly, the subject matter is one that has considerable editorial appeal and is likely to be of interest to a wide variety of publications. Secondly, it has an element of humour – something which will always help a picture to sell. Finally, it is a 'timeless' picture; while it was, in fact, taken many years ago, it could have been taken yesterday. The picture has appeared in numerous publications over the years, including women's magazines, child care publications, and a number of books. It has also been used for advertising purposes, and has earned well over £1,000 to date.

The right pictures for the right market

So how do you make a start in the competitive world of freelance photography? Well, first and foremost, you must decide which are the most likely outlets for your work, and then familiarise yourself with the market.

If you want to sell work, you must do more than simply produce good pictures. You must produce the right type of pictures – pictures that are right for the market.

An editor of a mother-and-child-type publication is unlikely to be interested in a photograph of a motorway under construction. Similarly, the editor of an engineering or building publication would have little use for a shot of a toddler – no matter how appealing.

To give another, less obvious example, mother-and-child-type publications tend to publish what are called 'situation' pictures. These are simply pictures showing a child in a particular situation – at play, doing schoolwork, laughing or crying. A posed studio portrait of a child, no matter how well taken from a photographic point of view, stands much less chance of being published than

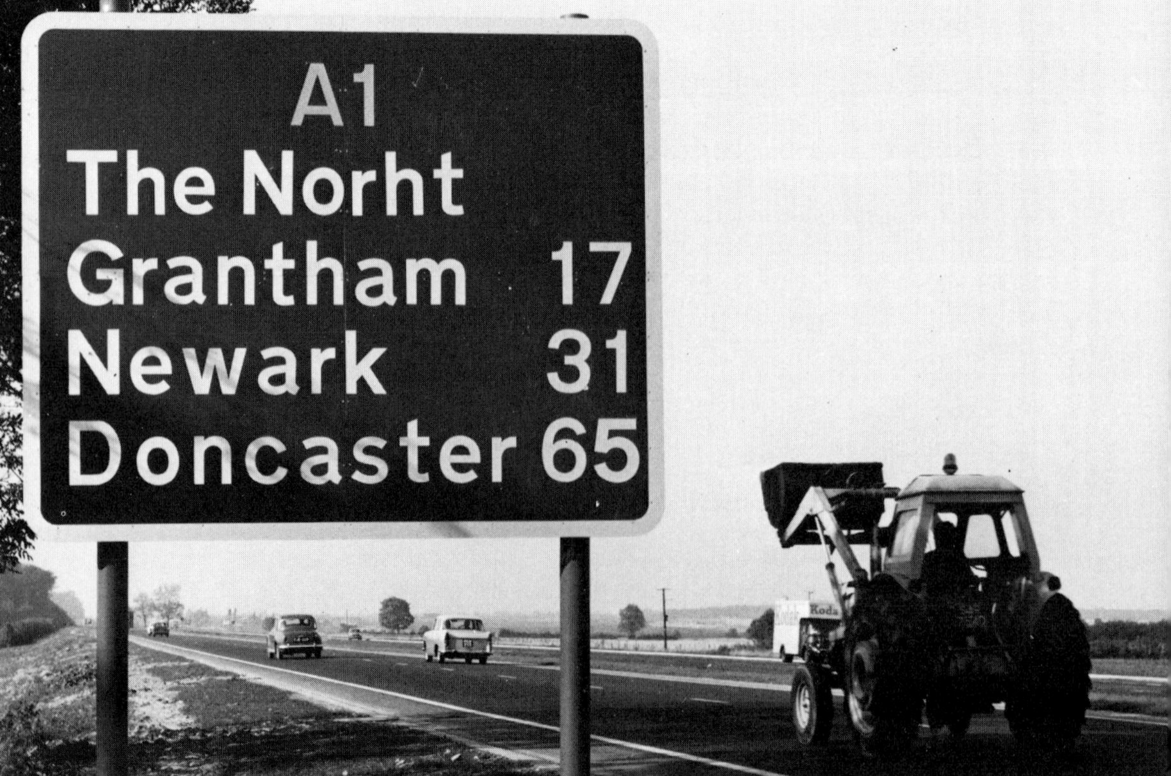

Pictures of unusual road signs and the like will always find a ready market. This incredible clanger has paid off handsomely for photographer Peter Jones. It was taken in 1971, but continues to sell to this day.

Among the publications which have so far used the picture are *Drive, Autocar, Woman's World*, the *Nottingham Post* and the London *Evening News*.

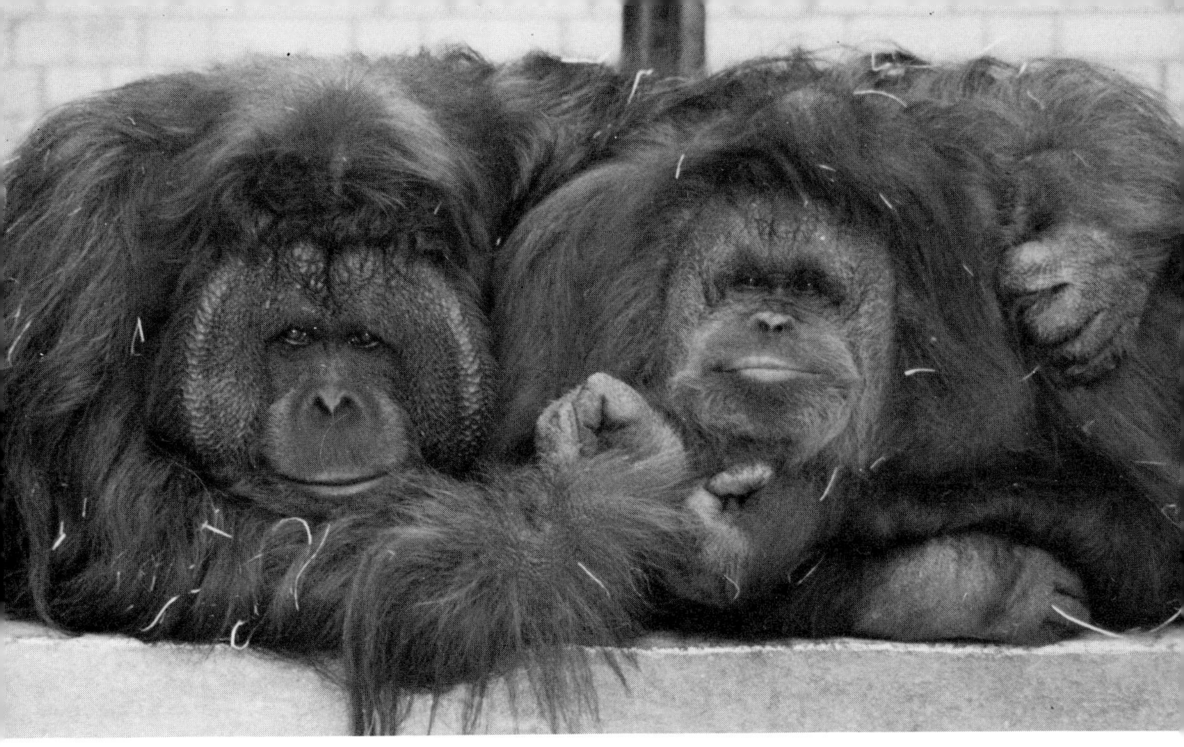

Another picture with plenty of sales potential. Wayne Paulo, a newcomer to photography and freelancing, photographed this contented couple at Chessington Zoo, submitted the picture to *Titbits,* and earned his first-ever reproduction fee.

does a candid shot of a child engaged in some activity. Pictures published in mother-and-child-type magazines invariably tend to illustrate particular aspects of child behaviour and child care.

Corny pictures sell

Pictures do not have to be earth-shattering to sell. Producing the right kind of pictures is more important than being a brilliantly creative photographer. An editor will not buy a picture, no matter how 'creative' or technically superb, if it doesn't suit his editorial requirements. So save your super-creative or experimental photographic work for the camera club – or the photographic press!

This is not to say that editors buy poor quality or technically bad photographs. They do not. Publications generally demand high quality work if for no other reason than the fact that poor quality photographs reproduce poorly. But as for 'creativity', there is more than a grain of truth in the old dictum that corny pictures sell. Nowadays, though, if you can bring a new angle to an old theme, you stand a better chance of a sale.

Start speculatively . . .

Some amateur photographers think that the best way to start out in freelancing is to write to editors offering to undertake assignments. But an editor is unlikely to offer an assignment to a photographer whose work is unknown to him. By far the best way of making a start in freelancing is simply to submit photographs speculatively. If you're after assignments, they'll come, once your work gets published and known.

Presentation

Photographs submitted to editors should be captioned with full details of the subject. Where possible, try to follow the old journalistic principle of giving the Who, What, Where, When, How and Why of the picture. Technical details about the camera and exposure are not required, except when submitting photographs to the photographic press.

Although captions can be written in pencil directly on to the back of prints, by far the best method is to type them on to a strip of paper which is then taped at one end to the back of the print. However, since captions normally become separated from prints before publication, you should ensure that your name and address appears both on the caption and directly on the back of the print.

If you're serious about freelancing, get a rubber stamp made with your name and address. Alternatively, those little self-adhesive name-and-address labels which are produced by various firms at about £2 a thousand can be used. Indeed, they may prove more suitable if you use resin-coated paper.

In many cases, a caption may not really be necessary, particularly in the case of a 'situation' picture. But it is a good idea to get into the habit of captioning all pictures you send. The very act of writing a caption can help to suggest a market for a particular picture. And it is true to say that many a picture has been rejected simply for the lack of a caption. Make sure your prints are properly trimmed and spotted and generally presented in as professional a manner as possible. For reproduction purposes, editors prefer 10 x 8in. glossy black-and-white prints. As far as colour pictures are concerned, magazines normally require transparencies, not prints. This is all to the good as far as the freelance is concerned, because transparencies are much cheaper to produce than colour prints.

As to the format preferred, at one time it was almost impossible to sell a 35mm transparency. However, that situation has changed dramatically in

Good pictures of animals are always in demand. And because this picture has the added ingredient of humour, it is likely to appeal to a wide range of publications including women's magazines, general interest publications and even newspapers. Photographer Raymond Lea can look forward to many years of continued sales with this picture.

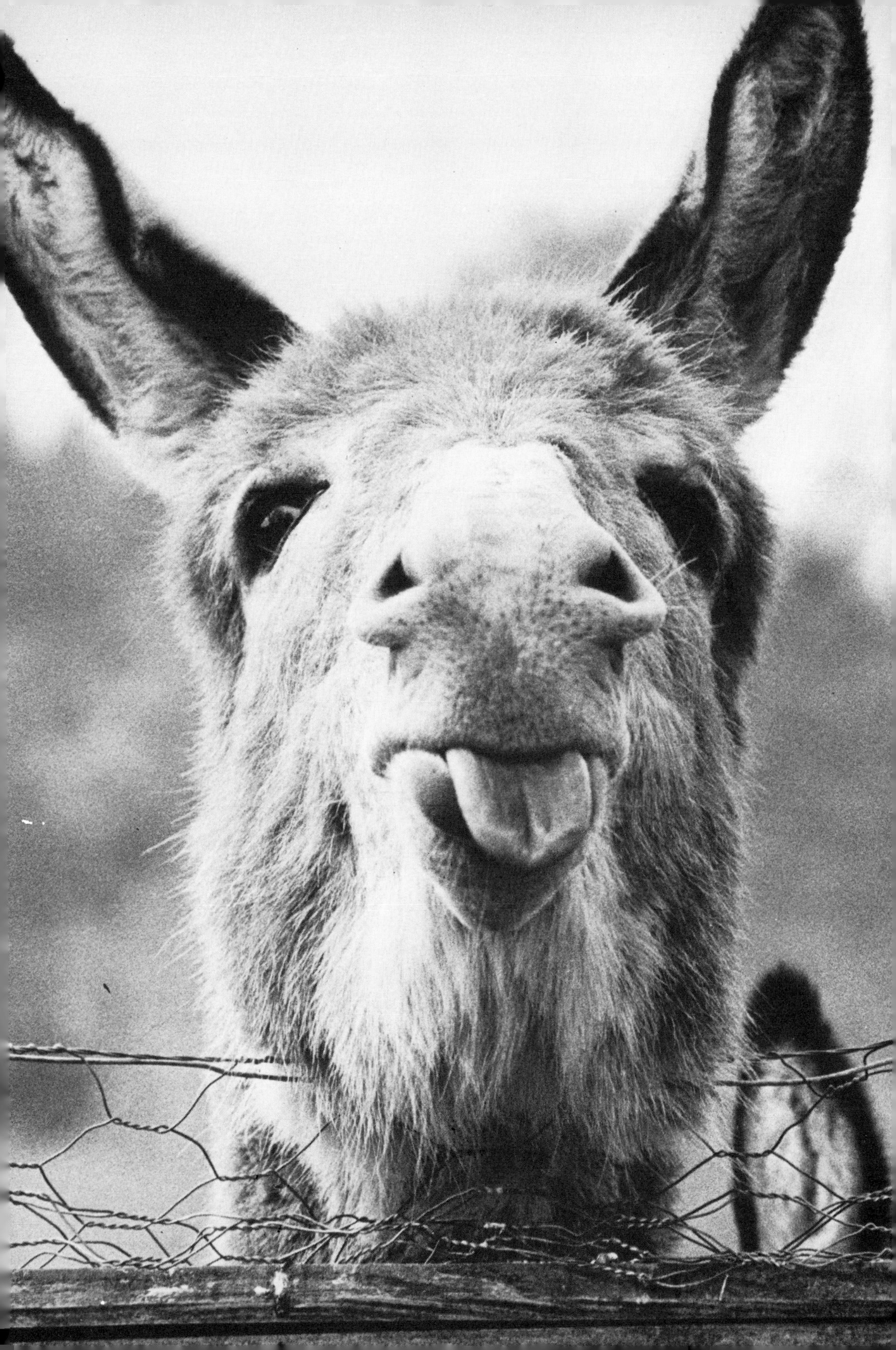

recent times, and you will find that just about every major national magazine now accepts 35mm. In addition, a large percentage of the smaller, specialist publications also accept this format.

However, a number of magazines still insist on large format transparencies and refuse to accept transparencies smaller than 2¼'' square. But these publications are dwindling, and I doubt if it will be long before all publications accept the 35mm format.

Of course, to be acceptable for reproduction purposes, colour transparencies must be of the highest quality – pin-sharp and correctly exposed with good colour saturation.

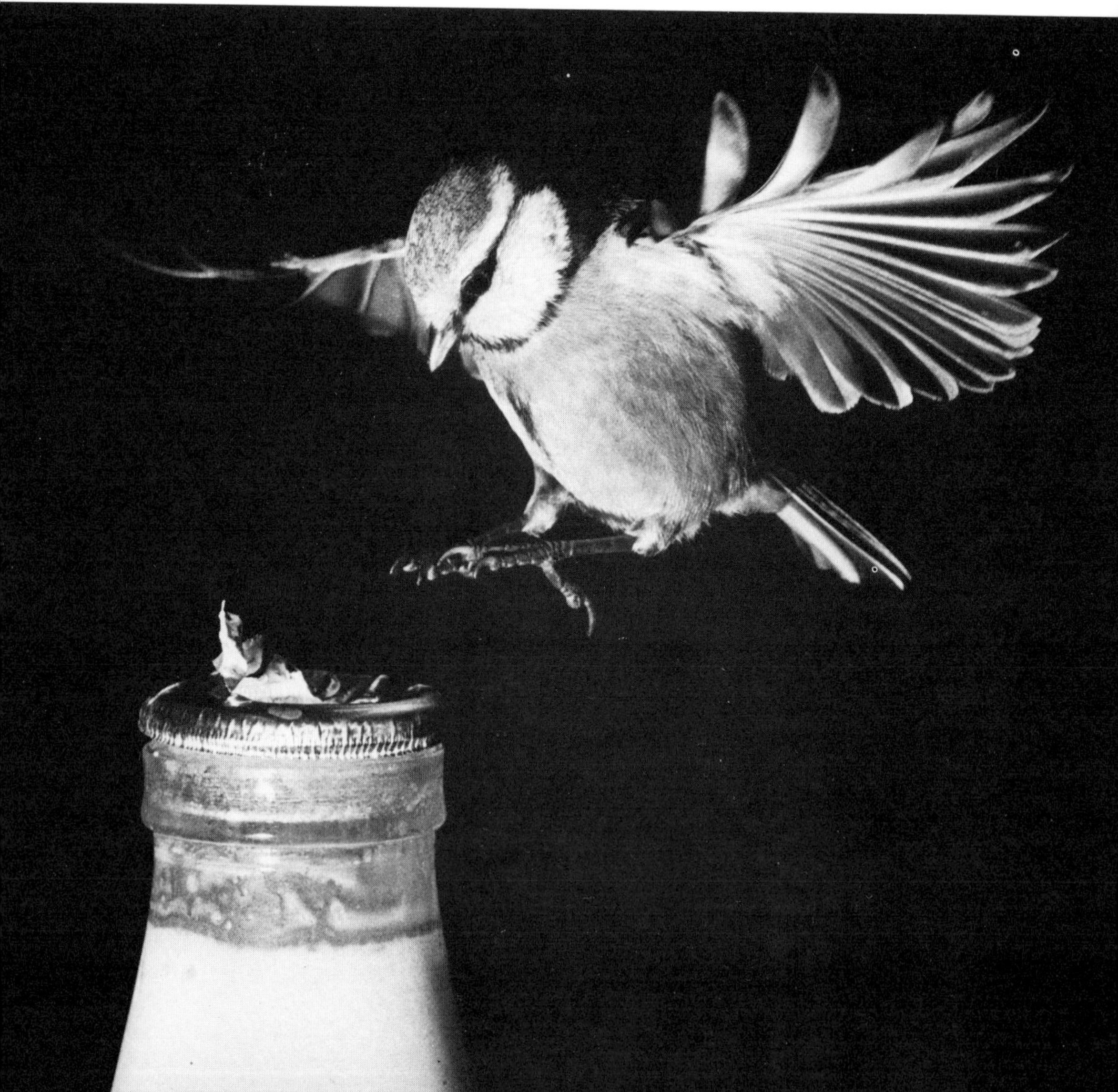

Submit sensibly

When you submit a picture to an editor, you would normally offer it for 'one-time reproduction'. This means that you are perfectly free to offer the same photograph to other markets. However, except in certain cases such as topical pictures or news items, it is not a good idea to offer the same photograph to competing publications at the same time.

For example, you would be unwise to offer the same picture to all the women's magazines at the same time. If you did so, and if, say, two of these competing publications used the photograph at the same time or within a few weeks of each other, any future work you submit is likely to be rejected out of hand. You are also likely to get yourself a bad name in the publishing world.

However, there is nothing to stop you submitting the same picture to non-competing publications at the same time. Indeed, this is the whole essence of freelancing: producing pictures that can be sold over and over again.

The rewards

Fees for published pictures vary tremendously, according to the size of the reproduction and the type and size of the magazine. A specialist publication with a relatively low circulation may pay only £3-£5 for a photograph, whereas, at the other end of the scale, a big-circulation national magazine would pay several times that amount.

While experienced freelances often set their own price by asking for a specific fee for each picture published, those starting out in freelancing are best advised to offer their work to magazines at standard rates. Once you start getting your pictures published by a variety of publications, you can expect and demand higher rates for your work.

However, the point to bear in mind is that you are not so much selling a photograph as a 'right'. A £3 fee may seem rather low, but what you are actually selling for that is the right to reproduce a photograph once. You are not selling your copyright and, as already indicated, you are perfectly free to sell the same photograph to other markets. Indeed, for this very reason, many professional freelances are happy to accept publications' standard rates for their work. They know that a single photograph, marketed properly, can earn a lot of money over a period of time. A good example of this is the picture shown on page 10 of the little boy in the water. Taken by successful part-time freelance Tony Boxall, it has earned well over £1,000 in reproduction fees having been sold over the years to numerous magazines, books, and other markets.

The point to remember when offering pictures for publication is that a highly specialist magazine with a circulation of only a few thousand and little or no

This appealing picture by Peter Hoare has been reproduced in a wide variety of publications including *She* magazine. Additionally, the original colour shot has been used on a record sleeve, and the picture has earned more than £250 in reproduction fees.

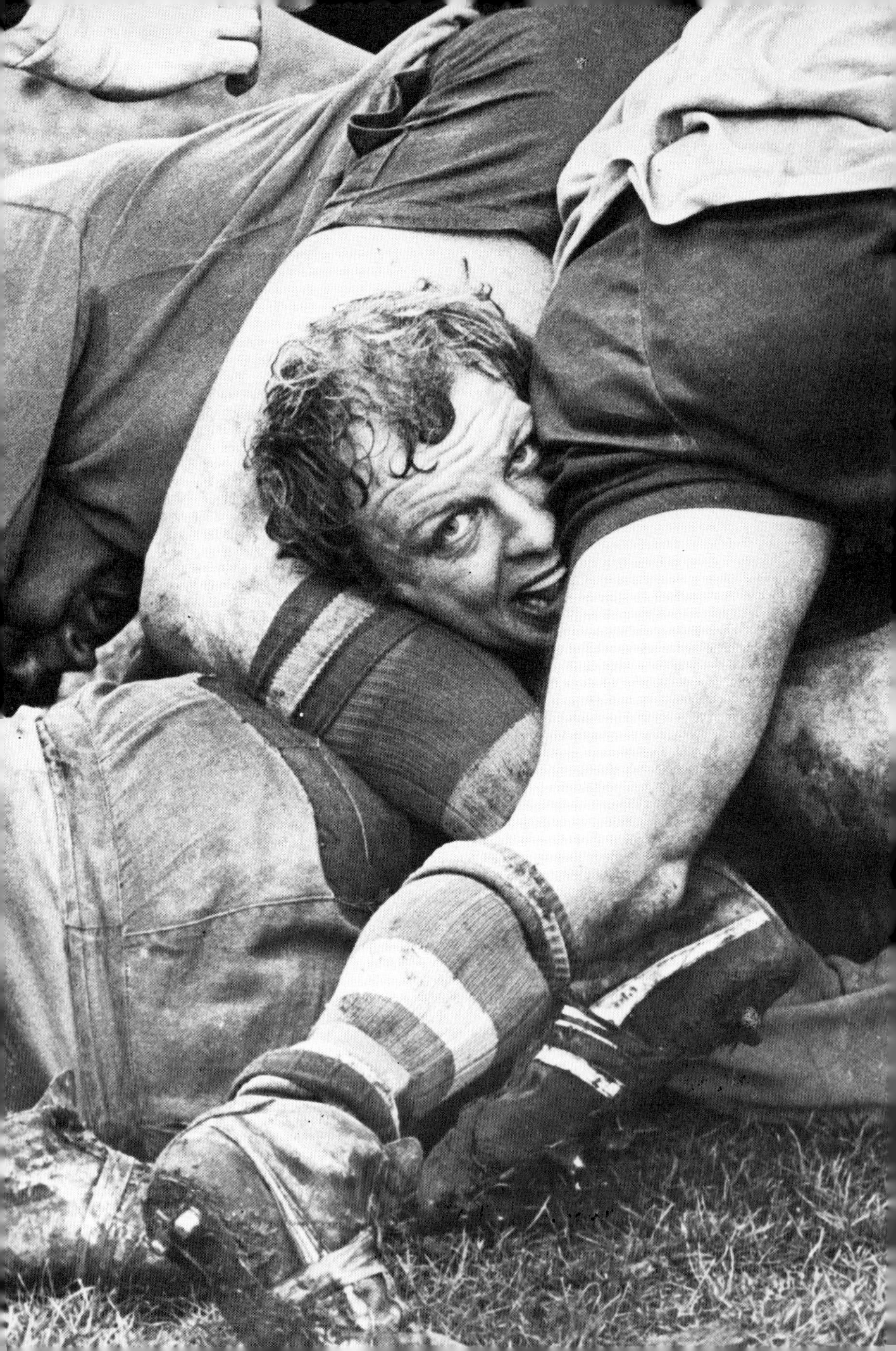

advertising revenue is not usually in a position to pay the sort of rates offered by a magazine with a large readership and plenty of income from advertising space.

However, having said that, it is also right to point out that editors can usually be persuaded to pay higher rates for material they particularly want to use.

A cautionary word about agencies

The subject is covered in more detail elsewhere in this book, but this might be a good place for a few cautionary words on the subject of agencies. There are many agencies which market photographers' work; most of them are entirely reputable and work on a 40% or 50% commission-on-sales basis, without charging any kind of 'registration' fee.

This latter point needs to be made, because a number of so-called agencies have started up in recent years, often offering a lower than 50% commission rate, but charging a 'registration' fee of anything from a few pounds up to twenty and more. As part of their service, they often offer a so-called 'press card', too. Genuine agencies do not charge registration fees, nor do they offer 'press cards'. Genuine press cards are available only to full-time professional pressmen; you can't get one for money alone.

And the simple fact is that the part-time freelance doesn't need a press card. Why make things difficult for yourself by trying to compete with the professional press photographer? The part-time freelance will make more money covering the sort of subjects not normally covered by the pro.

The monthly *Market Newsletter* published by the Bureau of Freelance Photographers features hundreds of outlets for the part-time freelance; in not one case is a press card necessary or even desirable. This business of press cards comes up quite frequently and it would be nice to think that it has finally been laid to rest. But every once in a while, yet another con-man gets what he doubtless thinks is an original idea; he wanders into his local printers and orders some cards with the word 'Press' printed on them. He places an ad in a photographic magazine and he's in business! At the BFP, we've exposed this racket several times in the past 15 years, and I'm glad to see that most photographic magazines now refuse to accept ads from people doing this.

While local newspapers do not usually present a very lucrative outlet for the part-time freelance photographer, David Bearne picked up several worthwhile fees with this picture following sales to two local evening newspapers and a weekly. It has also won a prize in a competition and has been re-produced in a photographic magazine. Another humorous picture which, suitably captioned, could find a market with a wide variety of publications.

Newspapers – not a good market

On the whole, local and national newspapers do not offer a good market for the part-time freelance. Indeed, many local newspapers do not even pay for pictures and seem to think that a credit line ('Photo by John Smith') is sufficient reward.

As for national newspapers, the competition here is fierce; Fleet Street is serviced by world-wide press agencies, professional freelance photographers, and, of course, their own staffmen.

But, again, why bother trying to compete with the professional pressman when there is a much bigger and more rewarding market available in those 5,000 magazines and periodicals?

In this book, we will show you how to sell your pictures to some of the many and varied markets open to both the part-time and the professional freelance.

This thrilling, one-in-a-million, climbing picture by John Woodhouse, taken at Stanage Edge in the Peak District National Park, has appeared in a number of publications. It was used to illustrate an article on rock climbers in *New Society* and has also appeared in *Climber & Rambler*. In addition, it has been been used in an advertising campaign by a manufacturer of climbing ropes.

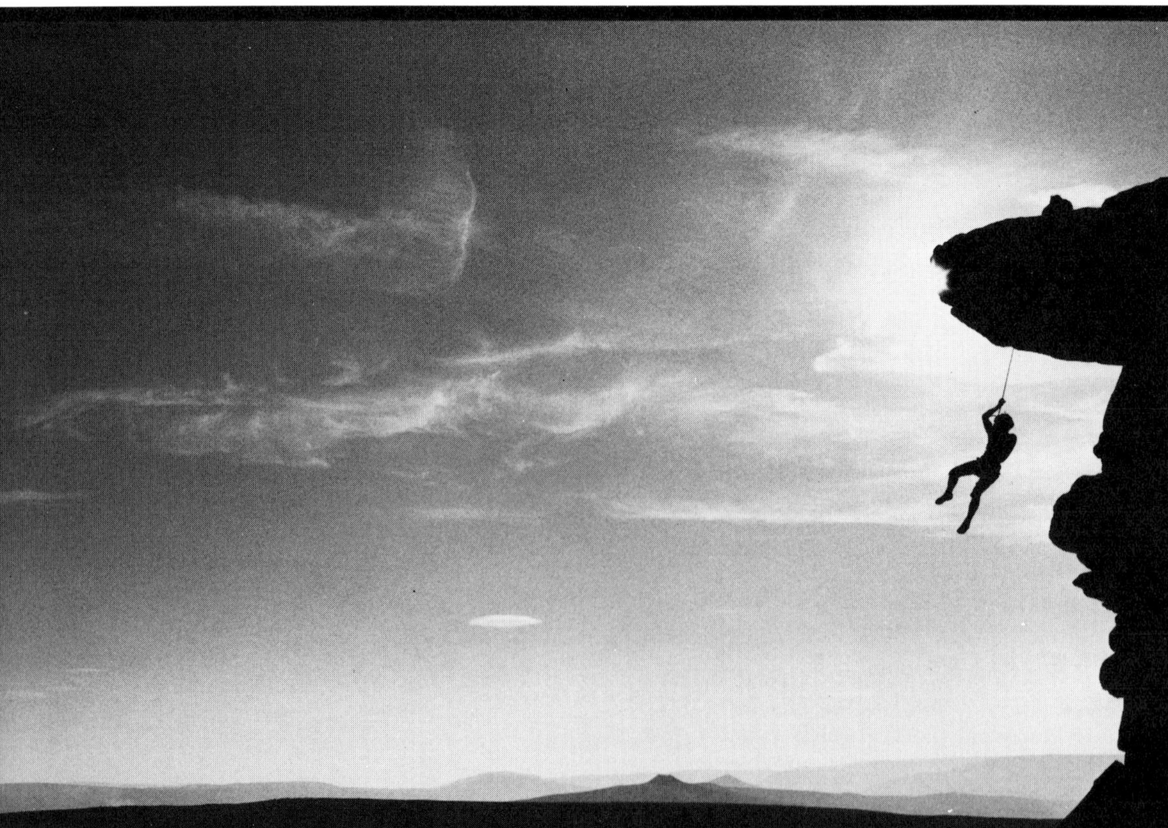

2

SHOOTING PICTURES THAT SELL & SELL

by Tony Boxall   The man who has earned more than £1,000 in repro fees from a single black and white picture explains his approach to freelancing and reveals the secrets of producing pictures that will sell again and again. Illustrations by the author.

I suppose I have enjoyed better than average success in making money from the sale of my pictures – and the first thing I can say is that there is more to it than simply the ability to produce consistently good prints or slides, important though that undoubtedly is.

In earlier days, much of my time was devoted to entering – and frequently winning – some of the many photo competitions which were found in newspapers, magazines and unlikely places such as food wrappers. Sadly, things have become more difficult for me as the years have passed because once your name is known in these circles it becomes a good deal more difficult to win. 'Not him again' – you can understand their attitude.

However, the hard facts of life which are to be learnt from trying to succeed in photo competitions underline many of the important principles in the production of pictures which you can expect to sell over and over again. To prove the point take a look at the picture reproduced here of the man on a donkey. Not only has it succeeded in photo competitions but it has been featured in a variety of publications including four photographic magazines, two books, and an advertisement, bringing in more than £200. Or the picture of the two dogs, which I took mainly because the subject appealed to me very much but which proved to be highly successful in competitions. It went on to enjoy similar success in the world of books, appearing in about six altogether, and a major publication in the USA. Also featured in four different photo magazines, it has so far made about £220 and I confidently expect it to earn more.

Timeless pictures with timeless sales

Lasting appeal or commercial demand can be achieved in a number of ways, but most of my pictures which have done well over a number of years are of the type which do not date. Of the pictures published in this book I do not believe that you could honestly put a date on any of them; the years have passed by but they seem as fresh as ever. Look at the two boys in the bath – I arrived home from work one evening to find my wife in the usual end-of-a-hard-day frame of mind with noises from the bathroom sounding like some sort of invasion by sea.

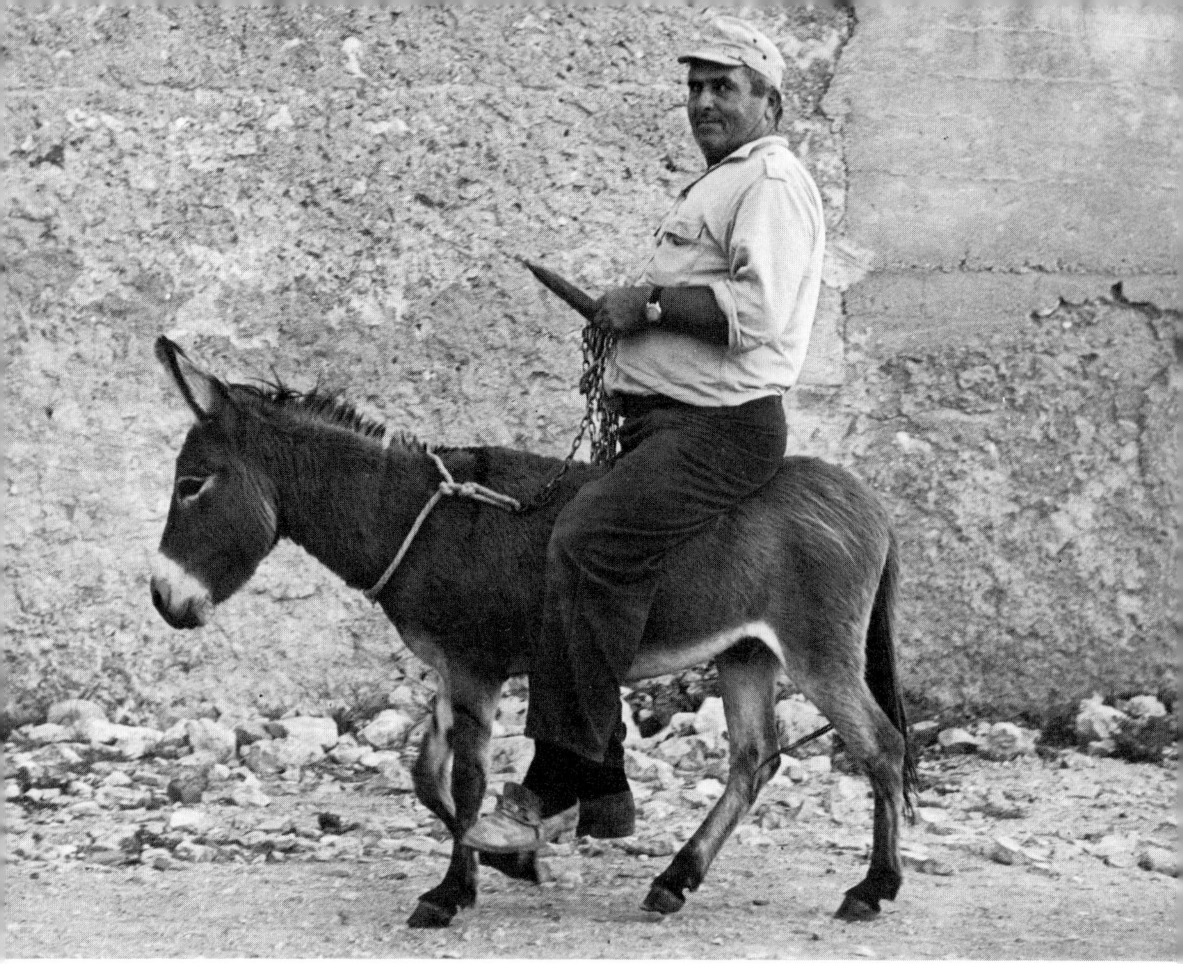

As well as picking up several prizes in photographic competitions, this picture has appeared in a variety of publications including *Weekend*. It has earned more than £200 in fees.

Up the stairs two at a time to sort out my two sons, but in place of the slipper I went for the camera and produced a nice little series of which this was one of the best. Two things you ought to know; one of my sons is a proud parent and the other is a big lad no longer in his teens, yet the picture could have been taken yesterday. If you are going to succeed as a freelance you will develop this feel for pictures which will be in demand, preferably over a long period of time. Children, animals, people in traditional dress, faces, buildings – the list of subjects which do not necessarily date is endless.

Looked at from the other angle, it is never a bad thing to take some pictures which will date because they capture events or ways of life which will retain interest over a period, or enjoy demand in the future, because of their rarity value. A good example is a series of pictures I shot of gypsies, who have a way of life which has largely disappeared. Yes, I know there are still people around whom we call gypsies, but these pictures are of traditional gypsies living in traditional horse-drawn caravans. They have earned money from books and magazines and I expect the pictures to continue to be in demand in the future for the reasons which I have mentioned.

A picture with obvious editorial appeal and one that will continue to sell for many years to come. It has so far appeared in six different books (seven if you count this one!), as well as in *Reveille* and four photographic magazines. Total fees: more than £220.

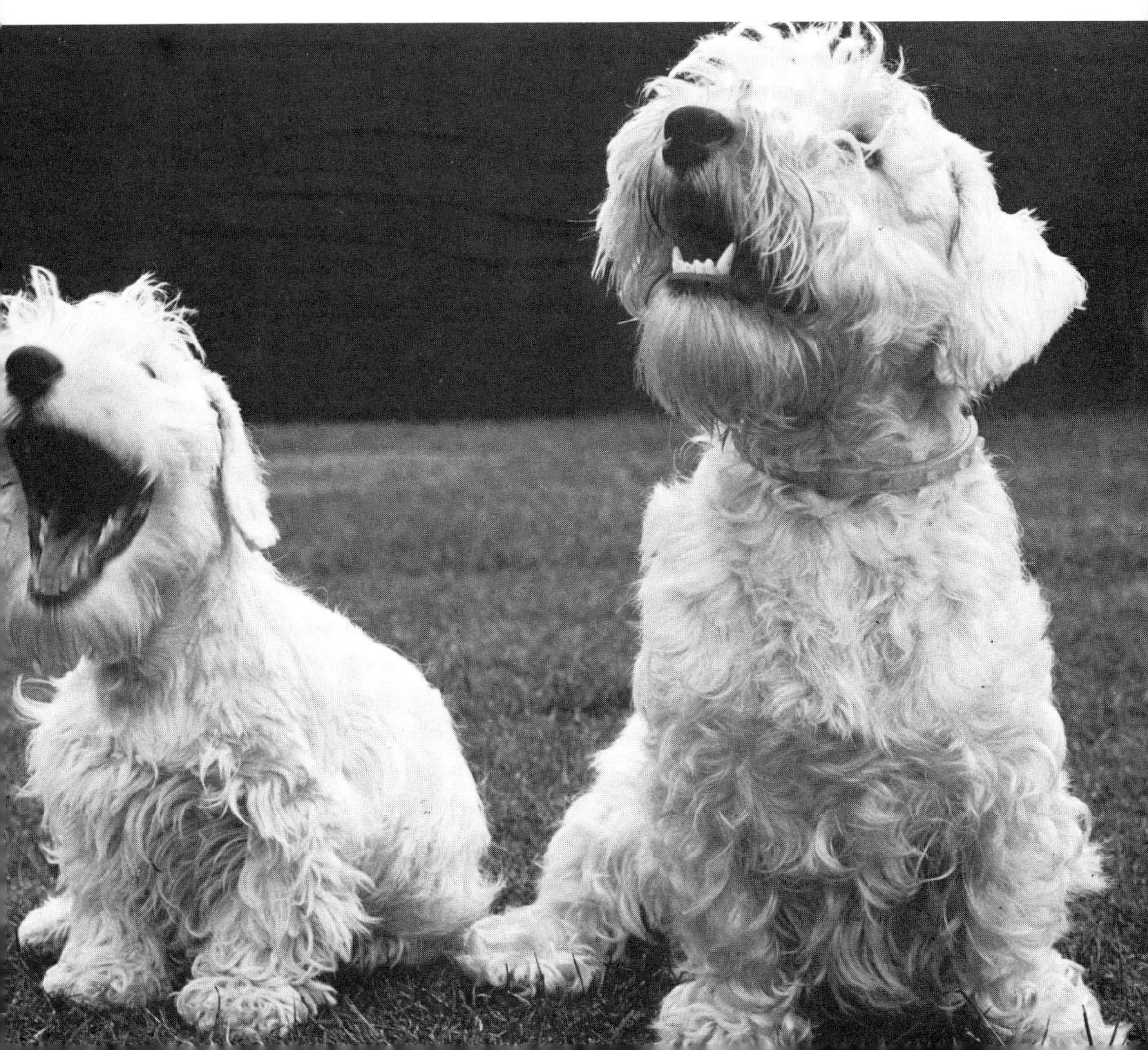

Give the market what it wants

Members of the Bureau of Freelance Photographers, of whom I am one, have a unique opportunity to see what pictures are wanted by various publishers and other organisations, and that can be quite an important part of a freelance's life. But as they stress at school when you are sitting the dreaded exams, it is important to read the question. The particular subjects specified are what they want, not something similar. Stick to the format requested, i.e. 35mm or 2¼'' square, black and white or colour etc., with a good coverage of the subject and sharp explicit pictures. I'm sure I do not need to say all these things, which have been stressed elsewhere, yet failure to provide what is wanted in the quality required is probably still the most common complaint from those who ask for our pictures.

When I am tackling a specific problem I usually try to take some additional shots, on the basis that if the subject is in demand in one quarter it is very likely to be required in another. This extra material can be sent direct to suitable publishers – for example, a series on pruning roses needed by a gardening magazine might well be accepted by another at a later date – or they may be

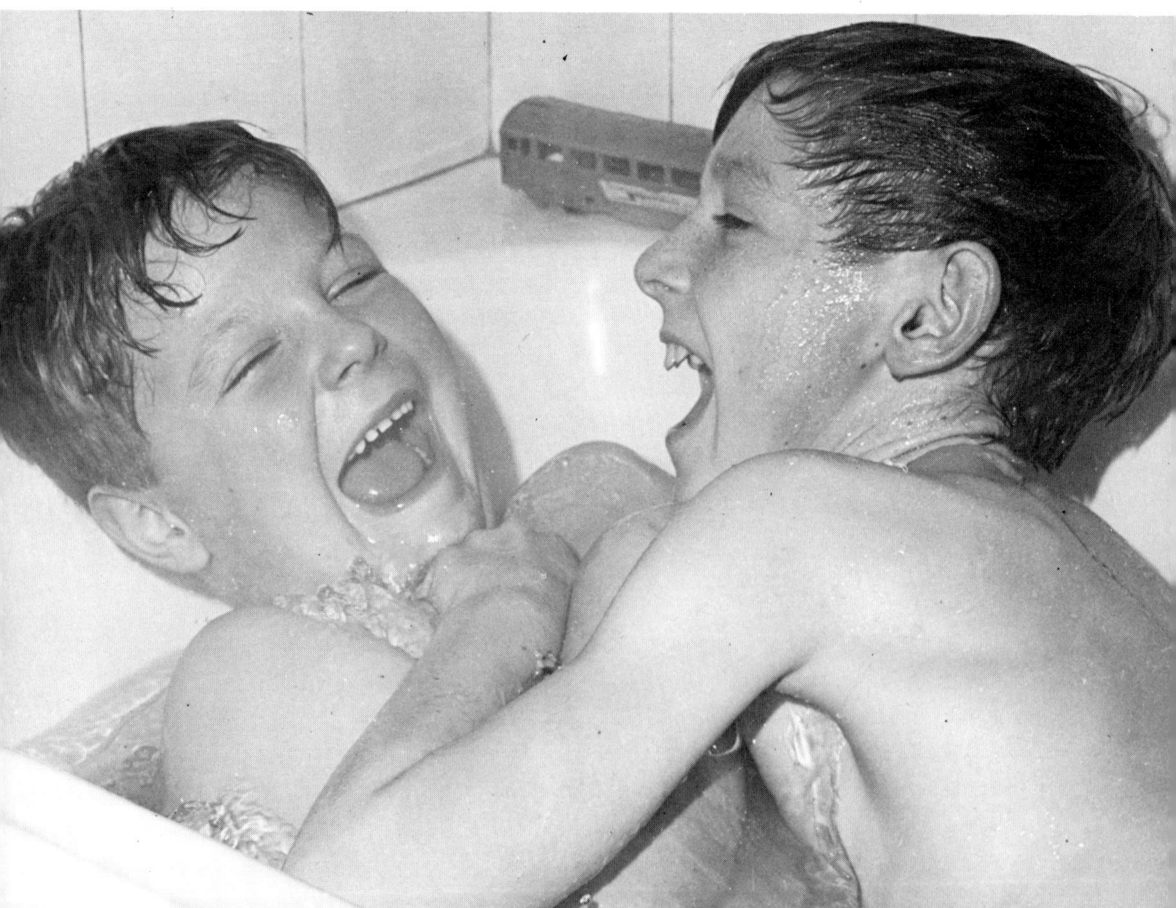

dealt with on my behalf by a photo library. This is a matter which I will cover later.

Earlier I mentioned that the Bureau is helpful in pointing freelance photographers towards suitable markets for their work, but if they are going to produce the sort of volume which I have over the last few years something more is needed. I think it is important to realise what the potential is, and the number of places and publications where photographs are demanded are innumerable. But let's be realistic, many of these needs are filled by experts who leave little room for outside supply, even if their trade organisations allow such practice. The daily press is a good example of this, and although I have on occasions been asked to help a national newspaper, generally speaking I accept that the full-time press photographers adequately fill the need. The local press is largely the same, although there are more opportunities here than in Fleet Street.

Photos that appeal to you too

In spite of the fact that much of my photography is now commercially orientated I would be sorry if the fun disappeared altogether. Many of the pictures which have gained success have in fact been taken simply because they appealed to me and because they portrayed a particular mood, way of life, or humorous moment. Such a shot was one I took of a workman digging out his mechanical digger with a shovel. I mean there was this mechanical monster, weighing several tons and capable in an hour or two of doing the work of a whole gang over a working week, stuck in the mud and powerless to move until its master had released it with his shovel! Well this fun picture was used in *Reveille* and *Weekend* as well as in various other magazines, books and a leaflet, making in all a sum of about £100 – with more to come, I hope. It's another of those photographs which won't date – not for a long time anyway.

The same comments could be made for the picture shown here of the man in Crete with a bunch of grapes, which I took simply because it was a character study which appealed to me at the time. I had no particular use in mind but I did not object, of course, when it was requested for inclusion in an encyclopaedia, photo magazines, a trade advertisement, two book covers, and in more than one magazine, including *Cosmopolitan*, making over £100 altogether.

The sea lion is another good example of a picture taken because it had appeal without particular objectives at the time. I loved the possibilities of contrasting shades in the water, and it still gives me a thrill when I produce another good print from a dateless negative from a few years back. Publications again read

Timeless pictures can sell for years. One of the boys pictured here is now himself a proud parent, yet this photograph continues picking up reproduction fees to this day. It has also succeeded in a number of photo competitions – winning cash prizes and a holiday.

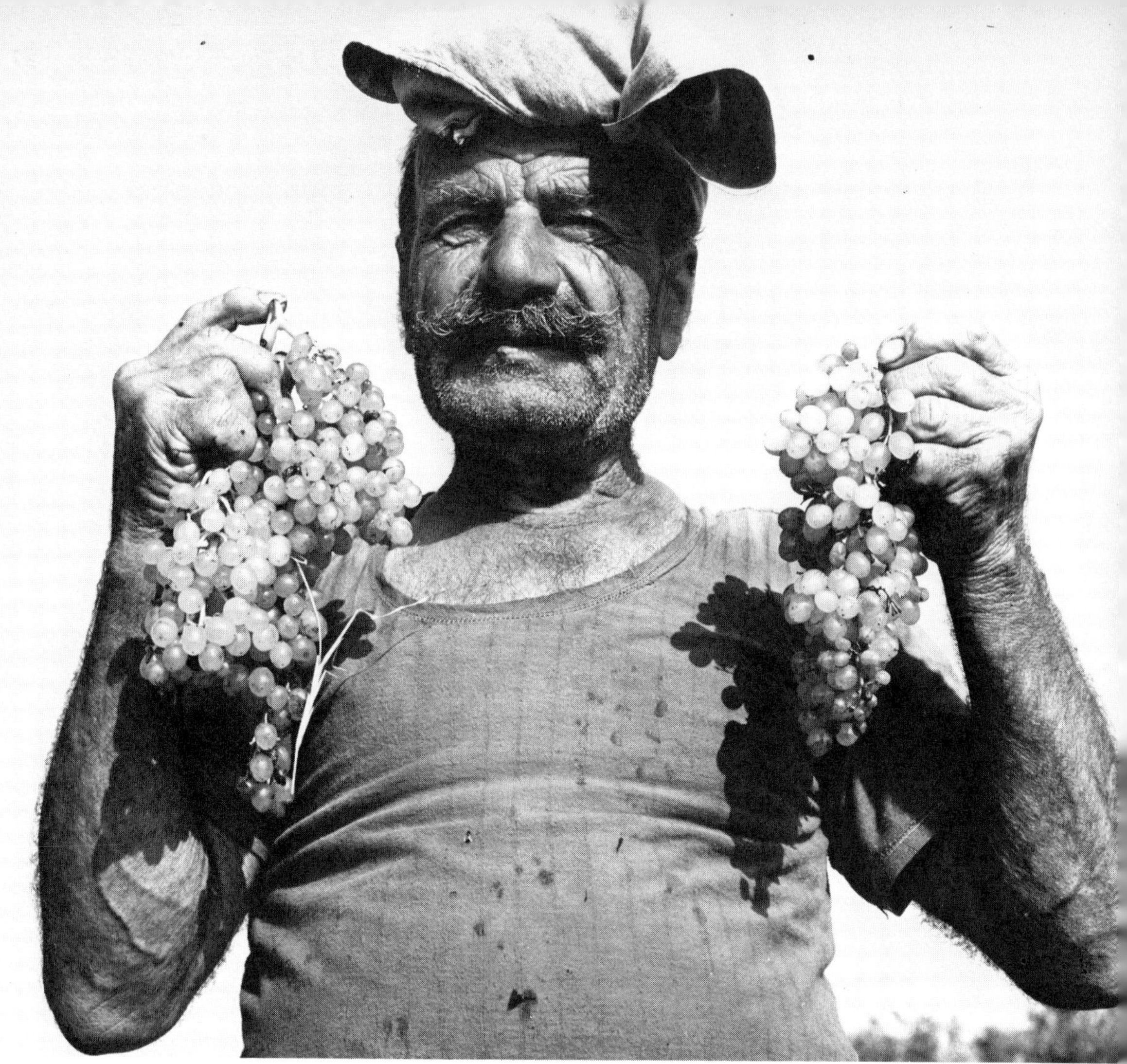

This picture was taken mainly for fun, without any particular markets in mind. However, it subsequently appeared in *Cosmopolitan*, an encyclopedia, was used as a cover on two different books and in a trade advertisement, chalking up more than £100 in reproduction fees.

like a shopping list, and to run through them is not to labour the point but to show what potential there is in quality work. This one has been included in a daily newspaper, several photo magazines, *Weekend*, *The Countryman*, trade press, an exhibition poster and in animal books, with a total of more than £100 in earnings to date.

Quality always scores

I take the view that if you are going to produce the goods is doesn't matter who buys them. My photographs, at least those which I allow to be circulated, are sharp, properly exposed and immaculately presented. I remember that at the height of his fame, Bobby Charlton admitted that very often circumstances forced him to shoot hard in the direction of goal with the sure knowledge that his power and timing would result in his shots finding gaps in the defence. I think that sums up much of my work as a photographer since my goal is success, but I often have no idea which part of the net I am going to hit. Produce consistent quality and other problems will tend to resolve themselves.

Using an agent for increased sales

This brings me to the point I made earlier about photo libraries. These people are experts because they know where the markets are and what they need. They are highly selective and will accept only the best material for their future demands. Obviously this last point is essential in libraries consisting of many thousands of photographs – only the best will do. That has become my criterion in much of my photography; will this photograph be accepted by the photo library? 'A good stock picture' is a description which those who know me hear quite often, and the subjects are too numerous to mention. People doing things, informative and interesting shots of sometimes quite ordinary objects, features of day-to-day life both here and in other countries, and pictures of lesser known parts of the world, of course.

Generally speaking the library will not be interested in ordinary landscapes, the type of pictures which might be placed in the family album, or in gimmicks. This suits me fine, because it means that most of my general work can be considered for a commercial application in due course even though I initially have no knowledge where. Let's turn to an example of my point and look at the water skier, which is another of those pictures which will not date, for some time at least. It was a subject which cried out to be taken for the pleasure of capturing the spectacular thrills of the sport. It has been included in two books, photo magazines, and more than one advertisement, in both black and white and colour, earning well over £100 already, and is still held in the library.

Love thy neighbour

Once you are seen about with a camera at home, and perhaps at work, your friends and neighbours soon become used to the idea that you are a keen photographer. They are not always complimentary I regret to say, and I have had some trouble with a neighbour who likes to leer over his lawnmower as I remove cameras and tripod from the car and shout 'David Bailey's back then' sufficiently loud to arouse the whole road. Nevertheless once they have seen some of your work – and take care not to feel too smug because the Instamatic brigade are fairly easy to impress – you will find yourself asked to produce pictures of children, houses, cats, dogs, and daughters just down from university. In fact a whole range of subjects, including weddings if you have really made progress, but here I would advise great caution since they are not easy, and the responsibility to produce the goods in often the most difficult circumstances is enormous.

One of my friends asked me to take a few pictures of her baby, and in her lounge I took several shots from a variety of angles in spite of the obvious hazards of baby powder on the lens and Smarties in the gadget bag. Then she asked for a few extra ones of the family pet dog, who was fairly freshly laundered and never far away. After that she went to organise a pot of tea and I took the opportunity to put baby and dog together, which was not hard as it happened. Mum was so pleased with the pictures which she had paid for that she was more than happy to agree that I might use the others in any way I chose. I could not have known then that through competitions and publications a picture of baby and dog would produce over £150.

More than one market

The picture shown here of bait diggers is another good example of a photograph taken with uncertain objectives even though it was obvious from the start that it would appeal to specialist publications. And it did of course, since *Fishing Weekly*, *The Countryman* and similar magazines printed it for what it was: a picture of men digging for lugworms on a beach. With a little help from my friends at the agency it was sold for use as a bottle lable, a T-shirt design, and in sundry advertisements and books to fetch a grand total of over £150.

Although they are not shown here, it is interesting to reflect upon the fact that two of my most used pictures were routine shots taken without much enthusiasm, but since used for a variety of purposes. One was a shot taken during a photo club tour of a sewage works and since reproduced in all manner of places, but not yet in a travel brochure as far as I know! The other was shot to finish off a roll of film exposed during a tour of a deserted house when I came upon an old piano. With very little film left the obvious points of interest were the inner workings of what had been a fine old instrument, and I spent some time selecting the best approach and filling the frame with strings and hammers. It has been a pleasant surprise that the resultant picture has been in demand for various books and magazines.

As well as appearing in several animal books, this picture has been published in *Weekend*, *The Countryman*, and several other markets, earning more than £100 in fees.

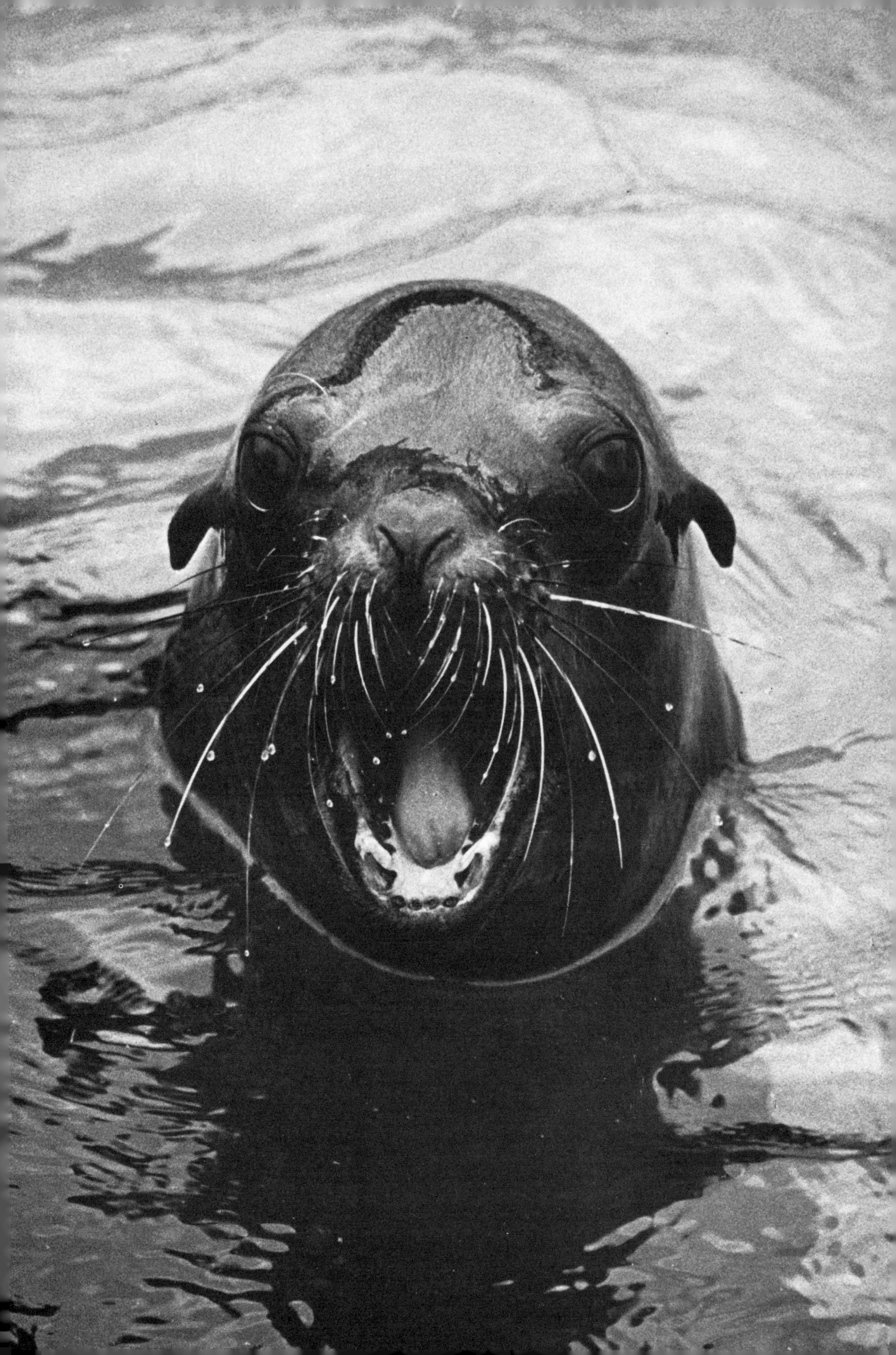

Loves and preferences

Generally speaking my great love is for black and white work, and in this or in colour I prefer to use the 2¼'' square format. There is much less opposition to 35mm than when I started taking photographs, and I expect that this is largely because the development of the smaller cameras with their sophisticated functions has made it very much easier to get good results. However, I believe that a good big'un will nearly always beat a good little'un, and the quality I get from my 2¼'' square equipment still gives me much pleasure and satisfaction. In fact I have tried a number of different types, but nothing has ever persuaded me to rely upon other than my Mamiya C330's with which I use 65mm, 80mm, 135mm and 250mm lenses. Still on the subject of personal loves and

A spectacular picture which achieves regular sales through an agency. It has been used as an illustration in two books, several advertisements and various magazines.

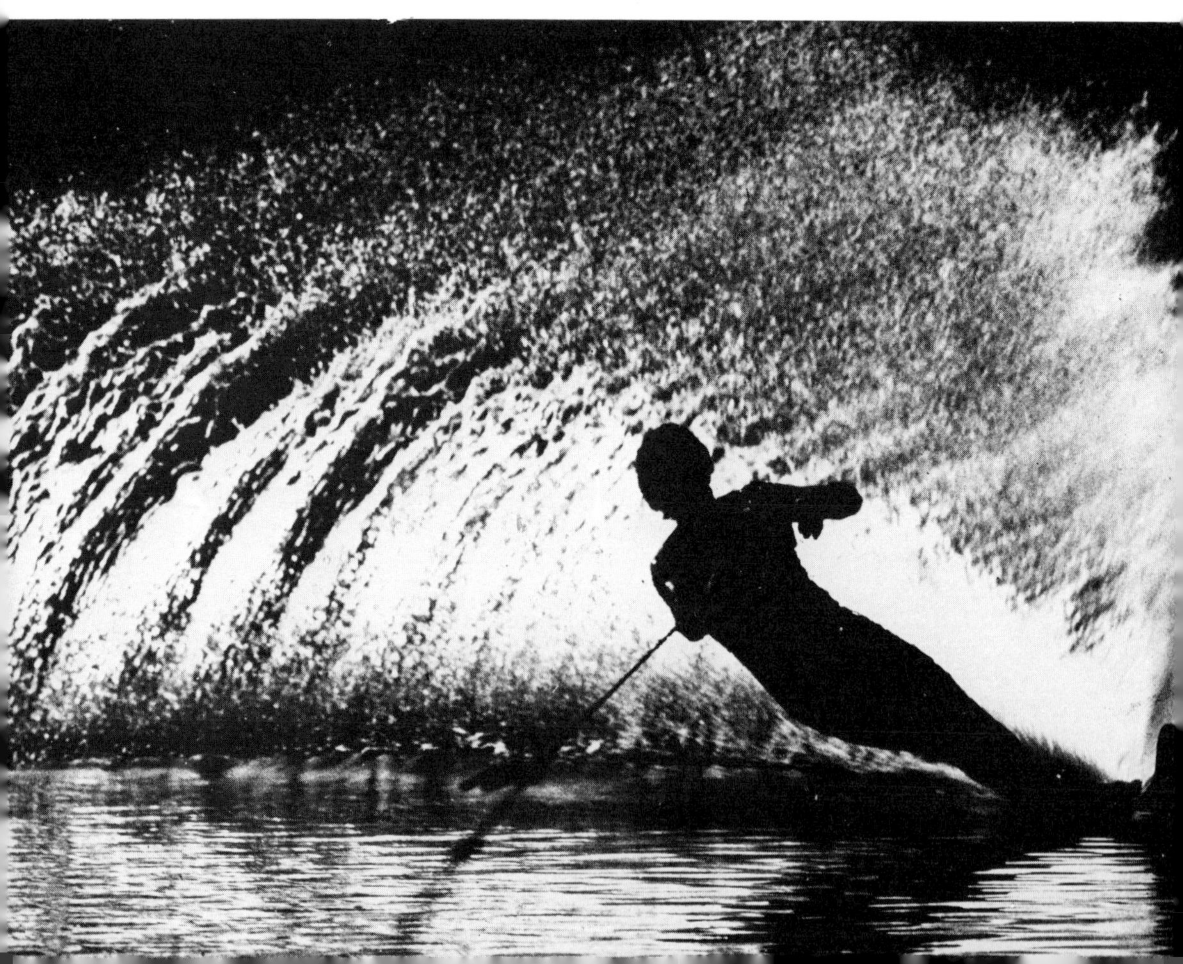

preferences, I almost invariably load Tri-X for black and white, and develop it in D.76 developer; and use Agfa CT18 for colour transparencies.

Take your time

One thing which I have learned is the fact that often the pictures in immediate demand are not the ones which can be obtained by rushing out with a freshly loaded camera. Shots of children engaged in a snowball fight, or of roses in glorious bloom, will often find a market when they are but memories, so it is important to take the pictures that are available at any given time, and to try to anticipate what will be in demand in the future when seasons and time have passed by.

Through an agency, this picture has been used as an illustration on a bottle label, a T-shirt design and in several advertisements. It has also appeared in *Fishing Weekly* and *The Countryman*, earning more than £150 in all.

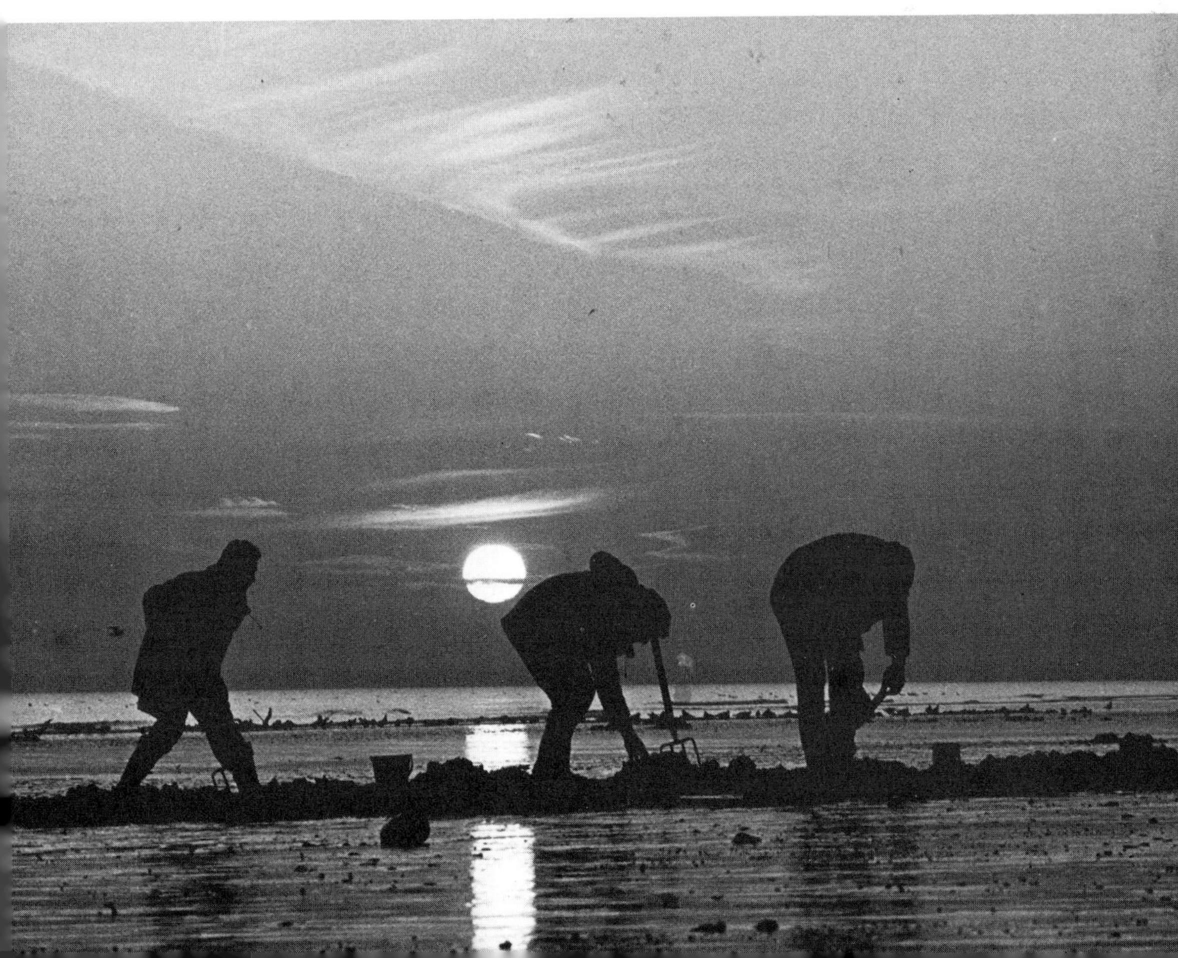

CASH FROM CONTESTS

by John Wade Every year, photo competitions offering lucrative prizes are organised by magazines, newspapers, companies, and others. Here, the editor of *Photography* magazine – who has himself organised and judged numerous photo competitions – shows how you can pick up some of those prizes.

There are photo contests everywhere, many offering mouth-watering prizes ranging from expensive cameras to luxury holidays. Some offer monthly cash prizes and, while it's true that you have to win the top position to get such a prize, it's equally true that the amount offered is often much more than a straightforward reproduction fee.

And if you win a piece of equipment, you can always sell it. Maybe that sounds mercenary and ungrateful to the organisers, but it does happen. There are people around who make a point of winning contests just for the sake of selling the prizes. Many of them have made deals with their local photo dealers even before the equipment is in their hands.

Alternatively, there is a very good chance that you might win a piece of equipment that you actually want – and that will save you money. You might even win a holiday for yourself and your family – and think of the money *that* will save you.

Keep your eyes open

In my position as editor of *Photography* magazine, I am involved with organising and judging a lot of photo contests. In 1979 our magazine alone ran seven major contests, four of which had a monthly heat with cash prizes, as well as top prizes at the end of the year. The value of all the prizes presented topped £4,000. On top of that, there were reproduction fees for many of the runners-up that were published in the magazine.

Multiply that by all the other photographic magazines in the country, each of which runs its own contests, and you begin to see just how much is on offer during the course of a single year. And that's just the photographic press. You can add many more specialist publications to that list too. From motorbikes to gardens, there is a magazine for every interest and many of them run photo contests. *TV Times* runs one or two a year with really top prizes. There are more women's magazines than any other single type of publication in this country, and the majority of them run a photo contest sometime during the year. Then there are the more obscure places like the back of cornflakes packets, tissue boxes, prepaid film envelopes. Big companies like British Airways run contests.

The *Daily Telegraph* and Kodak launch them. So does the National Trust. Keep your eyes peeled and you'll see them everywhere. Keep a watch on photographic magazines like mine; most contest organisers supply the photo press with details of requirements, closing dates, addresses where readers can get entry forms etc. and these will usually be printed on the magazine's news pages.

Less competition than you think

So, having found the contest you wish to enter, how do you go about winning it? There's good and bad news on that front. The bad news is that inevitably there will be a lot of entries. The good news is that the vast majority of those entries will be nothing short of rubbish.

It's sad but true that most of the people who enter photographic contests just don't stand a chance. That, in my experience, is the case with photographic magazines, which presumably are read by keen photographers. It stands to reason, then, that contests run by non-photographic magazines or organisers who are appealing to the general public will be receiving even more rubbish. Either way, if you are a reasonably competent photographer with a good eye for a picture, you're in with a very strong chance.

If you stick to contests aimed at the public in general, rather than at serious photographers – amateur or professional – you stand an even bigger chance. I know one keen amateur who wins around thirty contests a year, yet he rarely enters one organised by a photographic magazine.

On the other hand, there are those that make a point of entering and winning photo press contests. If you don't believe me, watch the published results. Irrespective of which magazine you look at, you'll see the same old names cropping up time and time again. The people behind those names are good photographers, but they're not necessarily exceptional. They have just learnt what it takes to win contests.

As an editor, I am sick and tired of seeing those familiar names. But if they deliver the goods and supply a better picture than anyone else's, I am committed to giving them a prize. I like nothing better than to find a new name coming in with good pictures, and I am sure there are many other editors who feel exactly the same.

If you want to join those names or, better still, knock one or two of them off their perch, your first job is to read the rules of the contest very carefully. Read them and stick to them. It's amazing how many people fail to do that one simple thing.

If the organisers say they don't want prints larger than 10 x 8 in., there is a very good reason. So don't submit anything larger than that size. If they say they want glossy prints, don't send them matt finish. If the closing date is the last day of June, don't think they'll stretch it to the first day of July just for you.

How to stop the judge

Let's look now at how photographic contests are judged. Knowing what goes on behind the scenes will help make sure it's your shots that appeal most to the judge.

You must first appreciate the sheer volume of pictures that come in. For this reason, none of them will be looked at very closely first time round. Prints will be in piles, picked up and thumbed through fast. Transparencies won't be projected. Rather, they will be removed from their envelopes, held briefly up to the light and slipped back in again. Ask most judges the subject matter of the pictures they were looking at a few seconds before and you'll find they have forgotten.

None of this sounds very professional. But believe me, the only reason the judges work this way is simply because they *are* professionals, photographers with a trained and quick eye who will see if a picture is worth a second glance literally within the first second of looking at it.

Every so often, one of those pictures, be it print or transparency, will stop the judge and he will shortlist it for a second look. Get *your* pictures on that shortlist pile and you're half-way there. The trick is to stop the judge, and there are several ways to do just that.

Give him quality. If you are entering prints for a contest – colour or black and white – go for the best possible quality. It sounds obvious, but so many contestants submit badly printed pictures. Surprisingly perhaps, black and white workers are the worst culprits. Mono pictures are so often under- or over-printed from negatives which are obviously under- or over-exposed. Photographers who attempt their own colour printing usually get it more or less right and transparencies are usually okay. But don't submit trade-processed enprints. There's rarely anything in the rules against it but, more often than not, the 'averaged-out' printing that the automatic machines in these processing houses turn out is totally inferior to a hand-made print. Enprints are acceptable, but they won't stop the judge.

Give him size. Check the maximum size for prints and make yours as near to that as possible. A good big 'un beats a good little 'un any day. That applies to transparencies as well. Inevitably you'll be submitting 35mm. But if you have access to a medium format camera and can turn out a 6 x 6 cm (2¼'' square) or 6 x 4.5 cm slide, your entry will stand out among the masses and, with luck, it will stop the judge.

Originality and beyond

Be original. Most of the pictures submitted will be pretty boring. If the contest you are entering has a set theme, don't delve into your files to find a picture that

This picture, by Conal Gannon, won first prize of £50 in a *Homes & Gardens* photo competition.

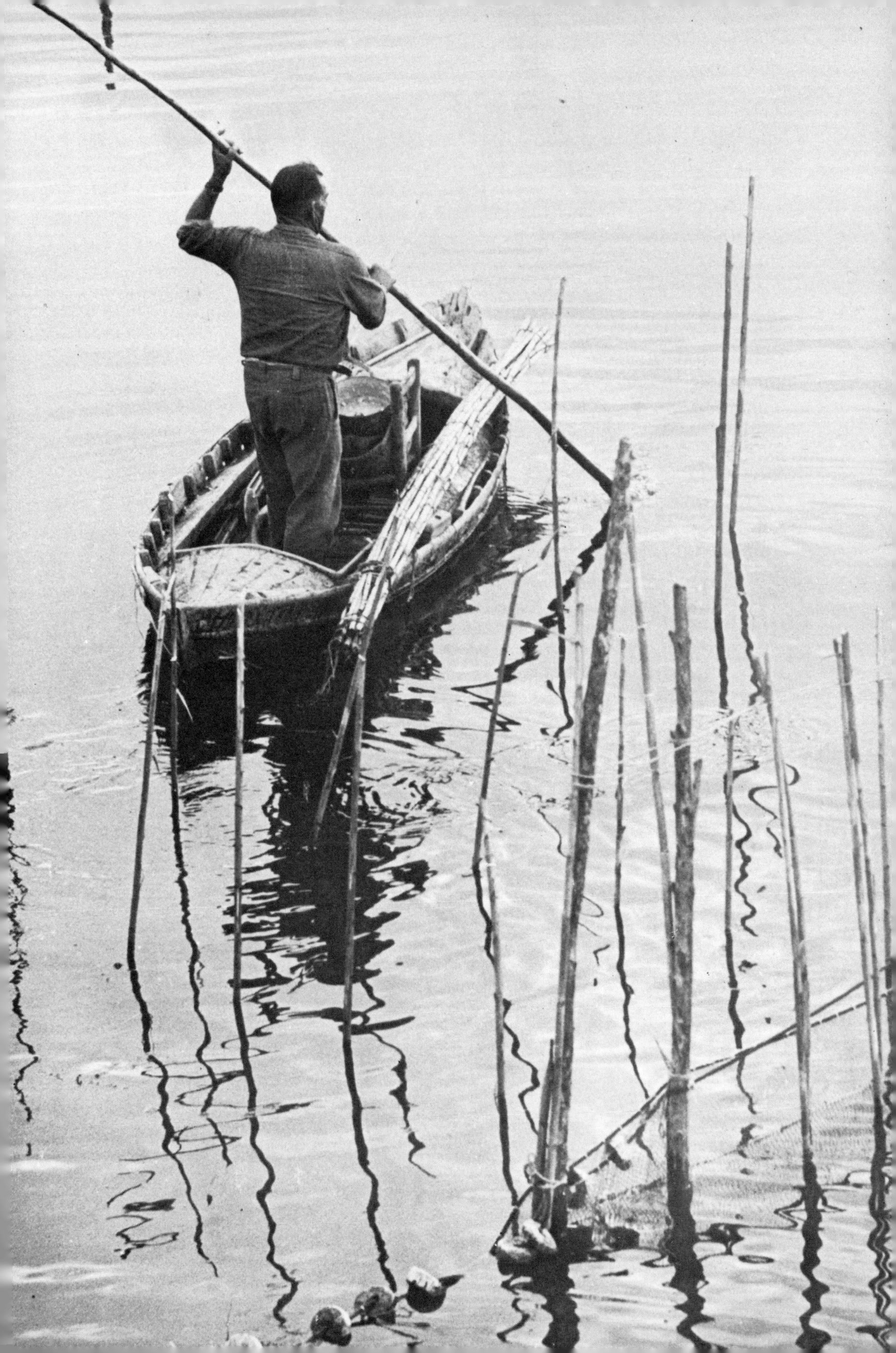

you think sort of sums it up more or less. A lot of the contestants will be doing that. If you can't find a picture in your files that *exactly* sums up the theme, think one up. Then go out and shoot it. If you can't do that, then don't bother to enter. Even though the majority of entrants will be submitting the wrong type of picture, there will be a minority who will be supplying pictures that are right on the mark, and they're the ones you have to beat.

Go one step further. Once you have decided on the type of picture you want to take for the contest, take a mental step back and look at the idea objectively. If it came to you in a flash and was easy to think up, it's a fair bet that a lot of other photographers have had the same thought. So, having come by your idea, add something to it. Go that one step further that the others won't bother about. Take your first idea and force yourself to improve upon it. The judge who has seen the same theme put across the same way ten times in a row is going to look extremely favourably on the eleventh picture that does the job better than the rest.

Have faith in your entry. If no one likes the picture but you, that's fine. It's your judgement that must count in the end. But if, despite encouraging noises from friends and relatives, you feel there is something lacking in the shot, then don't submit it. It's no use hoping the judge will overlook an imperfection you know full well is there. He won't. He's an expert and he'll notice it. That's why he's the judge.

If you have a picture that is suitable for a contest, it's often a good idea to prepare it some time before you want to send it, then to live with it for a while. If it's a print, prop it up somewhere prominent, in a place where you are forced to look at it all day. If it's a slide, then keep coming back and looking at it again and again. If it has that certain 'something', you'll know it. You'll get a feeling of excitement in the pit of your stomach every time you look at it. If that feeling is still there at the end of a week, it's a good bet that the judge will feel the same excitement when he looks at it.

The final judgement

Having arrived at a shortlist, the judge will now have a spread of pictures to consider for the top prize. These pictures are the best of the batch but, even at this stage, in an average photographic contest, it's rare that any one picture will leap out as an obvious and outright winner. All these pictures will be good; rarely can any one of them be called exceptional.

So in the end, it comes down to a personal preference on the part of the judge. If, for instance, there are three pictures of a dog, a girl and a landscape, all of which are equally good technically, the judge is bound to go for his own particular preference. If he likes animal pictures, he'll choose the dog; if he likes glamour shots, he'll opt for the girl; if he's more of a traditionalist, he'll go for the landscape.

It's unlikely that you'll know the judge or his personal likes and dislikes (if you do, capitalise on it!), so at this stage you have to make your picture stand head and shoulders above the rest *in spite* of personal preferences, rather than *because* of them.

There's no way that I, or anyone else, can tell you how to do that. At the end of the day, it must be your own flair and imagination that makes a better picture. What I can tell you, even at this late stage in the judging procedure, is the reason why the pictures that are finally rejected will fail.

The black and white pictures will fail through bad print quality. The colour prints will fail because they are either good subjects badly printed, or bad subjects well printed. The colour slides will fail because they lack that extra bit of sparkle, both technically and in the subject matter.

Despite all this, however, they *will* be good pictures. Good, but not great. No one can tell you how to make your pictures great, but knowing the failings of others will help you push yours just that fraction past theirs. And it is that fraction that will win you the contest.

No prizes for poor presentation

A word now about presentation. Don't send in tatty prints. I cannot emphasise that enough. It gives the judge the impression that the picture before him has been doing the rounds. And if it has been rejected from other contests, why should he give it a prize?

Make a fresh print every time you enter a shot for a contest. The time and cost will be worth it in the end. Pack it neatly with a sheet of cardboard in the envelope to keep it stiff.

Most contests ask for names and addresses on the backs of prints. If that's what they want, do it. Don't write the details on a separate piece of paper that will inevitably get lost.

If you are entering a colour contest with transparencies, then make them easy for the judge to view. For that first time round when he is shortlisting, he wants a way of getting the pictures out of their envelopes, looking at them quickly and putting them back. So don't make the wrappings difficult to get open. If the judge has to spend valuable minutes trying to slit Sellotape with a fingernail or unwrapping ten slides, each of which the photographer has wrapped in a separate piece of paper, then he will be exasperated before he has even looked at your picture. Don't encourage him to reject it simply because he doesn't want the bother of removing the wrapping again the next time round. Believe me, such things happen.

Slide boxes such as those returned with processed Kodachrome make quite adequate packing for your precious slides. Those transparent slide pockets that take sheets of twenty or so 35mm slides are even better for the judge's fast perusal.

Just as with prints, and for similar reasons, it's best to put your name, address

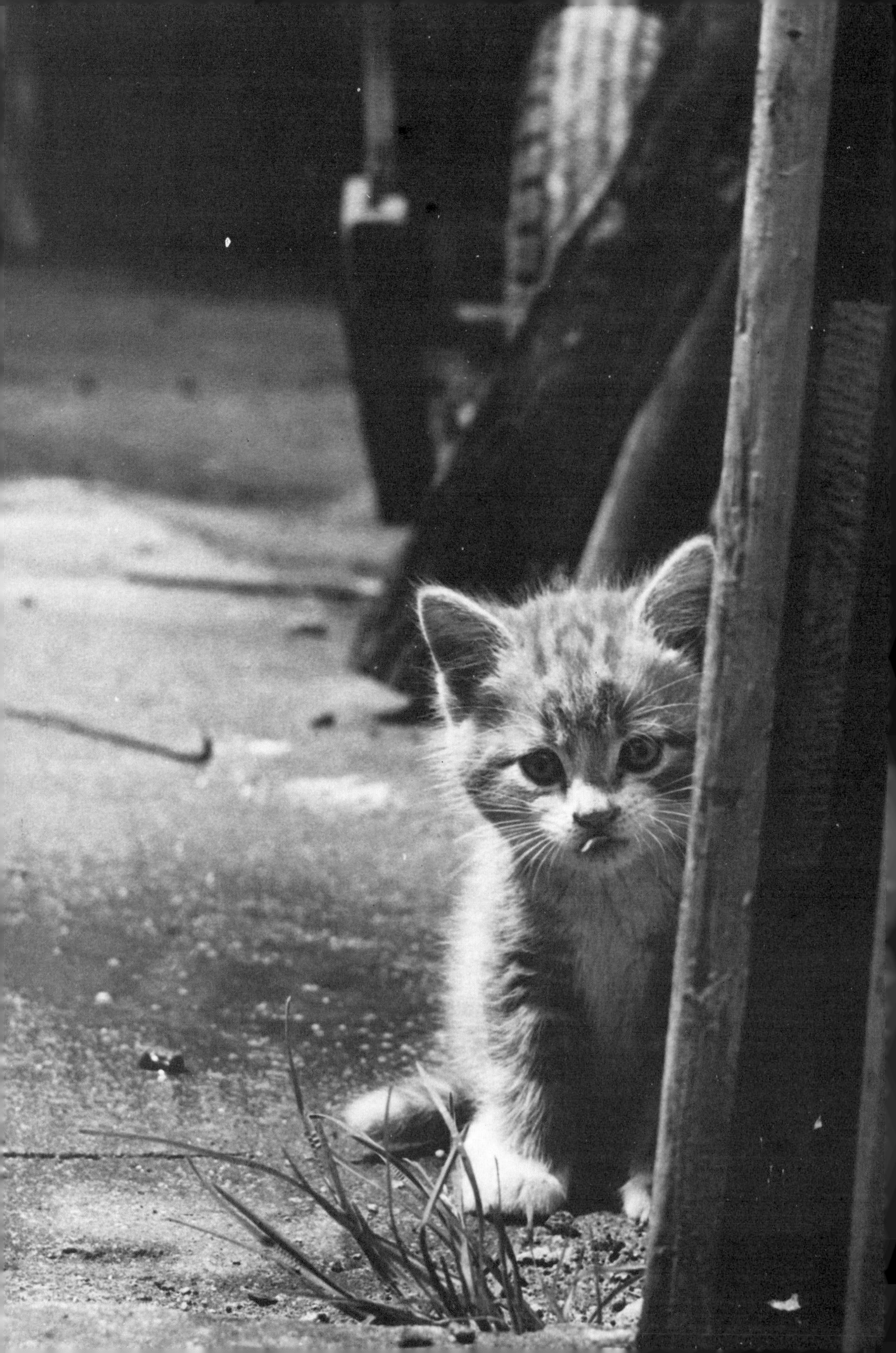

and any other relevant information directly onto the slide mount, rather than on a separate piece of paper.

Competitions to avoid

Finally, there is one type of photo contest *not* to enter, even though the prizes may look terrific. It's the one that claims copyright on your pictures.

To this end, read the contest rules very carefully. If one of those rules says something to the effect of, *All entries become the property of Brand X Trading Company*, avoid the contest at all costs.

The reason is simple. Let's say, for instance, that a baby food manufacturer is running a baby picture contest. Let's say that the prize is something stupendous – a holiday in the States or a car maybe. Let's say that the company gets 5,000 entries for that contest. Maybe 4,950 are no good. That still leaves fifty pictures that could be of use to them in their advertisements, illustrations on packets of baby food, promotional leaflets etc. If the contest rules claim the copyright on every entry, that means they can use those fifty pictures for any purpose they like without paying the photographers a penny.

So maybe one of those fifty pictures has won a photographer a valuable prize. That still leave forty-nine photographers who have lost the copyright on their pictures and who are losing a lot of money on account of it.

The company may appear generous in giving away such a valuable prize, but its cost has been covered a hundred times over by not having to pay photographers or picture agencies for the use of those pictures.

So watch out for that rule. You won't find it in any of the photo press contests, but you could find it in some of the trade-organised competitions.

Be a winner

Other than that, most photographic contests are fair game for the freelance photographer and if you have never thought of entering one before, it's time you tried your luck. Those that have already caught on to this most lucrative of markets are winning valuable prizes every week of the year.

Isn't it time you were among them?

This appealing picture won **V. Lakey** first prize in a *Practical Photography* competition. It would also be a likely contender for a prize in a competition organised by a baby food manufacturer, or indeed, in any competition with an animal or a humour theme.

SHOOTING KIDS FOR CASH

by Lorna Minton There's a world of difference between shooting child pictures for publication and simply producing pictures for the proud parents. The author of this chapter – whose pictures regularly appear in such publications as *Mother & Baby, Nursery World* and *Child Education* as well as in books on child care – explains the difference and sets out what publishers want.

If you have children, there must have been many occasions when you have felt like shooting them! Next time you feel that way, shoot them by all means – but use a camera! For it's on just these occasions, when the children make you feel you could strangle them, that the most saleable shots can be obtained. Think of the times when two of them are 'scratching each others eyes out', or fighting, or one is deliberately provoking the other by some means. If you can summon the presence of mind to fetch your camera, rather than intervene in the struggle, you will be giving yourself the opportunity of some very saleable pictures.

Shoot 'em doing something!

In the past, you have probably taken some excellent child portraits, and have been delighted with some of the natural expressions you have captured, coupled with impeccable photographic technique. Probably, you sold a few prints to the delighted parents, and you have begun to think, 'If I can take such appealing pictures of children, I should be able to sell them to a wider market'. Quite right to think in this way, but you will never sell any of your *existing* appealing pictures for general publication. There is a world of difference between the type of child pictures taken for the benefit of the parents, and those which are taken for publication. For the parents require an excellent likeness, and in general prefer the head and shoulders only to fill the picture frame. But a publisher, be he involved in magazines, books, greetings cards or whatever, will always require the child to be doing something, and for his activity to be self-explanatory without the need for a caption. The *last* thing a publisher is interested in is whether it is a good likeness; and in my experience, it is actually a help to sales if the child's face is not too visible.

Having said that, it is often possible to shoot both types of picture at one sitting, although you must first explain this to the parents and take care not to infringe the copyright laws. I will try to explain the method I use, for it might suit your requirements too. Firstly, I will only try to arrange a 'double session' with children of people I know. I then explain that I run a picture library of

This appealing picture, by Derek Holden, made the cover of *Nursery World*.

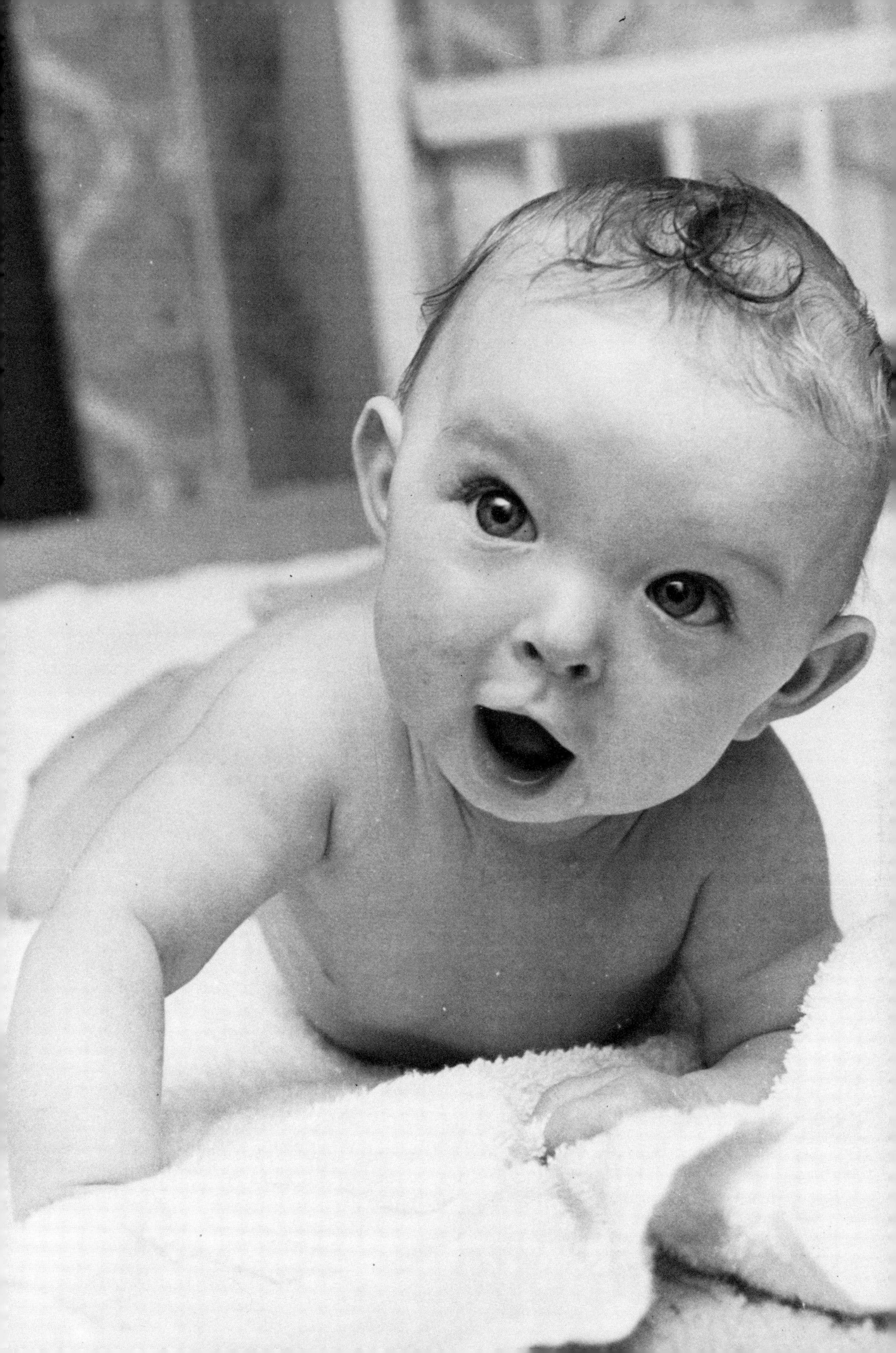

photographs suitable for publication, and that I would like to include pictures of their child. Naturally I do not charge them a sitting fee, for by so doing I would effectively be selling the copyright, but then I am not paying a modelling fee either. But I do offer to show them the finished prints, and if any should appeal, they can order copies at my normal re-print fee. The expense of the sitting and any financial risk is all on my side, but the resultant publication fees usually make a nice profit.

Once the sitting is booked, I spend some time thinking out shots with sales potential, and then at the time of the shooting, I can fairly rapidly set up my ideas and I can also take a few 'appealing portraits' with the parents' requirements in mind.

These pictures sell

By now you might be thinking, 'But what type of shots *do* have sales potential?' The answer is any type of activity which you can think of which could be used to illustrate an article in a magazine about children. To help you further, here are some examples of pictures which I have taken which have already sold:

1). A child sitting up in bed with a thermometer in his mouth;
2). A child cleaning his teeth;
3). Two children painting together;
4). A little girl with a doll's pram;
5). A toddler snatching a toy away from another;
6). A child rolling out pastry;
7). A small child trying to do up a sandal;
8). A child brushing his hair;
9). A toddler in a high chair trying to feed himself;
10). A child having his nose blown by his mother;

If you really study this list and try to imagine what each picture looked like, you will understand better what I mean when I say that saleable pictures show a child engaged in an activity, and they have no need of a caption for they tell their own story. The demand for pictures like those listed above seems never ending, and you could probably go away and shoot those same ideas all over again *and* sell them. Magazines like *Mother and Baby*, *Mother* and *Nursery World* have a perpetual demand for this type of picture, and book publishers use them too; for in particular there seems to be a constant flow of books published on child psychology, and these are the type of pictures that are used.

Black and white sells most

For all the markets mentioned so far, black and white is still the most widely used, and with printing and publishing costs escalating like everything else so rapidly, I would guess that black and white will continue to form the bulk of

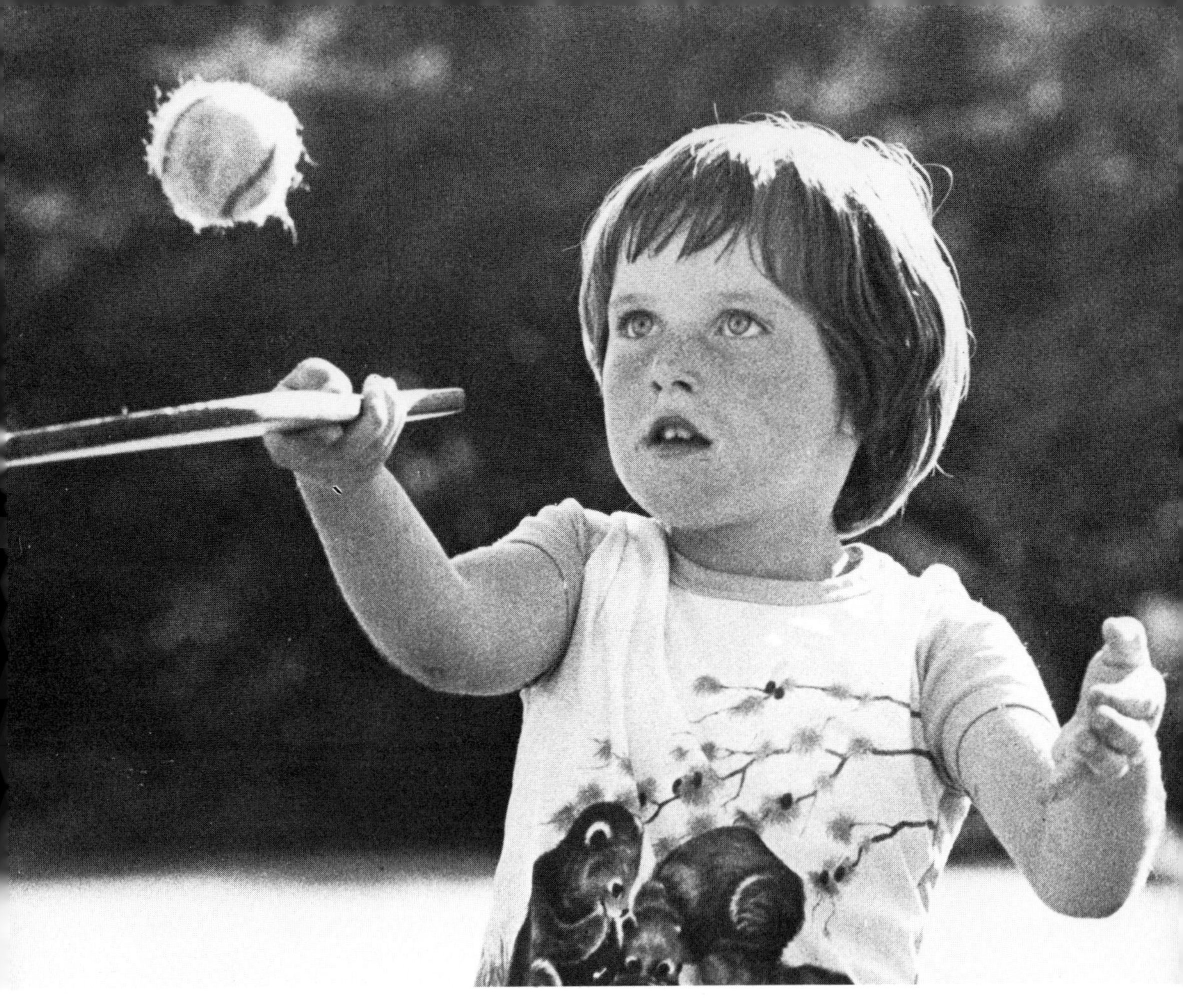

Editors want pictures of children engaged in some activity rather than formal portraits. This picture, by Valerie Bissland, sold to *Child Education*.

illustrations in magazines and books for many years to come. Specialist magazines, by their very nature, cannot expect a huge circulation, so they have to keep their costs to an absolute minimum. A coloured cover is usually invested in, because without it the magazine would become lost on the bookstall, but in most cases these covers are specially commissioned.

But colour sells here

Another good outlet for child pictures is the greetings card market, but you would be advised to study the card racks in newsagents and gift shops before you attempt to break into this market. Having perused the card shops, you will probably come away with several strong views and a lot of useful information.

You will find that children are only used for the 'children's age' range, and that the subjects favoured by the publishers are mundane and unimaginative. In other words, 'corny' pictures sell best. This is unfortunate for the photographer, and (speaking as a buyer of cards) boring for the customer, but I presume the card publishers know what they are doing! The type of pictures I personally prefer for greetings cards are action packed in the main – for example a boy on a bicycle going fast through a puddle, or a little girl being splashed by the surf – but whenever I submit a selection of pictures for this market, I take care to include shots such as a child stroking the nose of a pony, or a child on a hillside looking at the view, and *these* are the ones that sell.

But I shall keep on submitting the action shots, for I feel that one day I shall come into contact with a more enlightened publisher. Birthday cards for boys are the ones most difficult to find in the shops, and those that are available seem to feature adults rather than boys. Occasionally a card will feature a youngster, but invariably the youngster looks about twelve, yet the words say 'Happy Birthday five year old!' Since greetings card publishers often say they have more transparencies than they can possibly cope with, one wonders why they cannot make more accurate use of the ages represented. Perhaps I need to go and work for a greetings card publisher to find the answer!

For the greetings card market, the photographs must be colour transparencies and the larger the transparency the greater your chance of selling them. But there are one or two golden rules you must bear in mind when composing shots for this market. 1). The sky must be very blue; 2). The subject must be colourful and have plenty of depth of field; 3). There must be plenty of space at the top to allow the publisher to overprint a greeting; 4). The pictures must trim to a vertical format, for this shape can be displayed more effectively in the shops.

Bawling babies are best!

Having discussed some of the markets for pictures of children, it would perhaps be as well to outline the different methods of approach needed for photographing the different age groups of children. I will start with the youngest. In many ways babies are the easiest to shoot for they do not have the drawback of self-consciousness. In fact the opposite is true, for they are quite likely to engage in a staring match with you. Generally speaking, from a sales point of view, young babies are best photographed either yawning or crying, sleeping or feeding. Probably you are thinking that they don't do anything else! But staring blankly is one thing and smiling is another, yet neither of these expressions will easily sell.

The important thing to remember with young babies is that they sleep for the greater part of every day, and it is no use trying to wake them up for a photographic session, neither is it any good photographing when they are tired and wish to go to sleep. If their routine is broken, they will yell, and apart from a couple of useful crying shots, this is all you will get. This means, of course, that you will have to shoot when the baby is in a responsive mood, and not necessarily when the time is convenient for you. Older babies can be photographed in a much wider group of activities; in fact the list of activities with sales potential is endless. The following list should help you:–

1). Spoonfeeding;
2). Bottle feeding;
3). Learning to walk with a baby walker;
4). Crawling;
5). Building with bricks or beakers;
6). Playing in a play pen;
7). Having a nappy changed;
8). Sucking a thumb;
9). Chewing a toy;
10). Exploring an open cupboard;

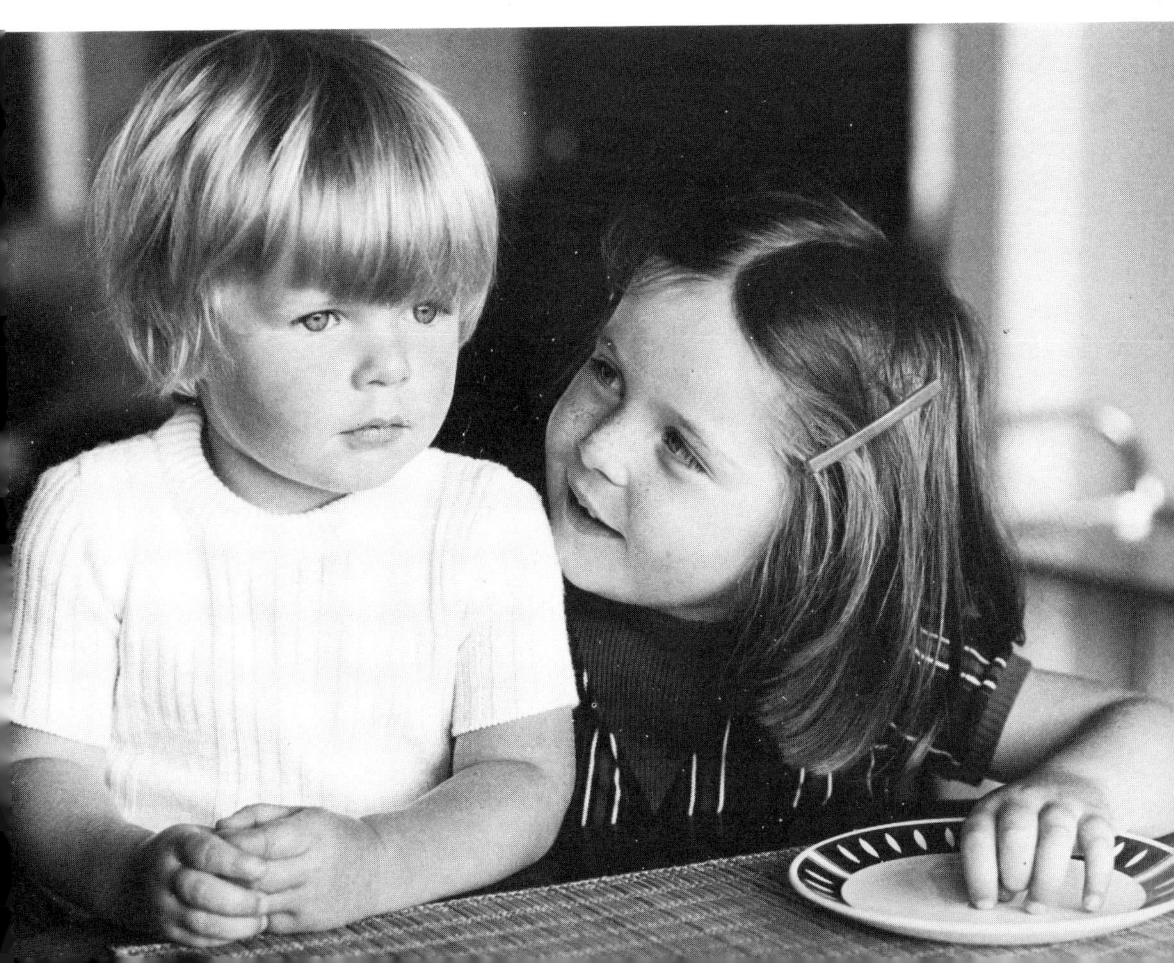

The type of situation picture which editors like to keep in their files to use as illustrations with appropriate articles. This picture, by Valerie Bissland, has appeared in *Woman's Weekly* and *Child Education*.

As I said the list is endless, but provided you have plenty of patience and time, none of these activities should prove difficult to stage. In fact the best way to get a toddler to play with something, is to set up something different out of camera range and try to interest him in it. Meanwhile you quietly set up the thing you want within camera range, and sheer perversity will cause him to want to play with that instead! By the time a baby becomes a toddler, child psychology plays a very important part of your photographic technique.

The easiest age to photograph

Once a child is walking and talking but still of pre-school age, he becomes the easiest age of all to photograph. You can explain to him what you want to do, and as long as you are prepared to answer a non-stop flow of questions while you are shooting, you will probably get some excellent shots that look unposed. This age group is best photographed playing with educational toys; e.g. building bricks or beakers; weighing things on scales; doing simple jigsaw puzzles, or playing with other children.

Shoot 'em in the classroom

The next age group is the school age child, and as with other age groups, it is essential that they are photographed engaged in an activity. With this age group the two best sellers are those pictures which indicate the seasons, and those which feature something educational. Examples of the first subject are: 1) Skipping (in summer clothes); 2). Playing hopscotch (in outdoor winter clothing perhaps); 3). Kite flying; 4). Fishing. The educational pictures could feature such activities as 1). Doing homework; 2). Walking to school (in school uniform); 3). Crossing the road via a 'lollipop' man; 4). Classroom work. This last item is probably the most difficult to obtain, for it entails special arrangements with the staff of your local school. If you explain to them what you are doing, they will probably co-operate, but by way of recompense, the least you should do afterwards is to present the head teacher with a set of finished prints.

But classroom pictures do have excellent sales potential, provided you make it clear in the pictures which particular subjects are being studied. Many educational books and magazines have articles on 'the difficulties of teaching maths', or 'English literature: how to make it interesting', or perhaps 'Helping with spelling'. These and many more topics like them are regularly discussed by writers and journalists, and editors usually like to 'break up' the monotony of a page of type, by using an appropriate photograph. Black and white pictures are required mostly for this market.

Fun with the autumn leaves. This picture, by Lorna Minton, has appeared in *Family Circle* and *Child Education* as well as in the photographic press.

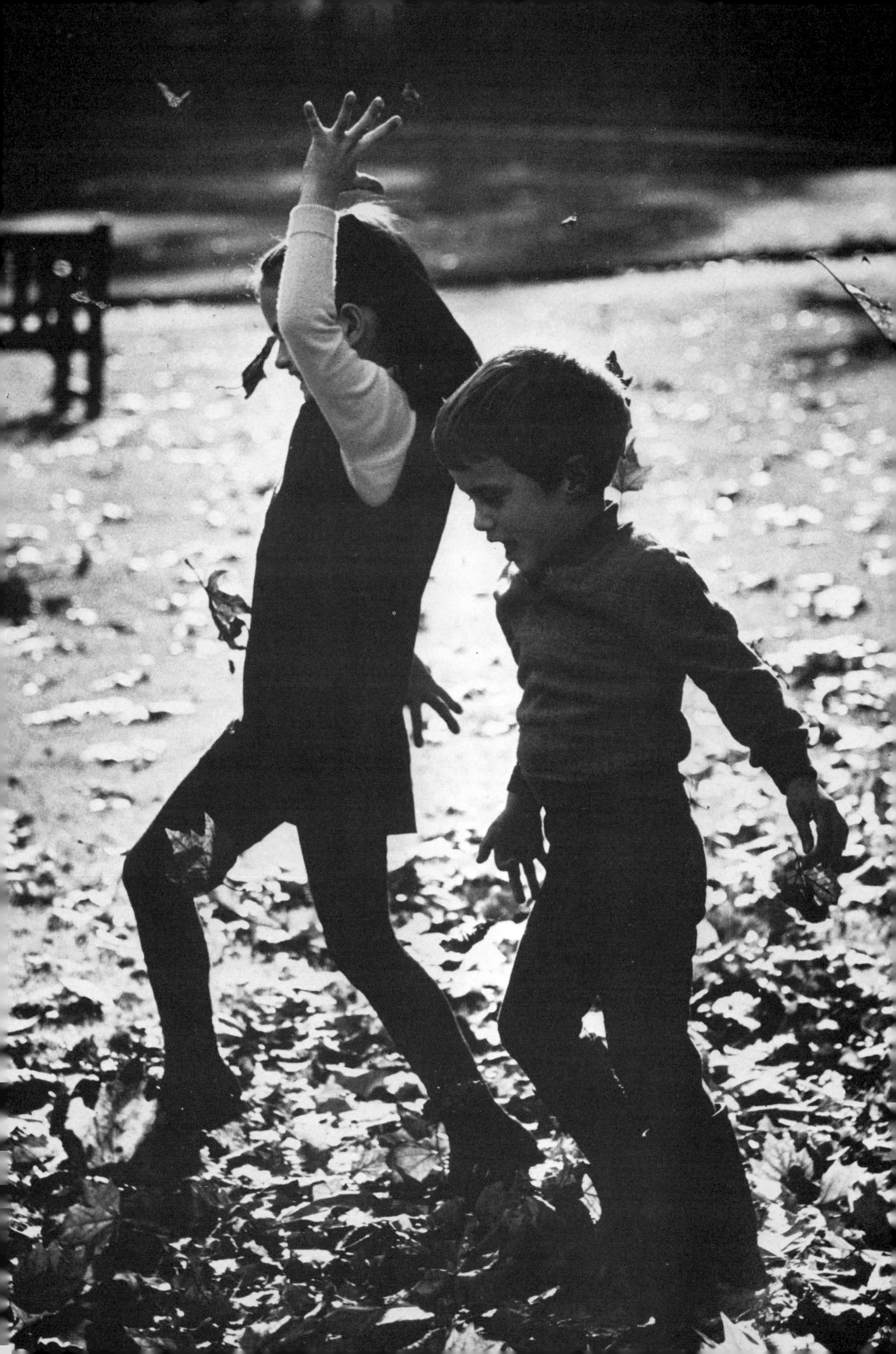

No kidding with ads

One market not yet discussed is the advertising market. You will have seen hundreds of advertisements featuring children modelling clothes, or playing with a particular firm's toy, but the chances of a budding freelance getting a commission for this type of work are rather slim. Manufacturers usually use the services of an advertising agent whose job it is either to specially commission a photographer, or more likely, to look through the files of several photo agencies for a likely picture to fit into his ideas for an advertising campaign.

Take careful aim

I think I have probably made it abundantly clear that regardless of the market you are aiming at, pretty pictures and portraits of children are out, whilst situation shots are in. But I must also stress again that when you are involved in a shooting session with children, you *must* have a clear idea of the particular market you are aiming for, and shoot accordingly.

CASH FROM CURIOSITIES

by Raymond Lea If you're an observant photographer, you can find curiosities everywhere. The author of this chapter has achieved considerable success selling pictures of everyday curiosities to publications such as *Country Life, This England, The Lady, The Field*, and many others.

Curiosity, 'tis said, killed the cat, but it is a very healthy characteristic for a photographer, particularly if he or she wishes to make some money from their hobby. There are so many ways of going about this, but one of the simplest and potentially quickest to reward is to photograph anything you come across which has curiosity value, and might therefore appeal to several of the papers and magazines open to this kind of material.

Photographing curiosities found in town and country within the U.K., and submitting them to such magazines as *The Field, Country Life*, county and gardening magazines, has been going on for so long you might well think that all possibilities had been exhausted by now. But the correspondence columns of these and many other publications continue to use numerous examples weekly and monthly throughout the year, paying useful fees ranging up to £15 or more. So there is no reason why you should not have some success. Of course, it can depend upon where you live. For example, town dwellers with little access to the countryside are less likely to find subjects suitable for country magazines, but there are plenty of oddities in most towns if you keep a keen lookout and know what to go for.

Curiously, the list is endless . . .

So, what are these curios? Well, their range is very wide and the best way to discover what is acceptable is to look through as many magazines as possible. But a typical list would include anything unusual in building design (in churches, farm structures, windmills, dovecotes, cottages and houses and so on); odd signs of the direction, inn and advertising variety; odd memorials; strange growth of plants and trees including topiary; birds nesting in unusual places; wells; pumps; stocks; clocks; artefacts made of wood, stone or metal; thatching; etc., etc. The list really is endless because this country remains so very rich in relics of the past, and there are also constant changes going on.

Thus it is worth photographing churches and schools which become redundant, chapels, barns and other utility structures which are turned into dwellings; buildings and landmarks which are threatened in some way or else are restored; old farm machinery which is put on display (very often at the

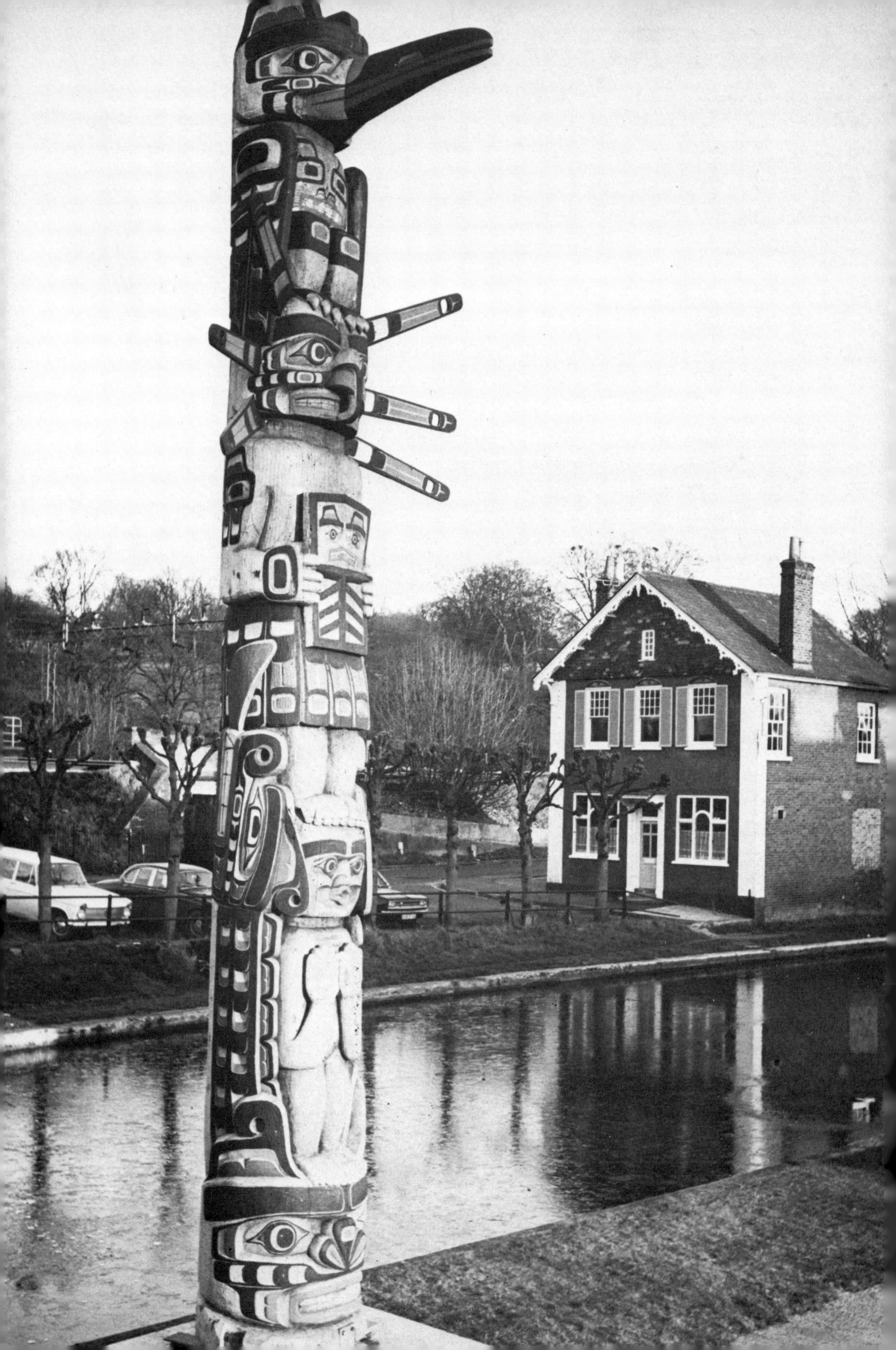

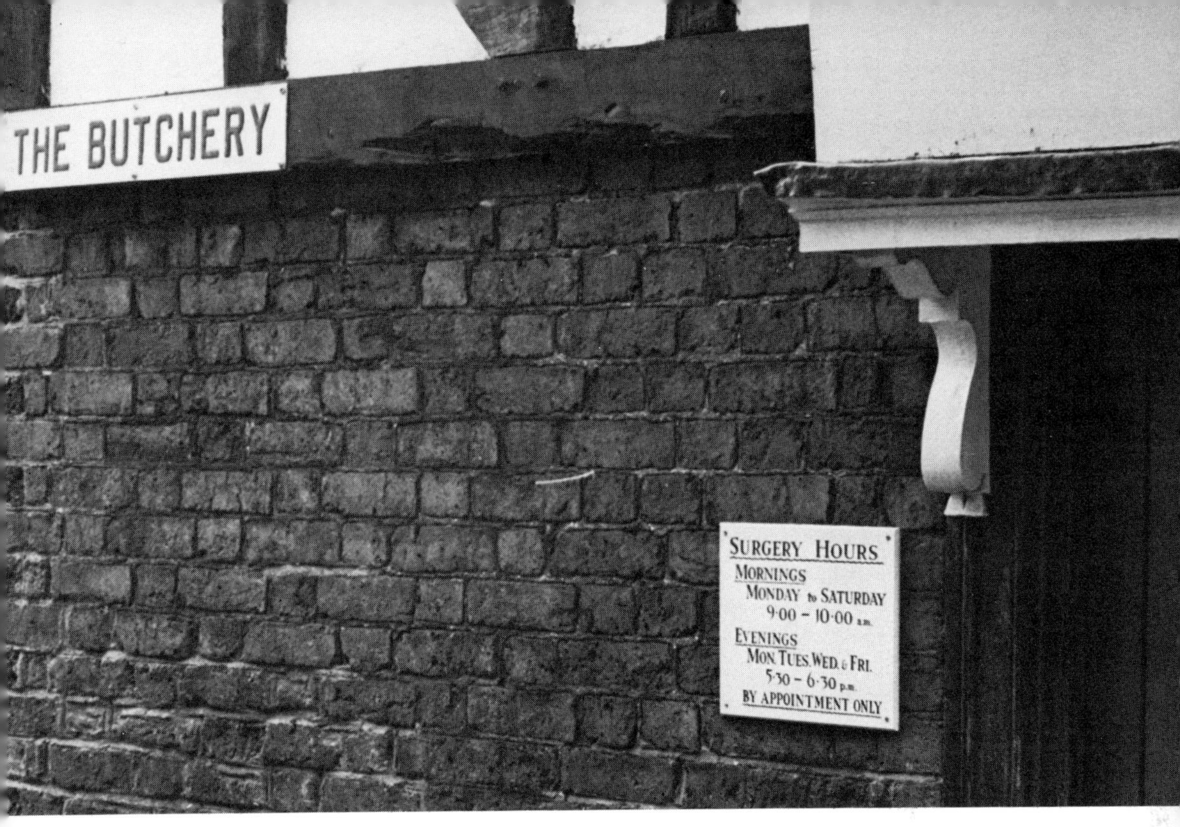

This example of 'accidental humour', spotted by L. A. Lunnon, has sold to *General Practitioner*, *Hospital Life*, *Nursing Mirror*, *Homemaker*, *Kent Life* and *Meat Trader*.

roadside); old carts and other unlikely objects which are used for planting flowers. There really is no end to the list of odd and unusual subjects which can be caught with your camera and sold to various outlets.

For example . . .

My list of successes over the past year includes new sails on a windmill, another that is being renovated, an albino sparrow (pure white) which visits my garden, a restored brick kiln, a dovecote made into a home, a village seat carved from an elm trunk, a corn exchange being turned into a theatre, a hedge with a gateway

This extraordinary totem pole – photographed by Raymond Lea – stands beside the Grand Union Canal at Berkhamstead. The picture has been published in *This England*, *Hertfordshire Countryside*, *Country Life*, *The Lady* and *Canal & Riverboat*. There are numerous markets for curiosities of this type, and this picture is likely to go on pulling in fees for many years to come.

cut into it (forming an arch), an unusual lodge, a resited Victorian drinking fountain and a set of weathervanes.

Obviously it helps in finding such a range of subjects if one can travel around a bit, but all these were obtained within an hour's drive of my home, as have been most of the hundreds of other examples I have had in print. And a good point about such pictures is that they can sell several, even many, times, just so long as you submit them to only one similar market at a time. If, for instance, the same picture or subject, taken from a slightly different angle, appeared close together in both *The Field* and *Country Life* from the same person, it would not go down very well. But you can certainly submit to another magazine after some months have elapsed. I have had pictures published up to 20 times because they appealed not only to country magazines but also to gardening and farming journals, specialist magazines and weekly newspapers. And many an odd picture gets into the photographic press!

Oddities in daily life

Indeed, there is another slant to this territory for the freelance, for there are many other oddities to be found in daily life which are worth photographing and submitting to the right markets. Very often they are a result of someone wishing to express themselves, such as a Dormobile which I photographed that has been covered with paintings in the style of a canal boat. I have also sold photographs of a scooter sprouting no less than 17 rearview mirrors, two Renault 4 cars that had been joined back to back to make one very long and puzzling vehicle (the picture is shown here); a Rolls Royce covered with advertising slogans and pictures (is nothing sacred?), and a clever collection of water driven models in a stream beside a country cottage.

Animals, loos and vicars

Then there are the 'funnies', such as a shot I have of a loo pan placed on top of an S bend road sign, and another sign in a churchyard which reads 'Reserved for Vicar'. It actually refers to car parking space, but I angled the shot so that there are only graves in the background and the sign takes on quite another meaning! Animals, too, can contribute some amusing, valuable material like the cat I photographed rubbing its chin on a 'Keep off the Grass' sign in Windsor Castle (published 6 times so far). Pictures like these are often kept on file by picture editors in case something turns up with which they can be paired, or else they contrive a suitably witty caption for use as a single.

Curiosities need captions

Captions are vitally important. For letters columns, of course, you have to write a letter providing concise but accurate details of location, origin, name(s) of creator, and history. Your reason for submission can be just the fact that it is unusual, or that the subject is in danger of being destroyed, or is to be repaired and re-used. Put relevant facts on the back of the print also (including your own name and address) and on pictures submitted without letters.

Be creative when you can

On the face of it, photographing curiosities might seem to be a pretty mundane use of your photographic skills, simply using your camera to record rather than to interpret and create interesting pictures. Well, it does depend to some extent upon the subject and the available lighting. For example, whereas on a dull day you might find your creative photography rather limited, it could still be

Raymond Lea's picture of the unique topiary chess set in the gardens of Haseley Court, Oxfordshire, has appeared in *Country Life*, *The Field*, *Amateur Gardening* and *Buckinghamshire Countryside*.

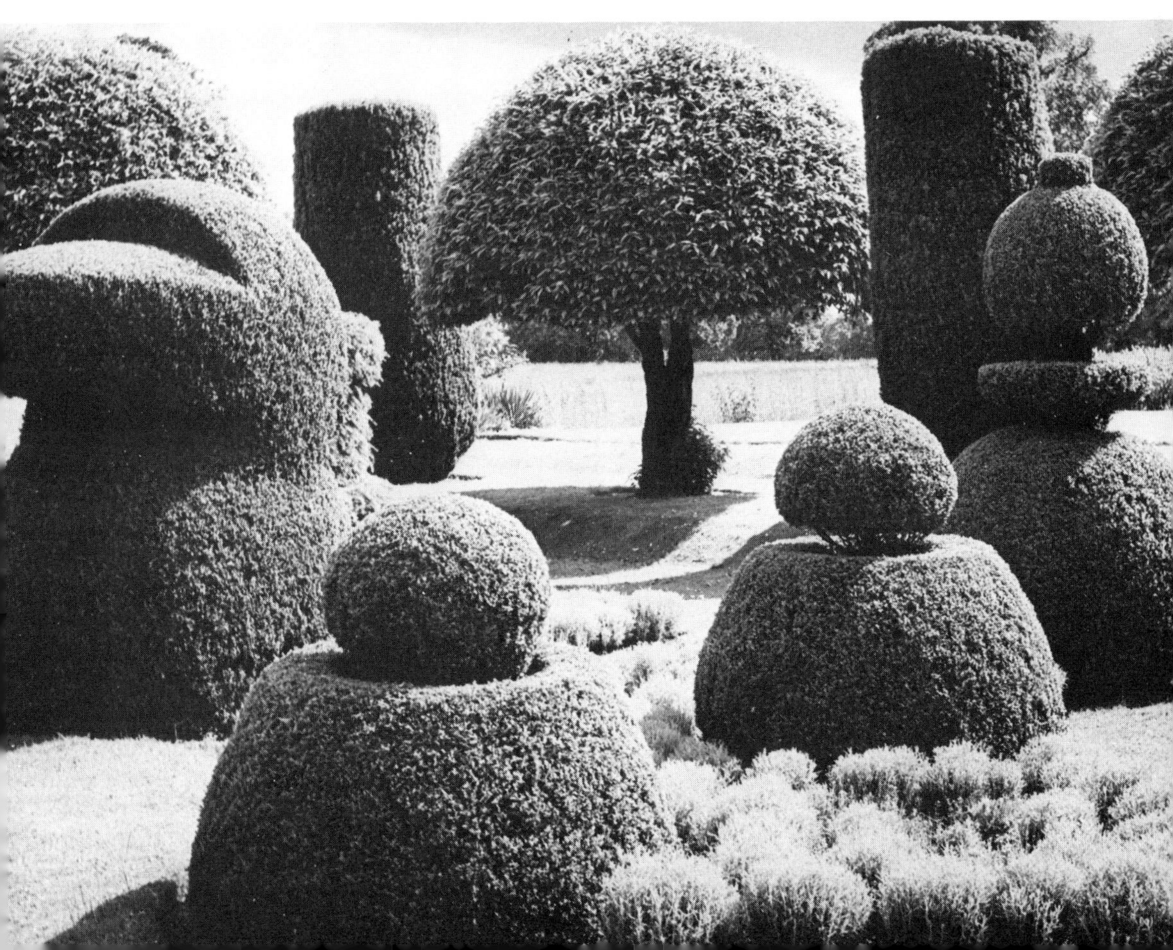

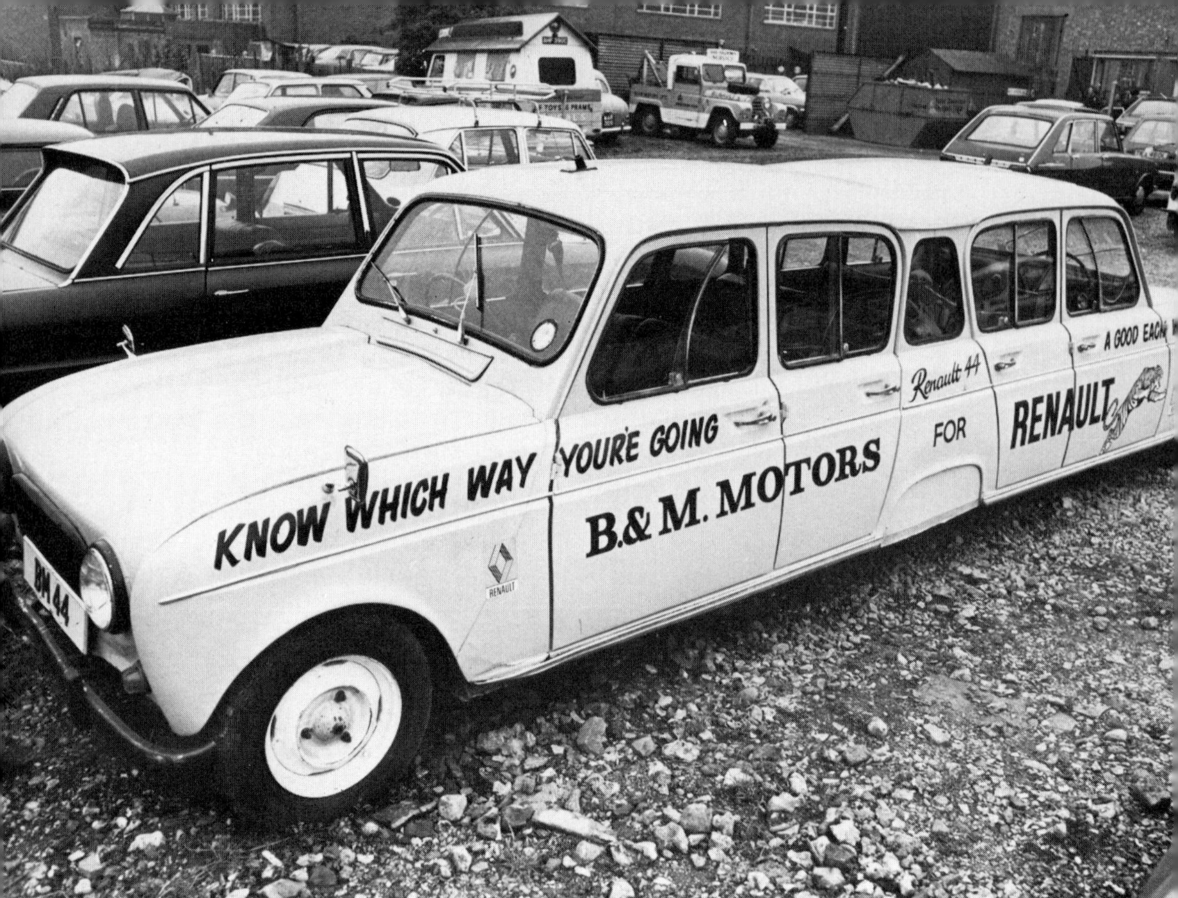

A rather startling sight for any pedestrian who may have had one over the eight! Raymond Lea's picture of this extra-ordinary double car has appeared in *Autocar* and *Amateur Photographer*.

possible to photograph any unusual subject you come across, even if the result is no more than a record. If the picture is a good one for the markets available, it will surely sell.

But when you are lucky enough to come across curios in good lighting conditions, make the most of them. Black and white pictures are invariably improved if the light comes from the side, so whenever possible shoot your subject – whether it be a block of almshouses, an ancient wellhead, a folly or a newly thatched roof – from a position which provides side lighting to pick out textures, and generally bring a feeling of life, depth and contrast to the result. Side lighting will enhance the features of a statue, for example, just as well as in portraiture, and you can also try shooting suitable subjects (such as monuments, strangely shaped trees, towers etc) against the light for a silhouette effect.

Shoot from several viewpoints

It is always a good idea, when possible, to photograph a subject from several viewpoints, since this will give greater flexibility when submitting to different markets. By really taking care over the way in which you photograph curiosities it is quite possible to produce excellent pictures which can stand a chance in competitions and as file pictures for the photo press, so do not dismiss this type of photography as being uncreative and hardly worth your attention.

A word about equipment

It is a happy aspect of photographing these curio subjects that very many can be taken quite adequately with a standard lens, either the type fitted to most SLRs or the slightly wide-angle variety found on compacts. If your technique is good and you produce really sharp negatives there is no reason why you should not obtain high quality whole-plate prints from less than half the negative area, which adds flexibility for taking quite small objects and those which are a little distant. A wide-angle of the 28mm type has its uses, especially when you cannot stand very far back from a subject, and a telephoto is necessary for picking out interesting details in buildings, for odd chimneys, weathervanes, clocks etc. Anything, in fact which cannot be approached close-to. In lieu of a telephoto lens you can hope for acceptable results matching a good SLR standard lens with a converter, giving a useful 100mm or so.

Alas, the tax man will be curious

One point to remember is that whilst you are allowed to submit for publication anything which you can photograph whilst standing on the public highway, you must not enter onto private ground to collect subjects. And, alas, fees received for the pictures you sell should be declared on your tax form! Above all, though, keep your eyes open, use your imagination and study the pictures that are published. Very often you can make a sale by following up someone else's picture with one of your own that makes an interesting comparison.

6

TRAVEL PHOTOGRAPHY
1: The Market

by John Tracy   If you're a keen traveller, keep your seat belt fastened for the next two chapters; this one considers the market for travel pictures while in the following one, Dennis Mansell outlines his personal approach to the subject.

The rapid expansion of the package holiday business in the past decade has resulted in a big demand for travel pictures. Every year, all the package tour companies need new pictures for their brochures. And with most operators now producing two brochures a year – one for summer and one for winter – the demand for pictures is greater than ever.

Competition between the various tour operators is also keener than it has ever been – and the wise operator appreciates the importance of good photography in selling his wares. He knows that it can make the difference between selling his full schedule of holidays or losing out to a competitor.

While some tour operators commission all their photography, most obtain their pictures from freelance photographers, mainly through picture libraries.

So what type of pictures do the tour companies want? Well, first and foremost, they want pictures of the areas they cover! This may seem obvious, but I have heard several operators complain of receiving pictures of parts of the world which are not covered in their holiday operations! So that is the first point to consider. Don't send a selection of pictures of, say, Albania to a company that doesn't cover that part of the world. (Actually, you can easily avoid that particular mistake by selling your pictures through a library – but more about that in a moment.)

Shoot pictures to sell holidays

The next step is to think carefully about the purpose of the photographs that appear in holiday brochures. Obviously, their main purpose must be to *sell holidays!* If you study the brochures put out by holiday companies carefully, you will soon see the types of pictures that are favoured. Since most people's idea of a good holiday is lazing around on a beach for two or three weeks, holiday brochures invariably include numerous beach scenes. Apart from those companies that specialise in particular age groups, or categories of holidaymakers (such as 'singles' and retired people), tour operators generally look for beach scenes depicting young couples and young families. But make sure that your

This picture, reproduced from a colour transparency, was shot by Dennis Mansell for travel brochure use. It depicts Golden Bay, Malta.

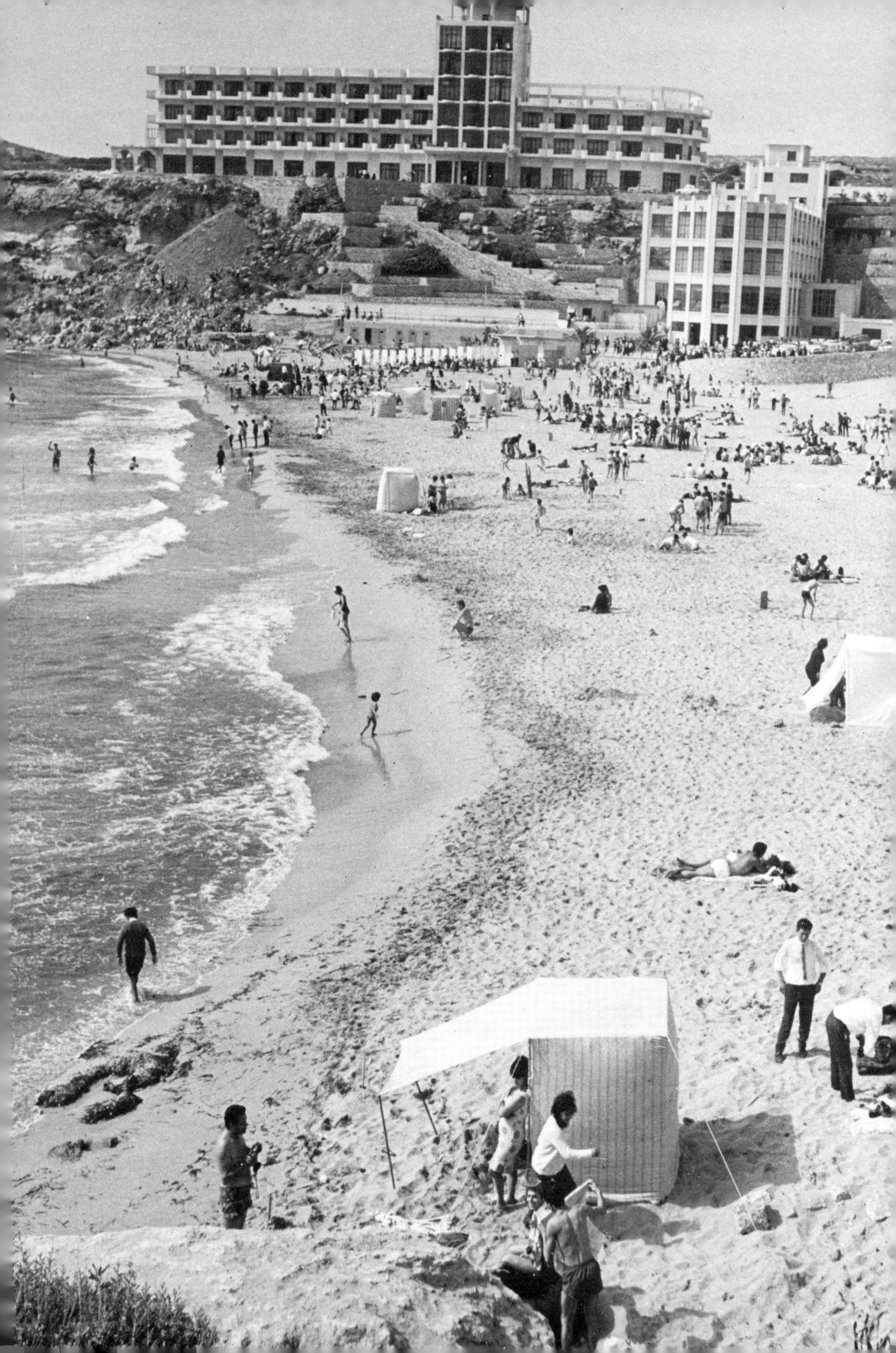

subjects are nicely sun-tanned! There's also a big market here for glamour shots, depicting attractive bikini-clad girls soaking up the sun.

Of course, not everyone spends their entire holiday on a beach, so there is also a market here for more 'creative' photography. Local views and local happenings photographed in an original way are likely to be snapped up by weary art editors tired of seeing the same old hackneyed scenes.

It is also probably true to say that the more exotic and far-away holiday resorts present greater photographic possibilities to the creative freelance hoping to sell to the holiday brochure market. After all, holidaymakers setting their sights further afield than Majorca and similar resorts want to see pictures which will give them an idea of what they may expect from a holiday in a far-flung land. Mind you, even tour operators specialising in more exotic places such as South America and the Far East, still tend to include a fair sprinkling of beach scenes in their brochures.

Approaching the market

So how does the photographer approach the market? Well, by far the simplest – and many would say the best – method is to place your travel material with one of the picture libraries. Although most libraries take 50% commission, tour operators invariably approach them first when looking for new pictures each year. Additionally, the good library will make sure that your pictures do the rounds of all the operators likely to be interested.

If you prefer to approach the market direct, you should simply send a list of the subjects you have available to the various tour companies, together with a few samples.

Other markets for travel pix

But of course, the holiday brochure market isn't the only outlet for travel pictures. There are any number of magazines publishing travel material. These publications are always interested in hearing from photographers who have a good selection of travel shots. But it's the photographer who can produce a complete travel 'package' who scores here. Editors are always in the market for 'travelogues' – well written and well illustrated features on life in other lands. This is an entirely different area from the travel brochure market. Although each publication has different requirements, generally speaking editors look for features that take the reader behind the scenes, that show how life is lived outside the tourist areas.

The restful, away-from-it-all quality of this picture makes it an ideal illustration for general travel features as well as holiday brochures. Picture by Dennis Mansell.

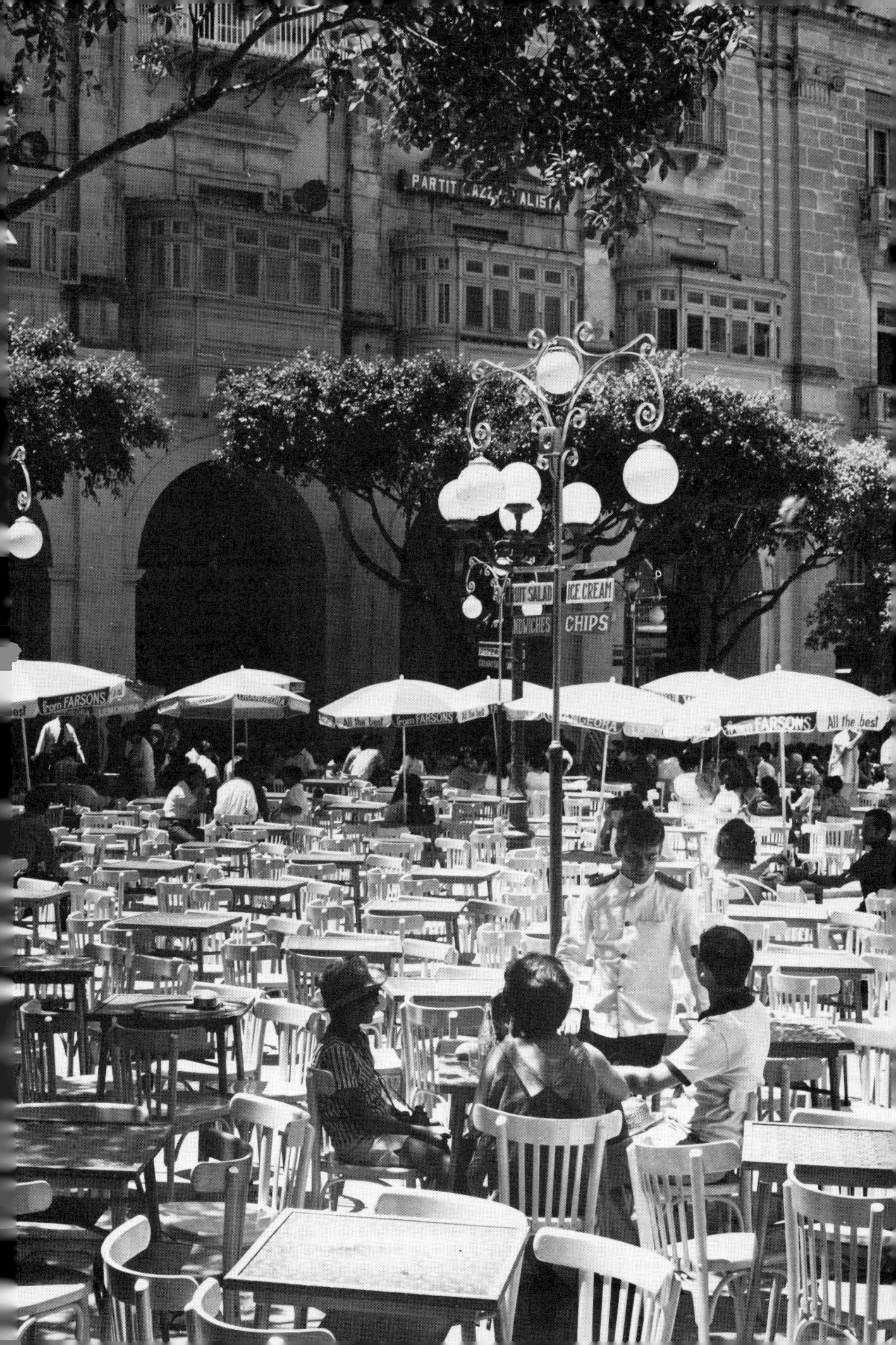

PARTIT LAZZARIALISTA
FRUIT SALAD
ICE CREAM
SANDWICHES
CHIPS
PIZZA
from FARSONS
LEMON
ORANGEORA
All the best

Of course, the posh Sundays frequently run features for the more sophisticated tourist, and the colour supplements offer a lucrative outlet for the well-produced travelogue, but these tend to be produced on assignment by 'name' photographers and writers.

Formats and equipment

The travel market is one field where the 35mm transparency has gained almost universal acceptance, with virtually all tour operators accepting this format for their brochures. Similarly, nearly all national publications which run travel features will accept 35mm although some do still prefer larger formats. The important thing is to ensure that the transparencies you submit are pin-sharp and have good colour saturation. But, as Dennis Mansell makes clear in the following chapter, saleable travel pictures can be taken with virtually any type of camera, using only the standard lens.

Nevertheless, aspiring travel photographers often make the mistake of lugging far too much equipment with them, with the result that they spend too much time fiddling with accessories and too little time taking pictures. This can also result in a lack of spontaneity in the pictures. The rule is: take only as much equipment as you need to produce the goods.

But whatever camera and equipment you use, do make sure you are thoroughly familiar with it before taking it on a trip abroad. I write here from bitter personal experience. On a recent trip, I borrowed a colleague's camera as my own was out of commission. I have to admit that I didn't take sufficient time before the trip to familiarise myself with the camera, and the pictures I brought back certainly reflected this. We learn from our mistakes!

We've said it before

Finally I make no apology for offering a piece of advice which you will find repeated elsewhere in this book and in many other books and articles on freelancing. It's this: you must study the market. If you aim to sell pictures to the travel brochure market, get your hands on as many brochures as possible – even if your travel agent does give you an old-fashioned look! Study the type of pictures preferred by the different operators.

The same applies to the photo-journalist who aims to sell travel features. Decide the magazine you want to sell to, and research it thoroughly. Study several issues; note the average length of travel articles, the number of illustrations used, and the writing style.

The travel market is highly competitive, and only by getting to know it thoroughly can you hope to achieve real success.

2: Don't Forget the Faces

by Dennis Mansell   The author's world-wide travel pictures have appeared in a wide variety of publications. Here he reminds us 'not to forget the faces when shooting places'.

Every freelance on a trip abroad will make sure he photographs all the major tourist attractions of the area – but many ignore the local people completely.

This is a great mistake, as there is a large market for people shown in their own environment. Pictures of this type are particularly in demand by newspapers and magazines to illustrate travel features. Whereas travel brochures will mainly want to show the physical characteristics of the resort, the press want photographs that capture the atmosphere, and usually human activity will do this.

People at work

Apart from the press, there is a constant demand from the publishers of books and encyclopaedias for pictures that show the working life of peoples in different countries. The easiest way for a tourist to get this type of picture is to hire a car and drive out into the country, where there is almost certain to be some form of agricultural activity taking place. Country people are usually friendly towards strangers, and will not object to being photographed if approached in the same spirit of friendliness.

It is perhaps the natural reluctance to intrude on a complete stranger by pointing a camera at close range, that puts most tourists off taking this type of photograph. There can be no hard and fast rule on overcoming this reluctance, apart from applying normal good manners and common sense. If in doubt – don't! I have followed this advice for a number of years without any trouble; in fact, in many cases I have chatted to my subject after taking a photograph and walked away later feeling I had left an old friend.

Be ready for action

A keen freelance will want to take enough equipment to ensure that he is covered for most eventualities. Don't overdo this however, and end up laden like a pack horse. For most subjects, saleable pictures can be taken with almost any type of camera, using only the standard lens.

Whatever equipment you do take, make sure that you have one camera with

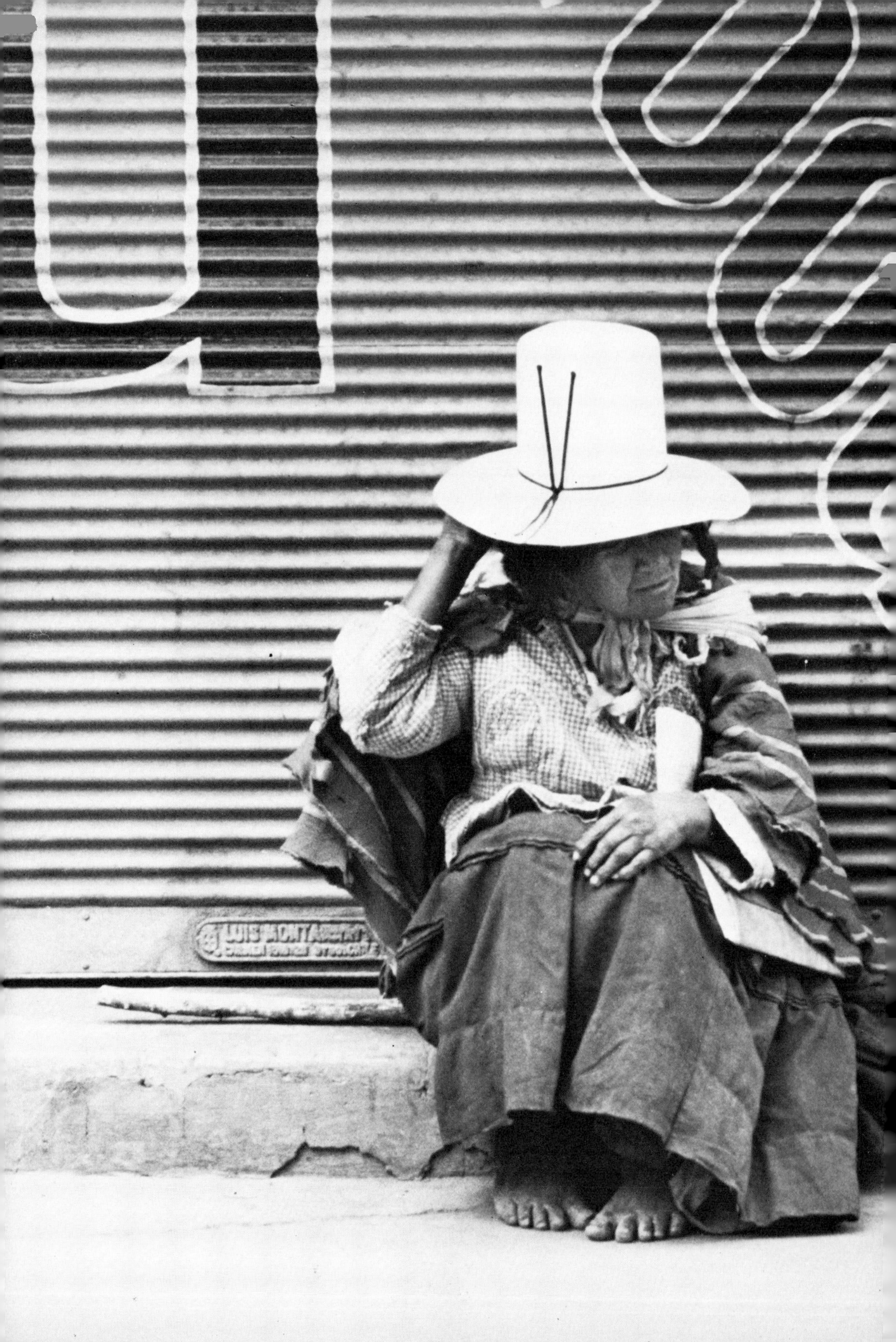

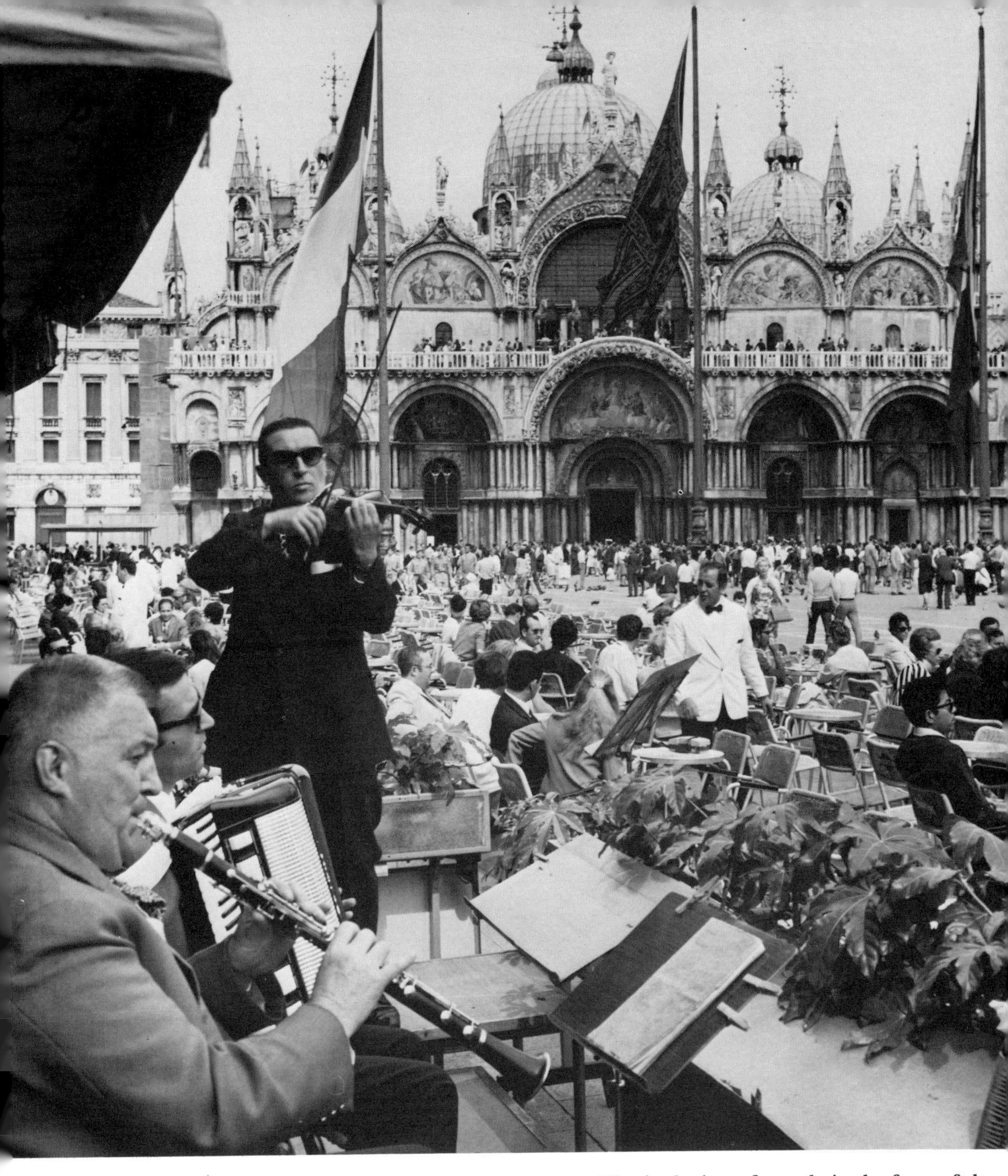

The inclusion of people in the form of the band in the foreground has made this shot of St. Mark's Square, Venice, much more saleable. It was first used as a cover on *The Lady*, and has since sold several times in this country and the United States. Picture by Dennis Mansell.

Capturing the atmosphere. Pictures of local people are often used in travel features and holiday brochures in order to capture the atmosphere of the place. This picture, by Conal Gannon, has been published in *Signature*, the magazine of the Diner's Club.

you at all times – the best pictures present themselves when least expected. In my own case when my Hasselblad equipment has been left at the hotel, I always carry an old Voigtlander Vito camera. This is a folding 35mm camera and really is compact, being easily carried in a pocket – or my wife's handbag if she doesn't notice it! Loaded with HP5 or Tri-X, it is normally set at f11 or f16, at 1/300 sec., focused at 12 feet, and can be used in seconds.

Many of the best subjects are found in a crowded city, a busy market, a street carnival or a sporting event. For these, a wide angle lens enables the photographer to get right into the crowd and capture the excitement.

Using wide angle lenses does mean working very close to the subject, with the result that they are more likely to be aware of the camera – and you. If you don't like this face to face involvement with strangers, then use a telephoto lens. A medium telephoto lens will give intimate results, with the photographer reasonably detached from the scene.

Posing problems

Generally there are two ways to photograph people; either to wait until the subject composes into the desired picture, or to get directly involved and pose the subjects. usually those taken without the subjects' knowledge are best, as often they become stiff and self-conscious when asked to pose. One way of overcoming this with a posed picture, is to take one and quickly wind on while offering your thanks and at the same time take another shot, which will usually be much more relaxed. One advantage of posing is that you know for sure that your subject has no objection to being photographed and will not cause embarrassment by creating a scene in protest.

However proficient you become at taking pictures unobtrusively, sooner or later some form of payment will be demanded for a photograph you have taken. Often a drink in a nearby bar will be sufficient, or if the subject is selling – the purchase of a bag of fruit or a small souvenir; but these are the exceptions, and normally a smile and a sincere thank you are all that is required. If you promise to send on prints, make this one of your first jobs when you get back home.

Although the wearing of national costume has disappeared from those areas visited by most tourists, they can often be seen during carnivals, religious festivals and other public celebrations. Apart from the colourful costumes, those wearing them are normally in high spirits and likely to respond favourably to the camera. It is quite easy to find out about these events, by enquiring at the hotel, the travel courier, or in many towns at the local tourist office.

So far in my travels I have not been to a country where there is a general reluctance to be photographed, which is the case in some parts of Africa and

Sponge Seller, Athens. This picture, by Dennis Mansell, has appeared in *The Observer*, *Woman's Weekly*, and various publications in South Africa, Holland, and the USA.

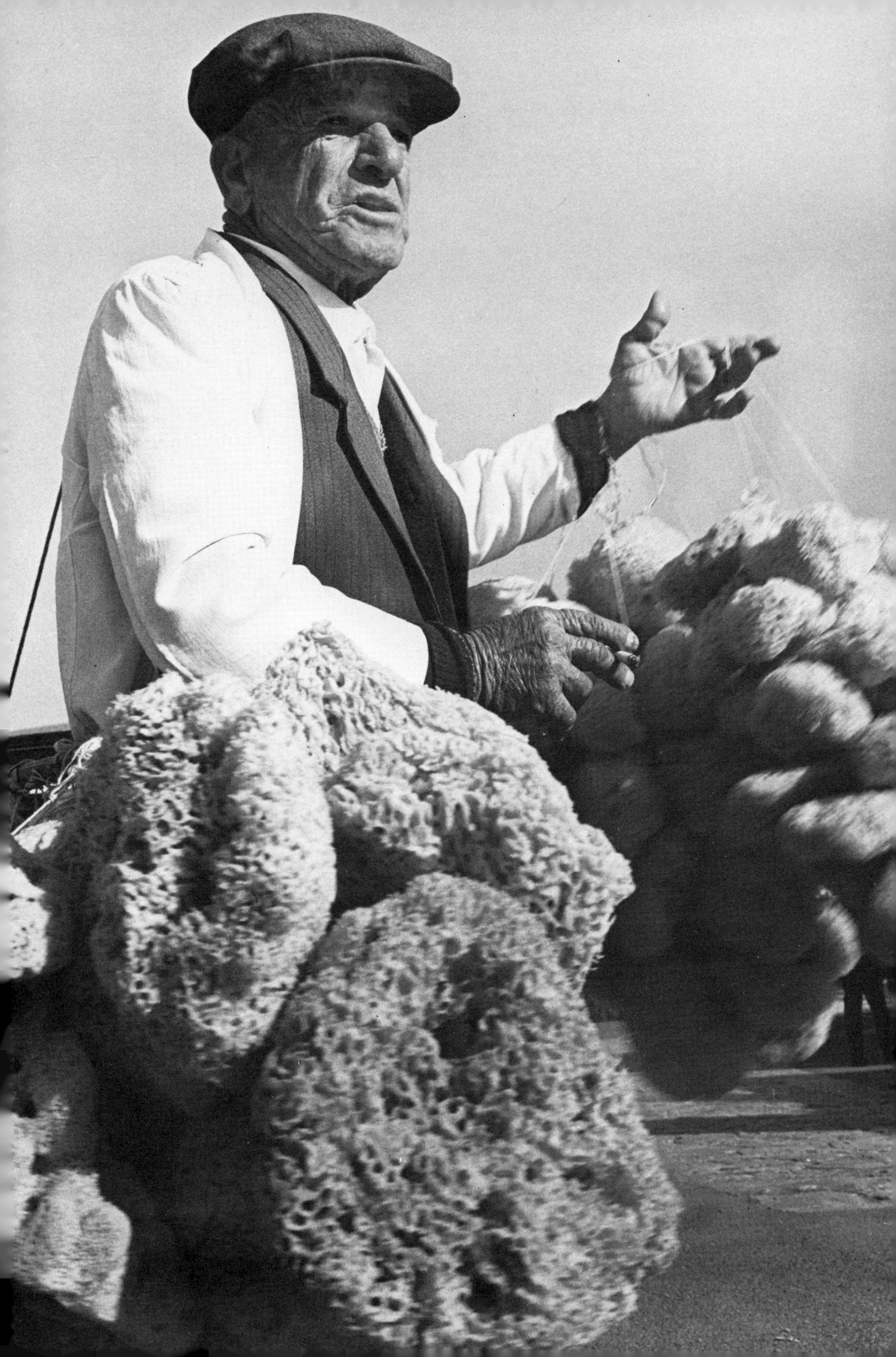

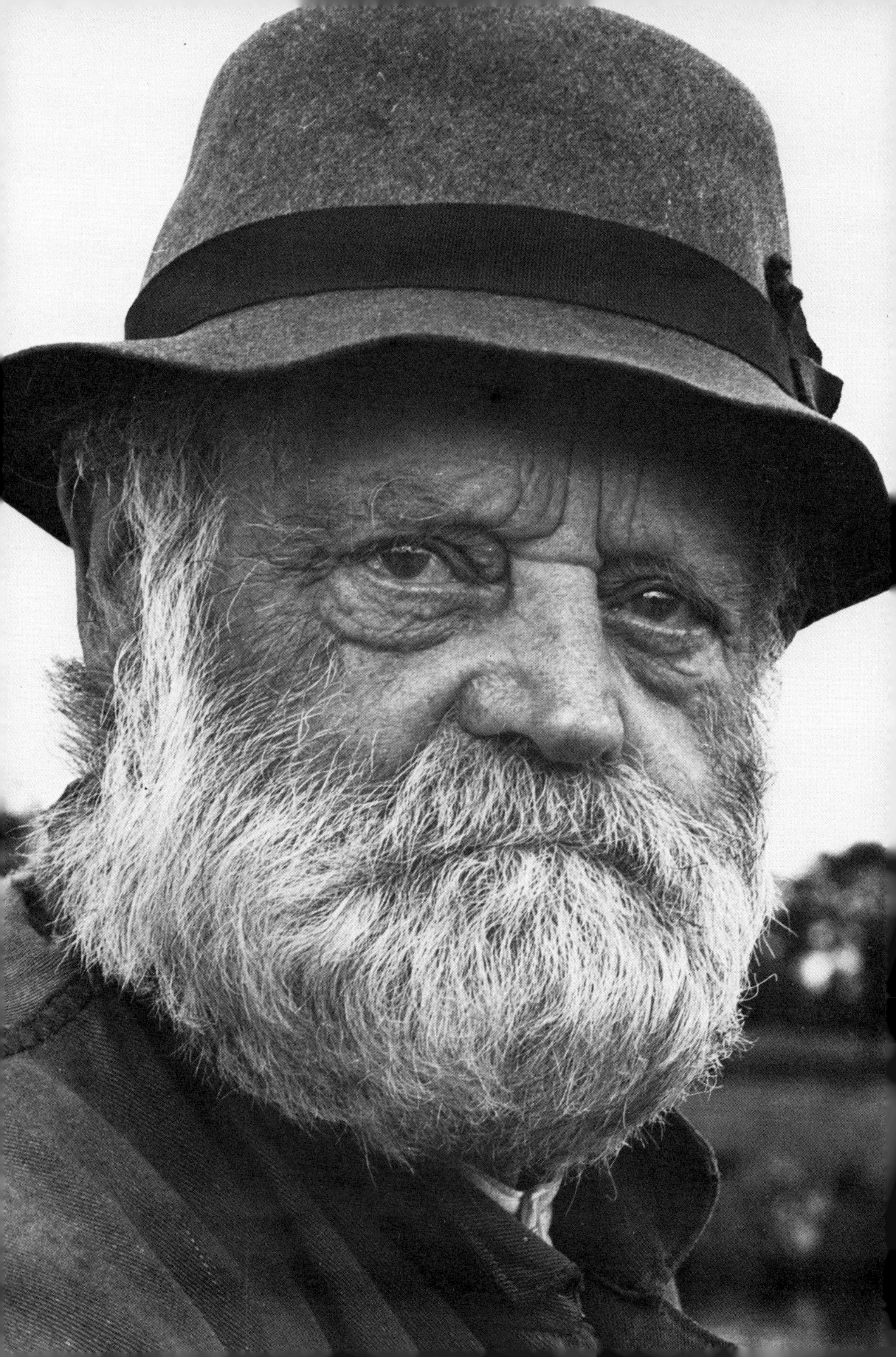

Asia, but obviously anyone travelling to the 'back of beyond' should be careful who they photograph. I play it safe by not pointing my camera at people who are obviously the worse for drink, and also avoid military personnel unless they are taking part in ceremonial duties, having no wish to spend part of my stay in the local jail.

Make the people pay!

Places, in the form of buildings, churches and scenery, will still provide the bulk of the subjects on your next trip, but try to include some faces – it could give a boost to your earnings.

Of course, you don't have to go abroad to shoot faces. This shot of the late Mr. Phillip Price, a retired Essex shepherd, has been used in many publications including *Farmer's Weekly*, *This England* and the London *Evening News*.

SHOOTING SALEABLE GLAMOUR

by Ralph Medland   The Glamour Market is very lucrative – and highly competitive. The photographer who discovered top model Jane Warner, and whose glamour pictures have appeared in the *Daily Star* and the *Daily Mirror* and in many other publications, outlines his approach to the subject. Illustrations by the author.

The dictionary definition of glamour is 'the supposed influence of a charm on the eyes, making them see things as fairer than they are.' Glamour photography is probably less easily defined. It can range from the all-revealing shots in 'girlie' magazines to pretty portraits on the covers of photographic publications; however, the common denominator is an attractive girl. The techniques used when taking glamour photographs for commercial purposes are varied, and often differ from the accepted ideas taught in photographic magazines.

Learning the game is best done by copying others. Yes, really! I used to take cuttings from newspapers and magazines – in fact I still do – building up a picture of each outlet's general style. Then I set about producing pictures that reflect this style. A professional photographer must be able to produce all types of work; not all markets want highly individual masterpieces. Every technique and style must be learnt if you are to survive in this highly competitive business.

Basic equipment and film

The correct equipment is essential, but each photographer has his or her own preferences. Personally, I prefer to use a 2¼'' square format camera for both black and white and colour work. However, 35mm colour transparencies are now accepted by all the major 'girlie' magazines. Any good camera capable of producing top quality, perfectly sharp results is suitable for glamour work.

Film stock should not present a problem since there is no point in going against the established and accepted standards. For 2¼'' square colour use Ektachrome 64. There is no difference between the 'amateur' and the professional stocks except the latter is sent out ready 'matured' and has to be used straight away or kept refrigerated, and is of course dearer. The reason for this is to ensure correct colour balance as Kodak intended, but the difference is not very critical and should not worry the glamour photographer. The main thing to watch is the batch numbers on the sides of the boxes; make sure that the

Sexy and provocative without being offensive, this is a glamour picture of the 'Page Three' variety. The model, Jane Warner, was discovered by the author and has since gone on to become one of the country's leading models.

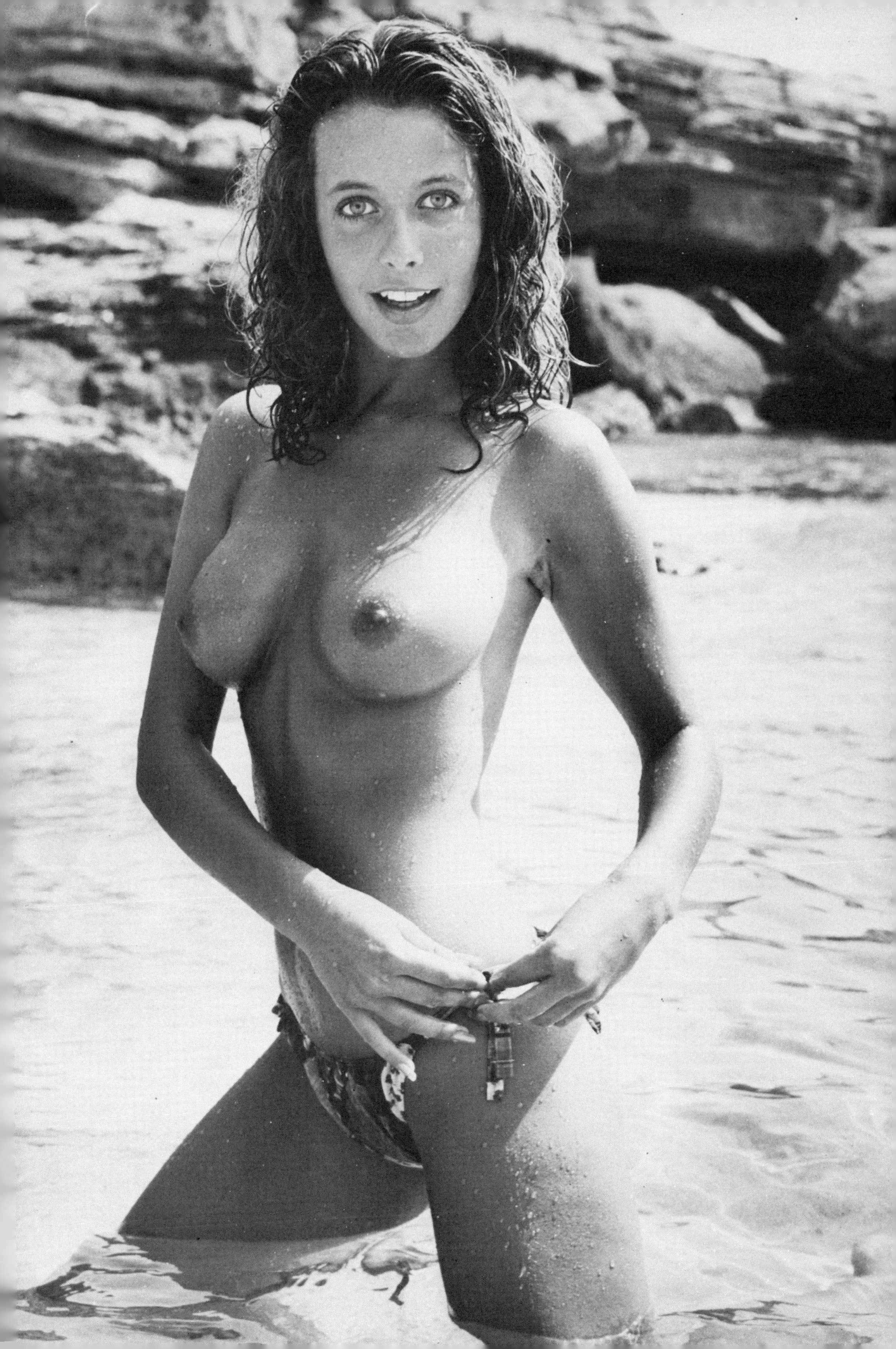

same batch number is used in any one setting, as there can be a slight colour shift from one batch to another. This may not be noticeable when looked at individually, but can be very evident if compared together. 35mm colour has to be Kodachrome 25 or 64 – those outlets that will accept 35mm will normally only do so if it is on these film stocks. The only exception is when grain is required for special effect. In these circumstances, the very fast films that are available can be used according to personal tastes, but do experiment first.

Black and white is very much a matter of personal choice; if you are using a black and white film and developer combination which gives good results, stick to it. If starting from scratch, I would advise a medium speed film such as FP4 or Plus-X developed in ID11 or D76 using the maker's suggested times. I prefer to dilute 1 + 1 using as a single shot developer and where the manufacturers give two development times (for different gammas), I use a time roughly half way between the two. This is fine for all general glamour work for magazine reproduction but if your sights are set on the national newspapers then a different technique is preferable. Newsprint is not capable of fine detail and glamour photos reproduce best when they have a biting crispness, but are *not too contrasty*. I have found the best way to achieve this is with slow speed film, Pan F or Panatomic X, coupled with fairly flat lighting and slight overdevelopment which gives good detail in the face and eyes, but is not too contrasty overall. This slow speed film also helps with making the giant enlargements required when submitting to this market, 20 x 16 in. being the order of the day!

The importance of lighting

Perhaps the most important aspect in glamour photography is the lighting. It is the lighting which depicts the mood, and the mood must suit the model and/or setting. As a generalisation, soft lighting is needed for romantic settings and sweet looking models, and hard lighting for raunchy, sexy looking models in the appropriate setting. When photographing nudes or partly dressed girls for glamour photography, it is important not to get confused with figure lighting. The latter attempts to depersonalise the model, whereas the object of glamour photography is quite the opposite.

In the studio, or anywhere indoors, there are basically two concepts; the natural room setting, and the obvious studio set with plain or contrived background. Build up the lighting one light at a time. Start with the main light, normally from the front, if necessary adding a second front light to lighten the shadows caused by the first, and possibly, a third light for effect. This last light can be a 'hair' light to edge-light the model in order to separate her from the background; alternatively it can be used to light the background. This basic set-up can be used with infinite variations far too numerous to mention, and in any case depend entirely on the merits of each situation and the photographer's own interpretation. The fill-in light can be replaced by a reflector board or sheet for economy, or even preference.

Studio set lighting can be exactly the same, the main thing to watch for here is shadows from the key light falling on the background. However, having said that, it is becoming increasingly popular for the shadow to be employed as part of the picture. A much used effect in the studio, particularly liked by newspaper photographers, is to place a light directly behind the model's hair to rim-light it. This is very effective when the model runs her hands through her hair or has a wind machine blowing her hair out. The latter item may be considered an expensive luxury, but can really pay off in producing very lively pictures.

There is one lighting set-up in the studio that is worthy of separate mention. This is used with the slow speed film and processing mentioned earlier. Have you ever noticed in the press how the models look like they have been drawn by an artist; the lighting looks flat and yet the edge line looks hard? This is done by lighting the model with two white umbrella reflectors at about 45° to the model in relation to the camera, and fairly close. The white background is at a suitable distance from the model so that the diffused shadows caused by the two umbrellas are out of the camera's view, or is lit separately. The effect can be pronounced by printing on grade 3 paper.

Outdoors the sun is your main light. If diffused by clouds, it is a simple matter of placing the model so that the sun is to the left or right of camera position behind the photographer. Again the background must not blend with the model; outdoors this is done by choosing a lighter or darker background. When the sun is blazing down, contrast is the major problem. Filling-in shadows can be achieved two ways, with flash or reflectors. The biggest drawback with flash is the recycling time, it slows the session down and this can make the model tense. It also leaves a hard shadow and looks a little unreal, so reflector boards or sheets are best. Boards are easier to set up and less affected by wind, but sheets are more portable; here, an assistant can be invaluable. Sometimes reflectors can be found 'in situ'; look out for large emulsion white buildings or white cliffs. A popular method at the moment is to place the model with the sun behind her and the reflector casting soft light onto her front. A suitable background must be used; if too light it will blend in with the model and not be separate from her. Harsh shadows can be used to advantage, particularly when a hard dramatic effect is required, but be certain the market you intend this type of work for will accept it; many will not.

Handling your model

The next problem is directing the model. The easiest answer when beginning is to use a professional model. She will know how to pose and have a good selection of props. However her fee will be high, her agent is unlikely to make a booking for her with an unknown photographer, and all markets will be flooded with pictures of her by established professionals. So an amateur model is really the most practical solution for the beginning glamour photographer. Do not ask an amateur model to start with standing poses; rather, get her to sit or kneel, and let her be natural but look out for rounded shoulders, bent backs and pro-truding tummies. Simple natural poses are what are required these days; therefore each individual pose should not present any difficulty. Direct the model from one pose to another by asking her to move one limb at a time. Also coax different expressions out of her. Very few models have a nice broad smile, but there is usually a very nice half smile which comes just as she relaxes the broad one, so watch out for this. A very popular look at the moment is the open-mouth expression; it is difficult to describe but it is almost a look of surprise. A check list of different poses or even a scrap book of cuttings is very useful and can be referred to throughout a session to prevent the flow drying up. If a girl has any aptitude for modelling she will soon start posing naturally.

One disadvantage of using an amateur model is that she is unlikely to have much of a glamour wardrobe. A professional model will turn up with about six skimpy bikinis, a selection of leotards; a dozen or so skimpy tops; some way-out high heeled shoes; a variety of scarves; necklaces; appropriate dresses; frilly panties and a host of other suitable accessories. The amateur will turn up with her one bikini bought for her Majorcan holiday last year; the evening dress she wears at her firm's social dance; a nightie she wears when Aunt & Uncle are staying; the panties she is wearing; and a necklace borrowed from Mum. It is therefore advisable to have some suitable items available, and this is where a wife, girlfriend, mother or sheer steel nerve comes in useful. You can get some very funny looks sifting through brief knickers in Miss Selfridge – unless of course you are a female glamour photographer! When buying for an unknown model, size could be a difficulty; fortunately most glamour models are about the same size, and if your chosen model is really suitable she will conform. With items that come in S, M & L buy the small size. In dress sizes 10 is the most common, and the average model is 34B-24-35. Height is less important but they usually range between 5'3'' and 5'6''. If your model varies in any way she will be slightly larger, but tight fitting clothes are an advantage in glamour photography.

Props and procedure

Props used by the photographer depend entirely on each session and the requirements of the end product. In a studio set-up, make sure that they are accessories to the picture and do not dominate. With natural room settings it is a matter of making sure the model and her outfit suit the mood of the setting. Once you have exhausted all possibilities in your own house, and friends' if you are lucky, then it becomes a matter of hiring locations, and this will set you back about £100 per day. It is therefore evident that ingenuity in altering your own home surroundings will pay dividends. As a general rule it is best to keep

A tasteful glamour shot of the type that might be used in a variety of newspapers and magazines.

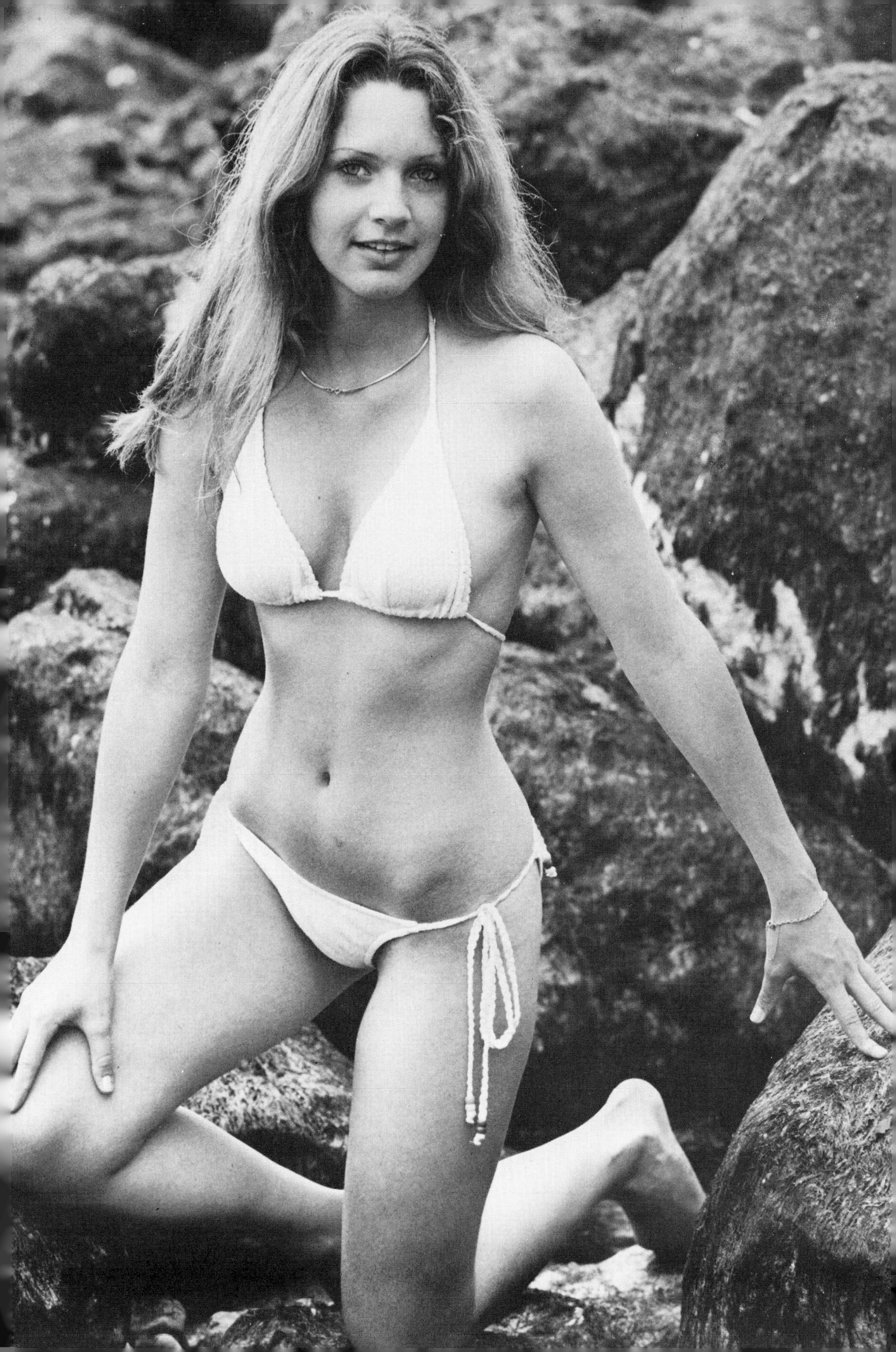

backgrounds and settings simple, avoiding clutter or 'overpowering' the model. One overriding factor will be the market for which the pictures are intended. The model/setting/lighting must be complementary to each other and the end result suitable for the market you are aiming at.

There are several factors which dictate the progress of a session. A photographer can work 'on spec' taking pictures to his or her own idea and then selling wherever possible. Alternatively he or she can be commissioned and be working directly to a client's specifications. In either case the final destination of the end result may well dictate the setting and subsequently the model used; or on the other hand a particular model can be selected first, and then the rest must be chosen to suit her. It is for this reason a professional glamour photographer must know all the basic techniques. In most glamour photography the girl's own image or personality is encouraged to come over in the pictures, but in certain advertising photos where glamour is used, the model's personal identity is lost and an image created totally orientated to the product. The model then has to be chosen on the basis that she can be transformed by make-up, lighting, etc. to suit the image required.

Commissioned work usually only comes after a photographer has proven ability, and this can only be gained by working initially on spec. Although this is less secure financially than working on commission, at least if a photograph turns out particularly well, it can be sold repeatedly with the remuneration coming to the photographer, whereas on commission the photographer settles for one fee.

Working on spec

To work successfully on spec it is necessary to be thoroughly organised. Research the possible markets, then organise the session as though you had been commissioned, the difference being that you will probably be shooting pictures for several possible outlets. Let us take a hypothetical situation: a general glamour session with a nice attractive model who has both face and figure going for her. A freelance photographer has to ensure he covers as many possible markets as he can, so he may well have a shooting sequence mapped out which might look something like this:

1. Head shots, plain background, large coloured sheet stretched on wall.
2. Head shots, plain background, sheet removed using plain beige wall.
3. Three-quarters and full length shots, french window background, some soft focus.
4. As above removing top clothing.
5. As 3 in bra and panties only.
6. Repeat 2 (beige wall) and 3 in panties only.
7. Nude against beige wall, using shawl loosely wrapped around hips.
8. Repeat above with light behind hair.

  9. Nude in french windows, using green plants in foreground.
  10. As above with soft focus, some demure not looking at camera.
  Shoot 1, 2 & 10 in colour only (also soft focus in colour only).
  Shoot rest in B/W & colour.

This is an abbreviated shooting plan based on the model changing clothes as little as possible, and the ability to move lighting quickly. With more complicated lighting and sets it would be rearranged, shooting one set at a time with the model changing clothes repeatedly. The sequence could be broadened to include more details concerning use of props and actual poses. You will notice the variety of work obtained. Magazine covers, sequences for glamour magazines, newspapers and calendar markets are all covered. There are a host of other possibilities.

Market research

The key to organising a session and working out a shooting sequence is market research. It is necessary to study several examples of each possible market, even contacting the picture editors concerned. Note the style used – most markets have a particular style and will not vary. For example the national newspapers use basically plain backgrounds, even outdoors; the poses are kept simple and not over sexy; and the pictures are cropped tight. One of the main complaints of editors is that submissions are unsuitable because they do not fit their style. This however does not mean that you should copy exactly what has been done before. The editor will want variety that fits in with the general pattern. Each magazine has its own individual 'feel'. Remove the title and you would probably still recognise it on the bookstands by its cover picture, layout and general style. To save wasting your time and money look for credit lines that crop up regularly in every issue. They are most likely staff or regularly commissioned freelance photographers, in which case occasional freelance submissions will automatically be rejected. Where the credit lines vary the chances are greater.

A good filing system is absolutely essential to aid the smooth running of a professional operation and to prevent duplication of submissions. In other words, the same or similar work must not be sent to competing markets, or a picture sent out as exclusive which has been published before. Submit prints and transparencies in a manner so that they can be unpackaged, viewed, then re-packaged with the minimum of fuss, and keep covering letters as brief as possible. Transparencies can be sent in sheet form or individually in neat black mounts, according to the number being sent. About five times the number expected to be published is the right amount to send. Where a single cover or B/W inside picture is used by a magazine send five or six pictures; where a magazine uses a spread of about ten pictures submit around fifty.

Sorting out pictures, typing letters, filing, cross-filing, subsequent re-filing etc is very time-consuming as is the matter of finding markets, and you may therefore consider an agency a worthwhile proposition. I deal direct with U.K. markets and have an agent in Germany and another in Spain for foreign sales. The problem with agencies is that they usually require a substantial amount of work from a new photographer before they will start dealing with him, and then it is necessary to keep up regular supplies. Also no payment is likely for at least six months, probably longer. The usual commission charged is 50%. On the plus side they will know markets you never knew existed, can sell the odd shot to some unusual places, and may even have some markets that deal with that agency exclusively and regularly.

Finding your model

Your stock in trade is models, and obtaining these is difficult until you are in a position to book professional models through agencies, and even then there are difficulties to start with. There are plenty of girls that want to be models, but very few have the right qualities required to produce saleable photos. I have always found the best local source for amateur models is beauty competitions. The only other method is the direct approach in the street or at a dance etc., but that is fraught with obvious problems, not a method I like. If a girl is suitable for sales to national magazines and is on the books of an agency, it will be a London one. Once you are established there is no problem, but if not, convincing the agent you are genuine is not so easy. In the first instance go along to the agent with your portfolio, including as many published pictures as possible, explain the type of work you want models for, and then expect to pay cash on the nail at the time of the booking. If your studio (your own or hired) is not in London you will also have to pay travelling expenses, which will include 50% modelling fees for the time the model spends travelling. Established photographers do not pay cash but sign the model's invoice book and settle monthly with the agent. Even then some of them go broke and models lose fees, so you can understand the agent's concern with new photographers.

Making your way

Whether working with amateur or professional models be sure to get a model release form signed; it is surprising what a model might object to at a later date. It is common practice with amateur, or part-time models to pay them a percentage of fees received, but this does present problems. It is likely to be at least three months before any fees are paid, and she may try to influence you as to which pictures are submitted and where, purely out of vanity. The ideal

Nowadays, most of the men's magazines published in Britain tend to go for glamour pictures of a rather explicit nature. The author, however, prefers to shoot pictures of a somewhat softer variety, like the one shown here.

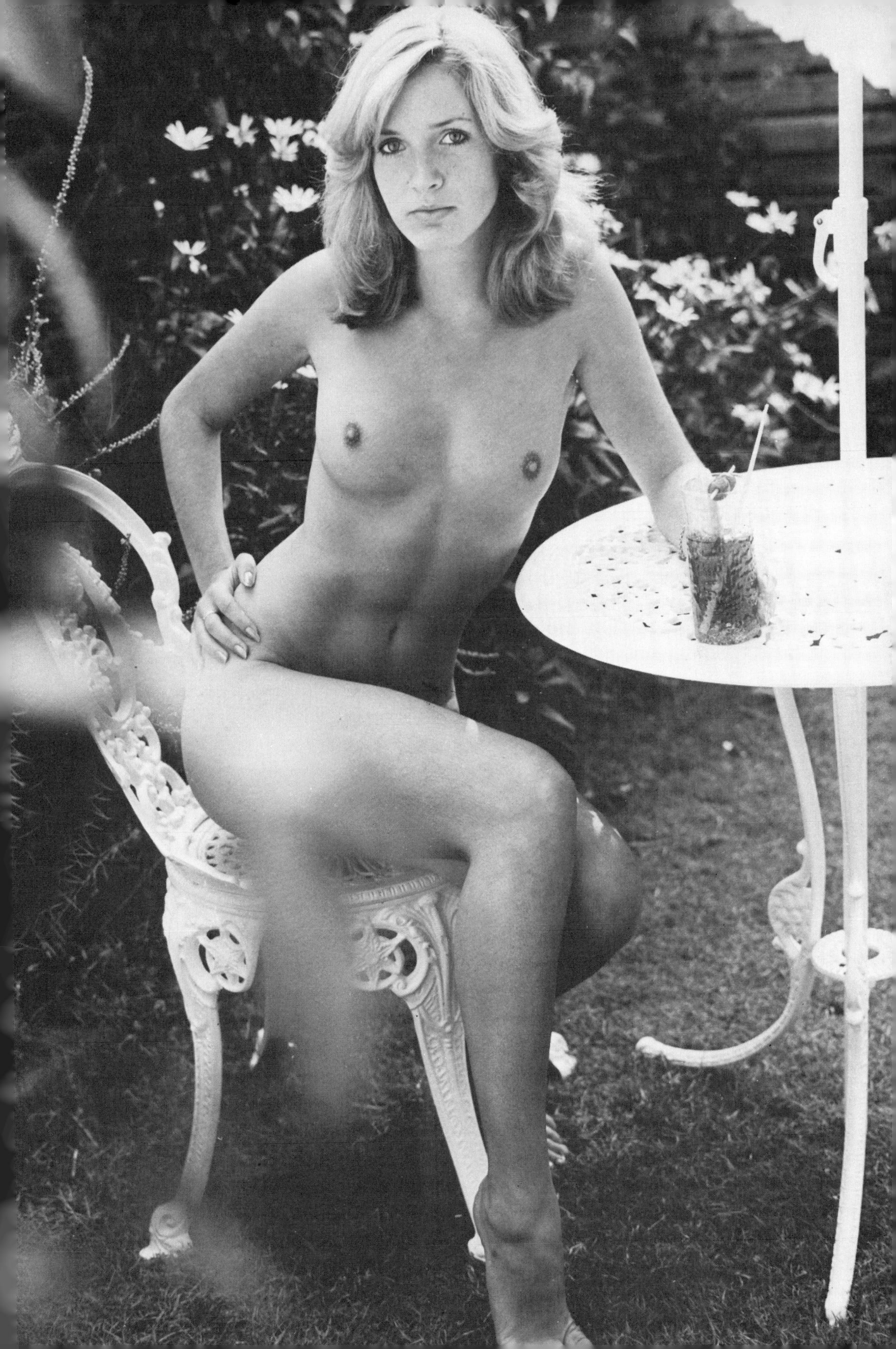

situation is to pay the standard going professional rate – then there are no problems. However, a photographer just starting a career cannot afford that sort of expense, particularly when he and the model are both unknown and the sales potential is that much less. Try to arrive at a figure that is reasonable to both you and the model, couple this with a few B/W prints from each session, and there should be no problem. It is not a bad idea to send prints to professional models as well. If your work is good they will welcome them, as they constantly need to update their portfolios and from time to time need pictures for their index cards. Surprisingly enough, professional models have difficulties in obtaining pictures from photographers, so if you can become known as a photographer who willingly supplies prints this can only be good.

Getting into the glamour photography business is not easy; in fact, it must be one of the toughest branches of photography. Going straight into the profession from school as an assistant or darkroom boy, learning the ropes, and most important making contacts, is by far the easiest. At that age living on the bread line can be fun, later on it is more difficult as responsibilities are taken on. I started selling pictures in my early twenties, learning by the 'suck it and see' method. In my efforts to get on I was drawn towards the shadier side of the business. This can easily happen and care should be taken; fortunately a quick think and a sharp turn around put me right.

My method of operation is simple. Find a market that appears to use freelance work and which I can tackle, take a series of photos that simulate the style and submit them. If rejected then study them in order to analyse why, and then repeat and re-submit. I keep this up all the time whilst I feel the market has freelance potential, or until there is an acceptance. Once a sale is made I can continue supplying at a rate which the outlet can use, and then start the procedure on another outlet. It is no good selling to a market, being satisfied, and then not following up.

Persistence pays off

Using the method just described, I have built up my markets and have had work published in the *Daily Mirror, Daily Star, Sun* (calendar), *Reveille, Stern, Amateur Photographer, Practical Photography* and many other magazines. Other outlets are puzzle magazine covers, holiday brochures, record sleeves, postcards and of course glamour magazines, the latter mostly abroad. It may seem unbelievable but Continental magazines require less explicit glamour work than their British counterparts. Of all the lessons I have learnt in ten odd years of selling photographs, there is one that overrides all others: constant study of the market coupled with sheer persistence pays dividends.

SELLING TO THE PHOTO PRESS

by John Wade   Who better than the editor of *Photography* magazine to show you how to produce material that the photographic press will buy . . .

Let's start by clearing up a few popular misconceptions. When I tell amateur photographers that they can write articles and take pictures for photographic magazines, there are a number of stock replies I have come to expect:–

'A beginner like me has no chance of being noticed among all the regular contributors who must be well known to editors.'

Wrong. Editors are always on the look-out for new talent. Photographic magazines have a ferocious appetite for features. Freelances who have been submitting work to the photo press for years have a habit of getting stale, running out of ideas, or quite simply giving up writing for that particular market. It is in an editor's best interests, then, to seek out and encourage new contributors. So don't worry about being a newcomer; you will stand as much chance of being accepted as the old hands provided you submit the right type of material.

'Editors must get hundreds of articles sent to them every day. I'm sure they end up with far more than they need.'

Wrong. Editors *do* get a lot of submissions, but very little of each morning's post will fit in with the style of their magazine, so it is quickly discarded. At *Photography* magazine, I probably buy no more than five per cent of all the articles that are submitted on spec.

But the contributors I do buy from, I buy from time and time again. And the vast majority of those contributors are amateurs. There's one very good reason why I buy their work so regularly: they are the people who have learnt to know what I am looking for. They provide it and I buy it. If you want to sell your work, not just to me, but to any photographic magazine editor, you must learn to do the same.

'I've already tried submitting an article to a magazine and they sent it straight back with nothing more than a printed rejection slip. They could at least have told me why they rejected my work.'

Wrong. Magazine editors are very busy people who have to keep to tight schedules. If they carefully analysed what was wrong with every article they rejected, they would inevitably end up spending more time dealing with rejections than with the work they actually accepted. It's not that they are rude, it's merely that they haven't the time.

The exception is when an editor receives an article which, although not quite right for his magazine as it stands, looks as though the contributor could turn out some suitable work with the right encouragement. In that case, an editor will often point the photographer briefly in the right direction and ask him or her to try again.

Start at the end!

So where do you start? The best place is at the end; with the magazine in which you would like to see your work published. It's the oldest trap in the world for an aspiring freelance to write an article or take a set of pictures and then look round for somewhere to sell his work. It's better by far to find the market first, then set out to write and illustrate an article aimed right at the heart of that market. That way, at least you are giving the editor the sort of material he wants. And with that, you are more than half-way there.

Study each magazine carefully, then choose the one you want to write for. Study that one in more depth. Get to know the sort of features they use, then find your own variation on their theme. Look to see which names appear regularly each month; these will be the regular contributors. From there, you can work out how much comes from general freelances such as yourself.

The biggest single problem any magazine editor has to suffer is lack of space. The more regular contributors, the less space is available for the general freelance. So you obviously stand less chance of selling to a magazine with a lot of contributors than to one with only a couple. Take all that into consideration before you even start to think about what you are going to write.

No need for good photographers!

Strange as it may at first seem, you don't have to be a good photographer to sell your work to a photographic magazine. If that sounds like a contradiction in terms, let me define what I mean by 'good'.

A good photographer, in this particular context, is someone like Snowdon, David Bailey, Patrick Lichfield or perhaps David Hamilton; men who share a perceptive eye, people who can turn the most ordinary subjects into works of art; photographers each with a unique imagination, who brand their pictures with an individual style.

Maybe you've looked at David Hamilton's work, compared his beautifully sensual pictures of young girls with your own attempts to photograph your wife or girlfriend, and felt like throwing your camera into the nearest dustbin. Well don't. Because, presented in the right way, your pictures could stand as much chance of being bought by a photographic magazine as those of the talented Mr. Hamilton.

No need for great photographs

A few years ago, photographic magazines were full of pictures. A feature would consist of around half-a-dozen pages with a single picture on each, coupled with the minimum of words. A profile of the photographer concerned, a description of why he took the pictures, his philosophy on life perhaps . . . little more. In fact nothing on *how* he took the pictures, or the techniques he used to achieve certain effects.

Today, things are different. With only a couple of exceptions, photographic magazines are now much more concerned with technique. In general, these magazines are aimed at amateur rather than professional photographers, and among those amateurs, there is a tremendous thirst for knowledge. When they look at an interesting picture, they don't want to know *why* the photographer took it, they want to know *how*.

Different magazines will have different requirements. Photographic magazines may all look alike at first glance, but closer inspection will show that they each have their own individual style. A few do still publish picture portfolios for their own sakes; others buy pieces on personal experiences in photography; but the vast majority use mainly articles with a 'how to do it' type of theme.

And that's why a picture of your girlfriend or wife can stand a good chance of being bought by a photographic magazine. Standing on its own as nothing more than a photograph for its own sake, it may not be considered very good. But use that photograph to demonstrate how a certain effect was achieved and you're on your way to a sale.

The photographs you produce don't have to be works of art, but they should be good illustrations of technique. That's what amateur photographers want to read about, so that's what editors buy. Look at the pictures shown here. They are nothing special pictorially, but they show the sort of work a photographic magazine will buy in the right circumstances.

Look at the twin landscapes, with and without clouds. The top picture shows an unexceptional scene which would never win a prize or sell to a photographic magazine in its own right. But contrasting the two pictures to show the effect of shooting with and without a red filter, makes it an ideal illustration for a photographic feature on filters.

The picture of the house on the hill could be used for several purposes in a photographic feature. It might, for instance, be used to show the effect of strong side lighting on a subject, illustrating the way it brings out texture and pattern. It could also be used in a feature on picture composition. The house is placed exactly on a third. It is minute compared to the entire picture area, but cover it with your finger and see how the picture loses impact by its absence.

The speeding car could have been used in a feature on action photography, showing how a slow shutter speed coupled with a panning technique can give a spectacular impression of speed. This particular picture was shot at no more than 1/30 sec.

The same picture could also be used in a piece on composition to show how a moving object must have space within the picture area to 'move into'.

The soot and whitewash effect could have illustrated a darkroom feature to show the techniques of using line film. In this case, the reader would want to know that the original shot was no more than one-third of a Tri-X negative, printed on to lith film, developed in lith developer to give a high contrast positive which, in turn, was printed again on to lith film and developed to give an even higher contrast negative. This negative was used to make the final print on grade four paper.

It didn't take exceptional skills or artistic ability to produce any of these pictures, yet each one would make ideal illustrations for photographic features.

Pattern, texture or composition . . . it could illustrate all three.

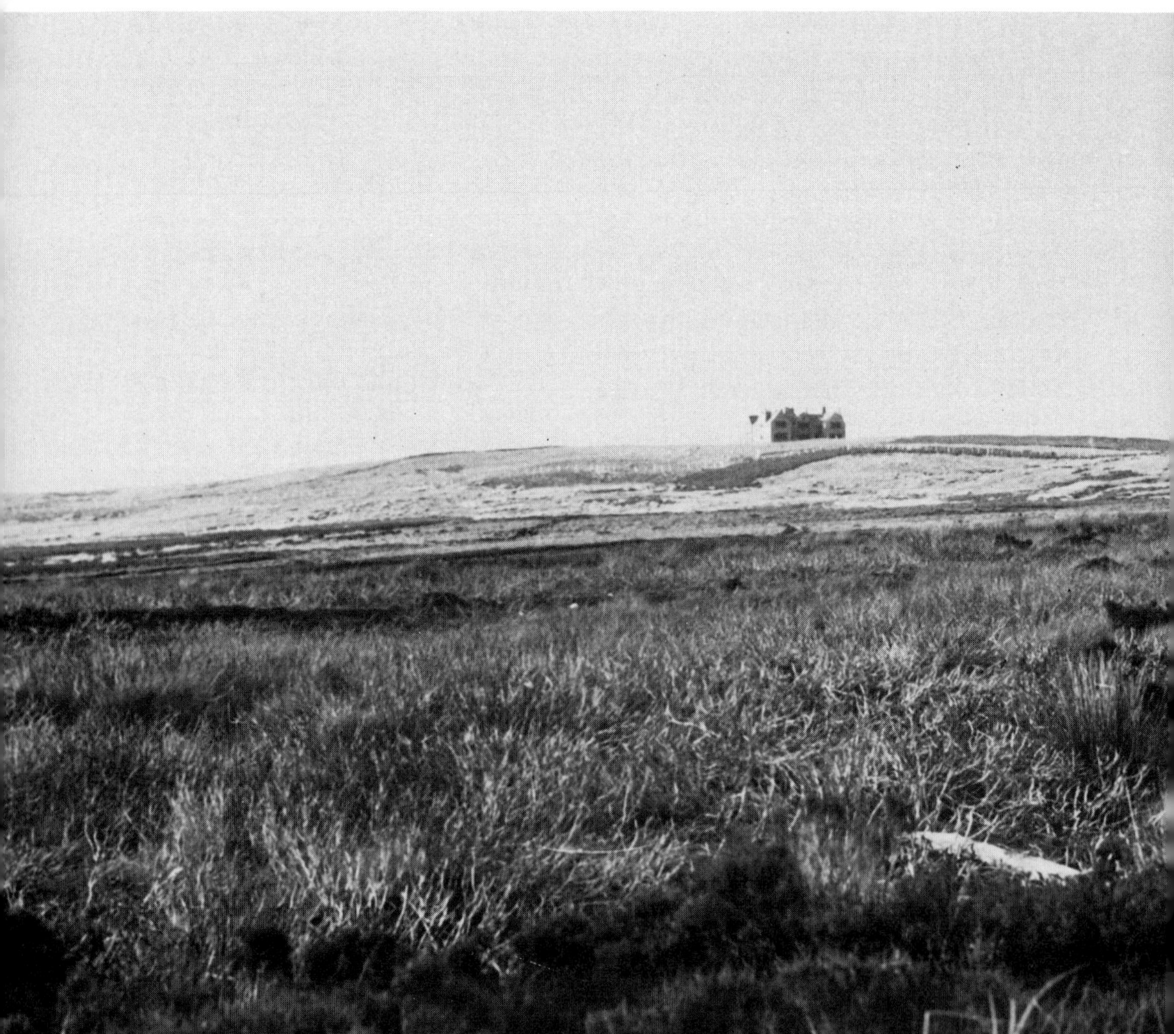

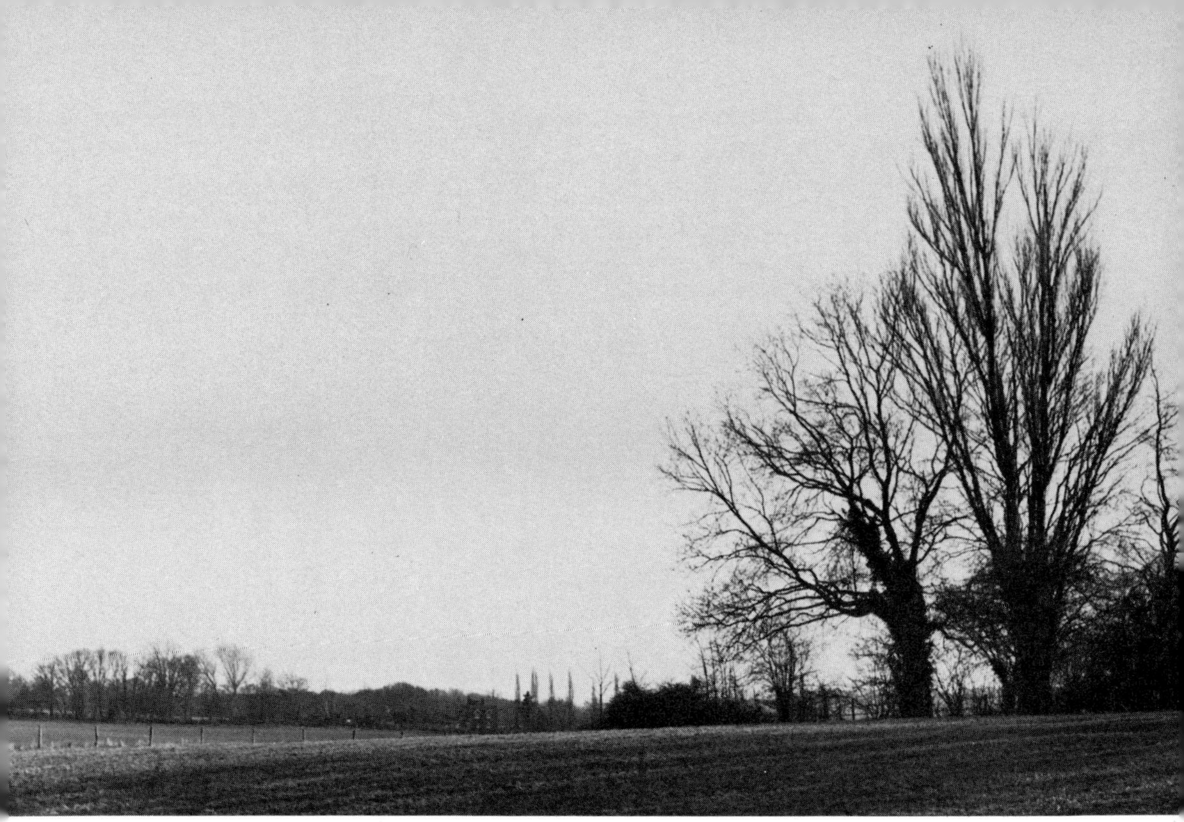

Contrast pictures like these are good for
filter features.

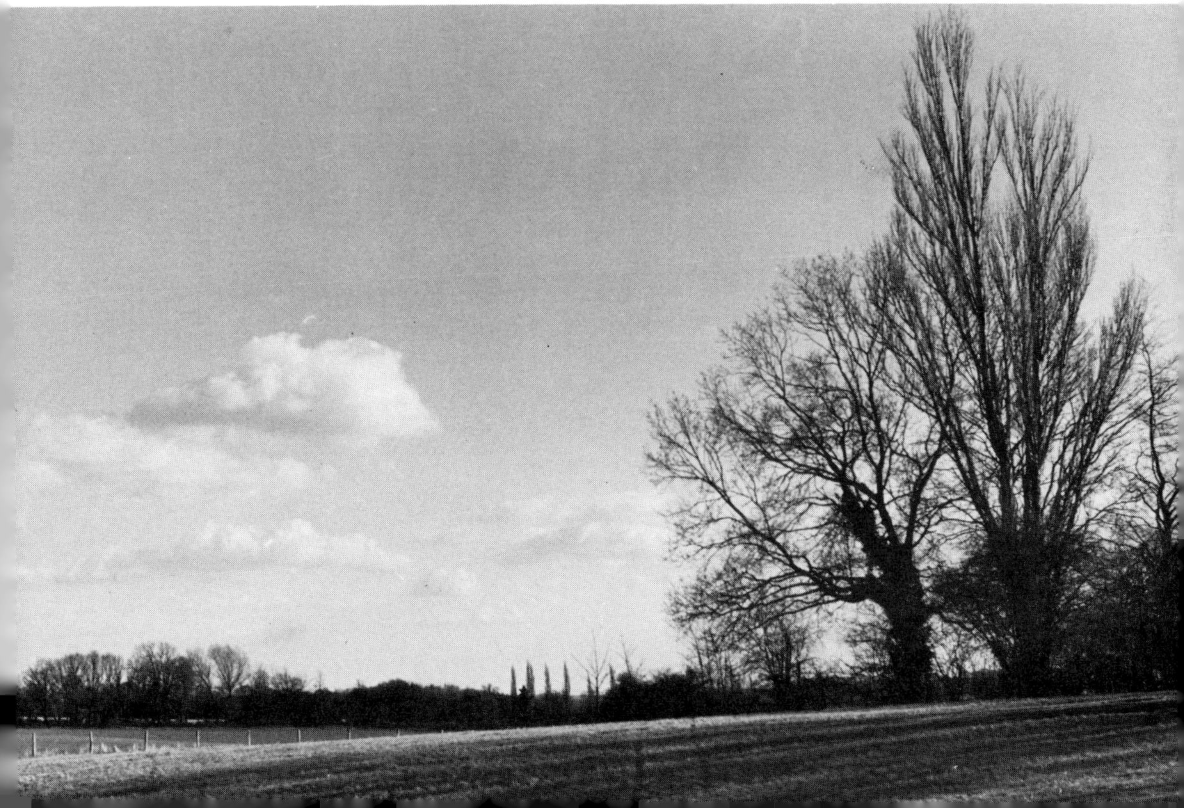

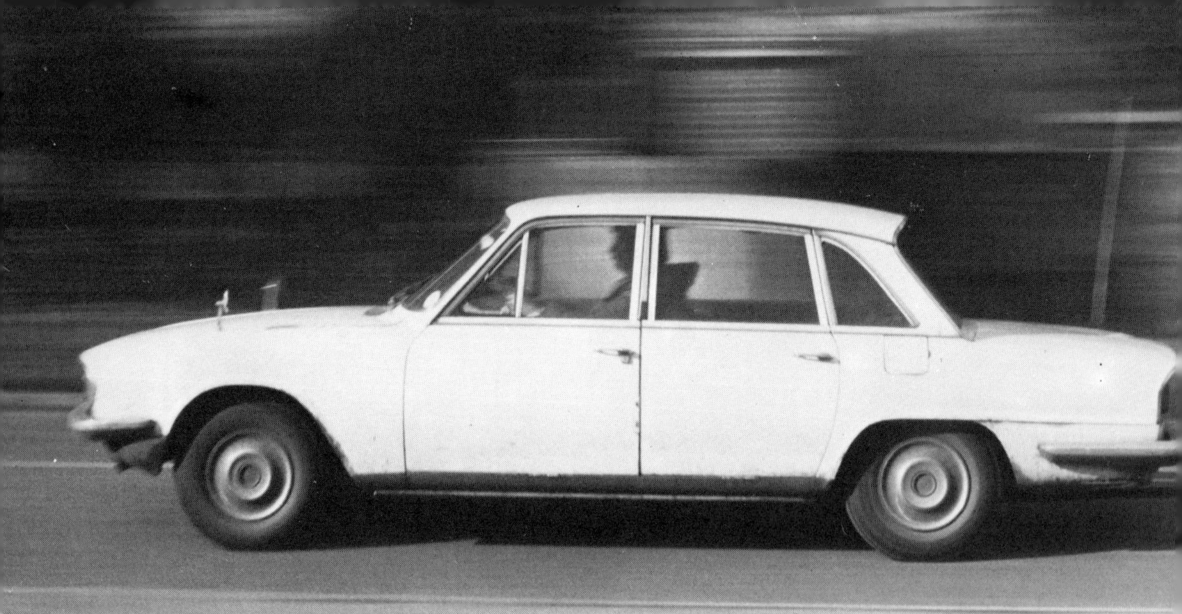

Anyone could take a similar picture, but it still makes a good illustration for a feature on action and shutter speeds.

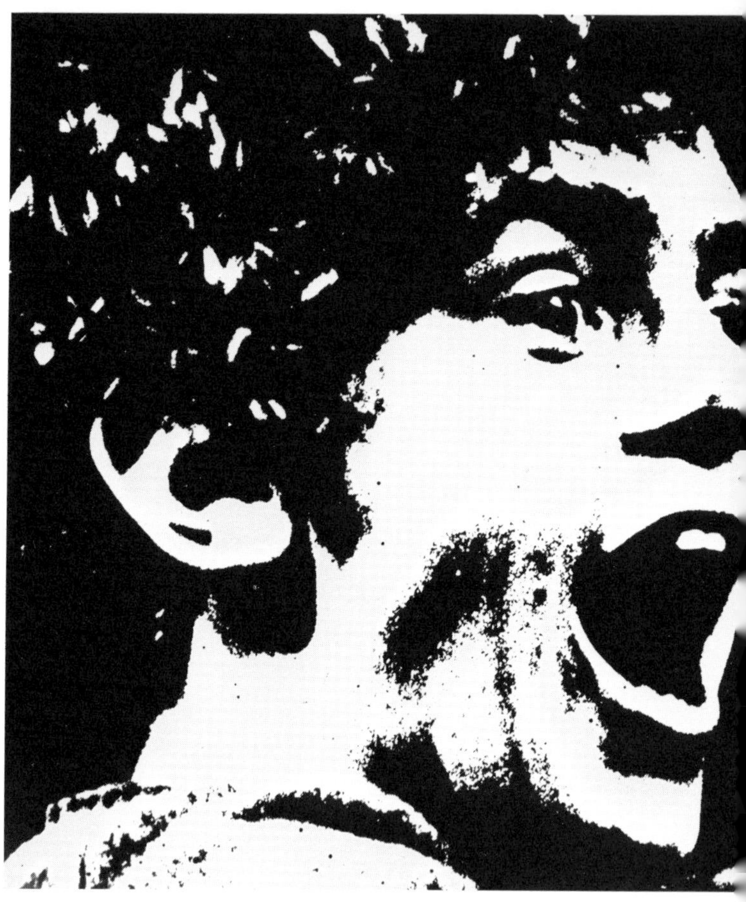

Describe how you produce a picture like this and you have the basis for an interesting darkroom article.

But a need for sound technique

Now we come to the part where you do have to be good. Artistically, your pictures may be only average; but technically, they must be spot on. It's amazing how many potential freelances submit articles to photographic magazines, accompanied by badly scratched photographs printed on the wrong grade of paper, or with colour transparencies that have been hopelessly under- or over-exposed.

If you are a professional photographer or a keen amateur, sound technique should be second nature. So, assuming you are capable of producing a technically acceptable print or transparency, let's look at the sort of article you are going to write.

The same old stuff . . . and when to submit it

It's sad but true to say that everything has been done before. Regular features appear in all the photo magazines, going into details of things like buying a camera, using a flashgun, getting the best out of your enlarger. All these subjects have been covered before and they will undoubtedly be covered again. The reason they are repeated so often is for the benefit of new generations of readers, newcomers to the hobby who may only just have started taking a magazine for the first time.

Most photographic magazines have their years roughly mapped out in advance. By the beginning of January, they will know exactly which topics they aim to major on each month throughout the coming year.

Editors will generally tell you what their requirements are. If you ask them, they might let you have a list of the year's topics. Submit an article on flash in plenty of time for their flash issue and you stand a good chance of acceptance.

Notice that I said, *in plenty of time for their flash issue*. A monthly magazine works a minimum of six weeks in advance. Two calendar months is a safer figure, so copy for the October issue will be going to the printer in August. That means the editor has actually been planning the issue up to a month before that – in July. So if you are submitting something purely on spec, you should make your first approaches at least three, and ideally four, months before the appropriate issue. In other words, don't submit a Christmas feature in December. By then, the magazine will be well into planning their Spring issues.

Inform the reader

When you come to write and illustrate an article, you should make it as informative as possible. Talk about cameras, lenses, film, exposures – anything and everything that is relevant to the particular subject you have decided to cover.

If you come up against something to which you don't know the answer, don't try to gloss over it. Nothing is more annoying to a reader than an article which raises a number of questions and then fails to answer them. So don't just rely on your own knowledge. Research your article. Ask people in the know. Refer to text books. Answer all the questions that need to be raised on the subject.

If, for instance, you are writing about flash, then discuss the advantages and disadvantages of direct and side lighting, contrast this with bounced flash, talk about flash as a fill-in for daylight, flash used an an effective super-fast shutter speed, special effects, the use of two flash heads, slave units, studio flash, brollyflash . . . cover the subject from every possible angle. Don't just tell readers how *you* take flash pictures, tell them how *they* can take them. Explain how they can improve on their own technique.

Show them too

After that, you can illustrate the points you have made. This is where your wife or girlfriend comes in. Set her up in front of a plain background, put the camera on a tripod and photograph her with direct flash, then again with the flash held out on an extension lead at 45 degrees to the subject and again with bounced flash. Develop and print your pictures, then caption them, explaining the different lighting effects you have achieved with the different types of flash.

That's the great thing in photographic articles. Don't just *tell* readers about the various effects, *show* them as well.

Or perhaps you fancy trying your hand at an article on filters. Get the facts first. If you don't know already, go to a text book and find out why a red filter turns a blue sky dark or why a yellow filter makes a lemon look white. When you know the facts, write them down. Then illustrate your article. Beg, buy or borrow a set of filters – yellow, green, orange, red, blue – and photograph the same scene through each. That will give you a series of pictures to show different effects.

Those are just two of the more common ideas, and the straightforward approach to them. Features written in this way stand a very good chance of selling. Unfortunately, they are *so* straightforward that there is every chance that the editor has already bought something similar and has it on file.

A different approach

You stand a better chance of selling your work, then, if you accept that the straightforward approach has probably been covered and look for a new approach to the old subject. Flash photography? How about a feature that demonstrates the effects of using flash out of doors at night, using the flashgun to 'paint' a scene with light. Filters? How about the unusual effects of shooting through three coloured filters on the same frame of film.

Those are two unconventional approaches to conventional subjects. The range of variations on all aspects of photography is limited only by your own imagination. And of course, there is always the rare contributor who does come up with an idea that is totally new. If it's interesting and he has described it well enough, it's bound to sell.

The sort of feature you *won't* sell is the 'what I did on my holiday' type of feature – and the same goes for traction engine rallies, carnivals and the like. Neither will you sell any type of article that the magazine runs regularly every month and which is written by a member of the staff or a regular outside contributor. Count test reports in this section. Photographic magazines get review cameras long before the new models reach the shops, so by the time you get hold of one, they have their test written and published.

Can photographers write?

Now we come to the actual writing. 'But I'm a photographer,' I hear you cry, 'I can't write.' Rubbish. If you can talk, you can write. Okay, maybe you can't express yourself on paper as clearly and concisely as a professional writer, but if the pictures are suitable, the idea is good, and you've got the salient facts down, then an editor will very often take time to doctor or even re-write your copy for the sake of running a good feature.

When you come to write it down, just imagine you are describing the appropriate technique to a friend at the local camera club. Write it the way you would talk about it. Describe exactly *how* the pictures were taken and *why* the techniques involved work.

Never be afraid of going into too much detail. An editor would far rather trim an article that is too long than find he has one that, while interesting on the surface, is too short on essential details. Cutting copy is easier than expanding it.

How to impress an editor

First impressions count for a lot when an editor opens a submission from a freelance he has never heard from before. So present your article simply and neatly.

Type your copy. Or, if you can't type, have someone do it for you. Write on one side of the paper only and leave a double space between the lines.

Start the first page about one-third of the way down, leaving the area above blank. This is to allow space for the printing instructions. Number each sheet in the top, right-hand corner. Put your name and address in the top, left-hand corner of the first sheet. Write 'm.f.' at the bottom of each sheet to show that 'more follows' and when you get to the end, write 'end' at the bottom of that sheet.

Write picture captions separately. Some editors like individual captions stuck to the back of the appropriate photograph. If you do this, use Sellotape and fix the caption at one end only, making it easy to detach. For the same reason, never gum captions to photographs or write them directly onto the back of pictures. Most editors prefer the captions written together on a separate piece of paper. Number each caption, then number each print appropriately, in pencil if you are using fibre-based paper or *lightly* with a ball-point if you are using resin-coated material.

When the manuscript is completed, take a fresh sheet of paper and type the title of the article in the centre, together with your name and the number of words in the article. Leave a few spaces and, beneath that, add your address and, if possible, a daytime telephone number. That's your title page. Clip it to the manuscript with a paper clip.

The ideal size for prints, black and white or colour, is 10 x 8in., though no one will complain if your pictures are marginally smaller or larger. Print them on glossy paper; it's better for reproduction.

Any size from 35mm up is suitable for transparencies. If the quality is exceptional, even 110 could prove acceptable. Don't glass-mount your slides. Leave them in card mounts and, ideally, slip them into plastic slide wallets – the type that holds a dozen or so at a time. That allows the editor to look at your work quickly and take the general standard in at a glance. Save him time and you're on your way to winning his heart.

An even better way of presenting transparencies is to take a sheet of black card and cut away a series of apertures through which to display your transparencies. Since you'll probably want them back, mark your name and address clearly on each mount.

Pack your slides and/or prints in an envelope, together with a piece of stiff cardboard or hardboard to prevent your prints getting creased in the post. And *always* enclose a stamped addressed envelope with adequate postage, not just for a reply, but for the return of your article as well.

Now you have to write a covering letter. Take the trouble to find out the editor's name. Give him the idea you really want to write for *his* magazine. Whenever I get a submission that begins 'Dear Sir', I can't help wondering how many other magazines have seen and rejected the feature before me. When I see 'Dear Mr. Wade', I automatically feel that this is something exclusive to me. Little things like that mean all the difference for first impressions.

Your letter should be short, sharp and to the point. It's amazing how many freelances send in bad quality work, then try to justify it in a covering letter. Your work will stand or fall by its quality. The editor doesn't want to know how difficult it was to take a certain picture, unless that difficulty is part of the feature's subject matter – in which case the explanations should be in the copy, not in the letter. If the quality is second-rate, it won't be published, no matter how difficult it was to capture in the first place.

A contributor recently wrote me a four-page, hand-written letter demanding an immediate reply and complaining about photographs that other editors had managed to lose. It went on to say: 'I don't take anything startling, exciting or unusual,' and added: 'Your previous editor said my work was very good but boring.'

Having ploughed my way through that lot, it isn't surprising that I felt little enthusiasm for looking at the contributor's feature. But I did read it, only to find that my previous editor had been dead right.

That's the sort of letter you should never write. Something like this is far better:

Dear Mr. Wade,

I enclose an article on photographing insects which I hope you will consider for use at your normal rates. I also enclose a stamped addressed envelope for its return should it prove unsatisfactory and look forward to hearing from you in due course.

Yours sincerely,

That says everything that needs to be said. Everything else should be in the feature itself.

Get it in focus

Remember: Choose a magazine, buy it, study it, get to know its freelance needs, then write for that particular market. Go for the original approach to a subject. Keep your copy clear, concise and informative. Present your work neatly.

If you are a keen amateur photographer, there's no reason why you shouldn't sell your work to the photo press. But don't just take my word for it. Try it and find out for yourself.

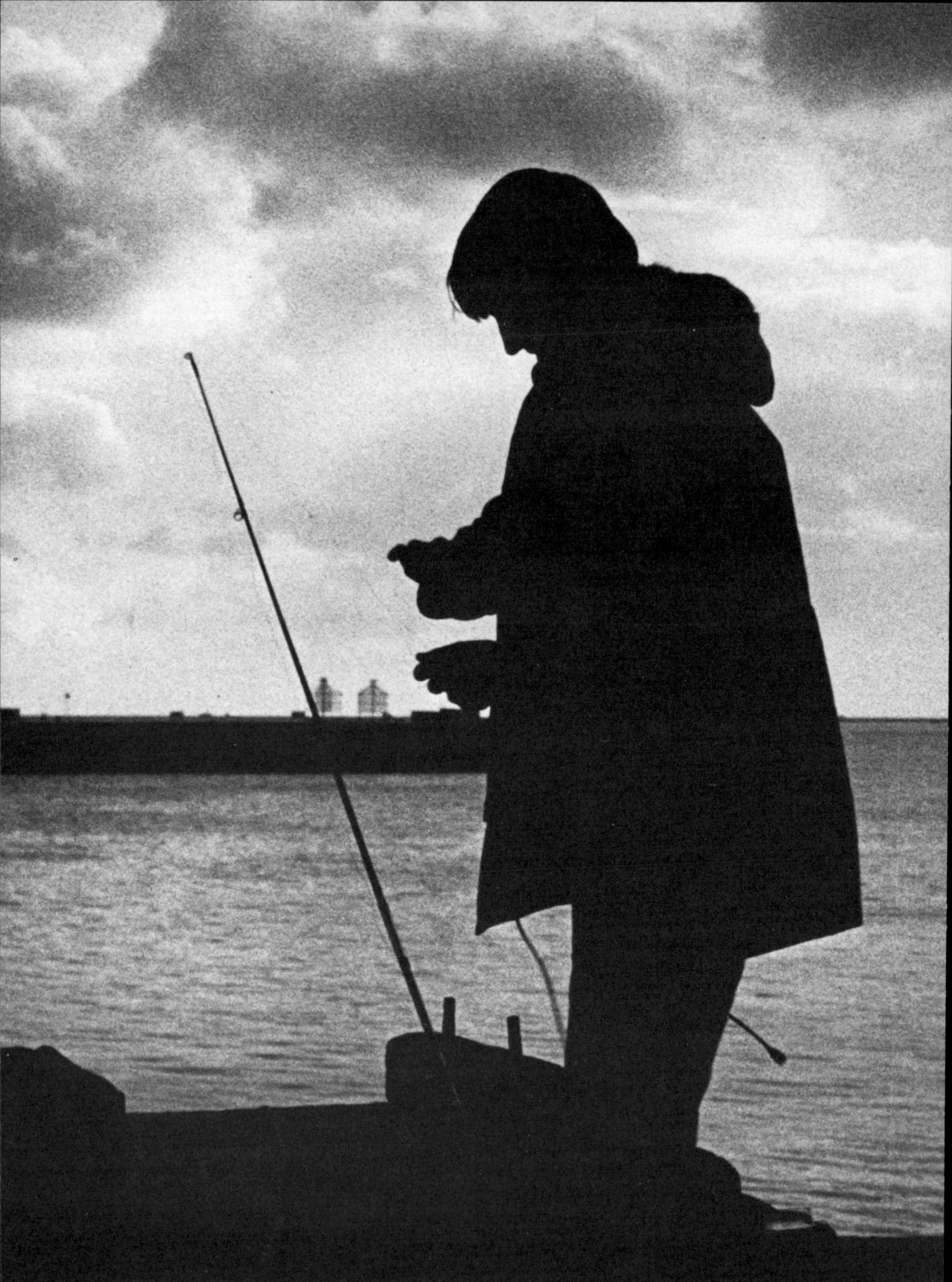

10

ANGLING FOR FREELANCE SALES

by Ray Forsberg An established writer and photographer whose work appears regularly in all the major angling publications, tells you everything you need to know to sell to this market.

Before I write one word on the subject of angling photography so far as techniques, equipment and locations are concerned, let me first define what I consider to be the essential attributes which go into the make-up of that extremely rare bird: a successful piscatorial photographer.

To fish or to photograph?

There are top class photographers who occasionally angle, and shoot some film when doing so. Conversely, there are expert anglers who also carry a camera to record their exploits at the waterside.

But the genuine 50-50 angler/photographer, who is equally conversant with a camera as he is with a fishing rod, is definitely in the minority.

Ideally there should be an equal balance of both angling and photographic interest in the nature of the person behind the camera. Too much of the fisherman in him will prevent him from even thinking of photography whilst the fish are biting and the action is red hot. Such a person finishes the day with a bulging keepnet or boat full of fish – and no pictures . . . He never gives a thought to stopping to record his exploits when the light is at its best.

The other side of the coin reveals exactly the same faults; but in reverse. Here we have a camera-toting angler who can seldom, if ever, settle down to any serious fishing. Therefore he is never in the fortunate position of being able to photograph a catch of his own. He is merely a photographic riverbank or shoreline prowler who must constantly rely on the catches made by other anglers to provide him with good picture material. A photographer who adopts this approach can often be quite successful for a limited period of time, provided he sticks to locations where there are lots of anglers catching fish regularly. But not on remote stretches of riverbank, out at sea miles away from land, or when featuring exclusive, private waters. The whole success of angling photography hinges on a self-sufficient, Do-It-Yourself approach.

The type of picture that angling publications like to keep on file as a general stock illustration. The dark foreground makes the picture particularly useful as far as the layout artist is concerned since it can be used to carry reversed-out lettering – an article title, for example. Picture by David Beare.

One of the greatest disappointments which can be suffered by a newcomer to angling photography is to be unexpectedly approached by an interested editor, for whom he has previously done some good work, and be offered a lucrative, commissioned assignment which has to be turned down because he is not sufficiently well versed in the art of angling.

You can't fool a fisherman

Like most other highly specialised outdoor pursuits angling receives its fair share of coverage in a variety of popular magazines, holiday brochures, greetings cards and adverts; apart from the obvious outlet of the angling press. However, the general standard of angling photography put forth on what I would call 'The Ordinary Public Market' is at times pathetically out of tune, due to certain errors which creep into the pictures. These may not be apparent to the layman, but alas, bring gales of laughter from real, observant fishermen – and sighs of consternation from those who have been concerned with the production of oftimes photographically perfect, but piscatorially putrid angling shots. To illustrate my point: A few years ago a certain manufacturer of outboard motors had an advert for their products published in a whole con-glomeration of outdoor sporting magazines. The shot showed two well developed, bikini-clad young ladies about to set off on a fishing trip in a sailing dinghy with the famous outboard motor, crisp and beautifully sharp, right in the foreground. A wonderful advert – on the face of it. Unfortunately, as the firm later discovered to their dismay, the two fishing rods held by the models had the fixed-spool reels mounted upside down. A foolish, glaring error which had passed all the non-angling photographic staff who were only concerned with the technical perfection of the print. If only the advertising experts had invited an angler to view the prints before the advert was done, they would have saved themselves a lot of ridicule and embarrassment.

A brief glance at any selection of 'Fishing Scene' greetings cards and calendars will usually reveal a number of obvious errors which cause genuine anglers to roll around with laughter, rather than being enchanted. A recent example I have come across depicted two young boys supposedly coarse fishing by a beautiful stream, but clad in yellow oilskins (complete with souwesters) and wielding short, thick, sea fishing rods with boatfishing reels attached, complete with hawser type line! Book publishers should know better, but I recently saw a very well done fishing book cover depicting an angler with his tackle all set up neatly by a reed fringed river. Unfortunately, the picture maker had forgotten one vital thing; although the angler had three or four bright green plastic bait boxes grouped around his feet quite conveniently, so that he could easily reach them – clang . . . clang . . . The boxes were completely empty! The lids were off and the bottoms could be seen as unsoiled as the day they left the shop. A sad omission which screamed aloud to any angler picking up the book that the cover was a fake. This angler was most decidedly not fishing. Just going

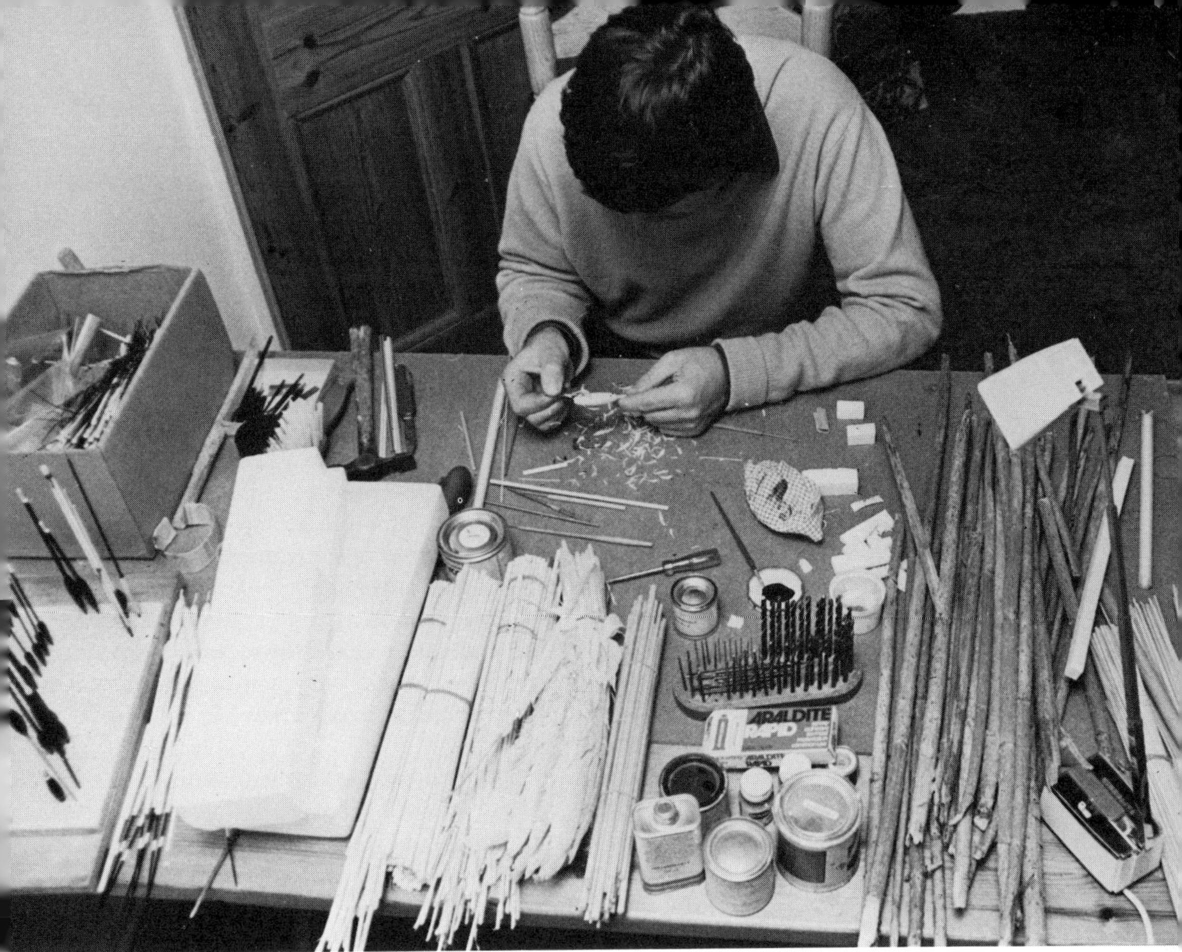

A key illustration in a series of pictures on float making. The series appeared in *Angler's Mail*, earning a total of £165 for photographer Edwin Grant.

through the motions of it, with a set of tackle, on a 'mock-up' photographic session.

But truly the most hilarious error I have ever seen appeared in a mail order catalogue. The tackle which was being advertised in the colour shot was for reservoir trout fly fishing. There stood the proud captor, in the bows of a rowing boat, with the trout fishery in the background. Under one arm he had a fly rod with the correct reel and thick fly line. A box of artificial flies was by his side on the thwart and he had the correct kind of short handled, flip-up fly fishers' landing net, plus a deerstalker hat with a collection of both dry and wet artificial flies stuck into it, all of which produced a genuine looking effect. But, bloomer of all bloomers; smilingly, he held aloft by the gills – A COUPLE OF VERY STIFF, DEAD MACKEREL! Someone, somewhere, had blundered . . . Was the switchboard operator or typist sent off to the fishmongers for a couple of rainbow trout? And not knowing what they were, or finding them unobtainable, innocently brought back a couple of very pretty, mottled backed mackerel as a substitute!

The moral, therefore, in all angling photography, must be, if in doubt, find out. Don't take a chance on anything not being noticed if it is incorrect. Errors of the most subtle kind will be picked out quite easily by experienced anglers.

Who fishes where

After that rather lengthy, but most necessary, discourse on the subject of being very careful with regard to the technical correctness of angling pictures, let us now approach the three different categories or branches of the modern angling scene. We must define which is which, and – of great importance – investigate the different types of location where each separate kind of angling is practised.

By far the greatest number of anglers in this country are those known as 'coarse fishermen'. The name has nothing to do with their appearance – although when viewed collectively, I admit they do look a somewhat raffish breed (myself included)! These devotees generally practise their sport in fairly safe riverside, lake, pond or stream locations, which are not hazardous from a personal point of view, or as far as the camera gear is concerned.

The second category, which are known as 'game' fishermen, are the trout and salmon fraternity. They also operate on what I will term 'safe' locations: rivers, streams and in recent years, the ever growing water storage reservoirs, some of which are almost the size of inland seas. Whilst this type of angling is quite safe, when the fishing is done from a bank, the trend towards trout fishing in boats on large reservoirs brings with it a certain element of danger to the camera and its operator. On large expanses of very exposed water a three foot 'sea' can be whipped up by a strong wind quite suddenly and without warning.

Finally, we have the ever growing branch of piscatorial performers known as sea anglers. A hardy breed, whose sport ranges over a wide variety of locations from safe, gently shelving sandy beaches to formidable rock and cliff marks, where the angler-photographer will need nerves of steel and the agility of a mountain goat. In addition to this there is the sea boat fishing scene. Both inshore, from small outboard powered dinghys; and offshore, from purpose built angling craft, which are without doubt the absolute 'killers' of photographic equipment. Especially when the sea is rough, the action is hectic; there is water and salt-laden spray flying everywhere and the cameraman can hardly keep his footing on slimy, wet, heaving decks.

Calculating the risks

From hard, personal experience over the course of about twenty five years slipping and sliding around on muddy river banks or staggering about in a boat at sea; with driving rain, sleet, snow, sand and dust ever ready to ruin my

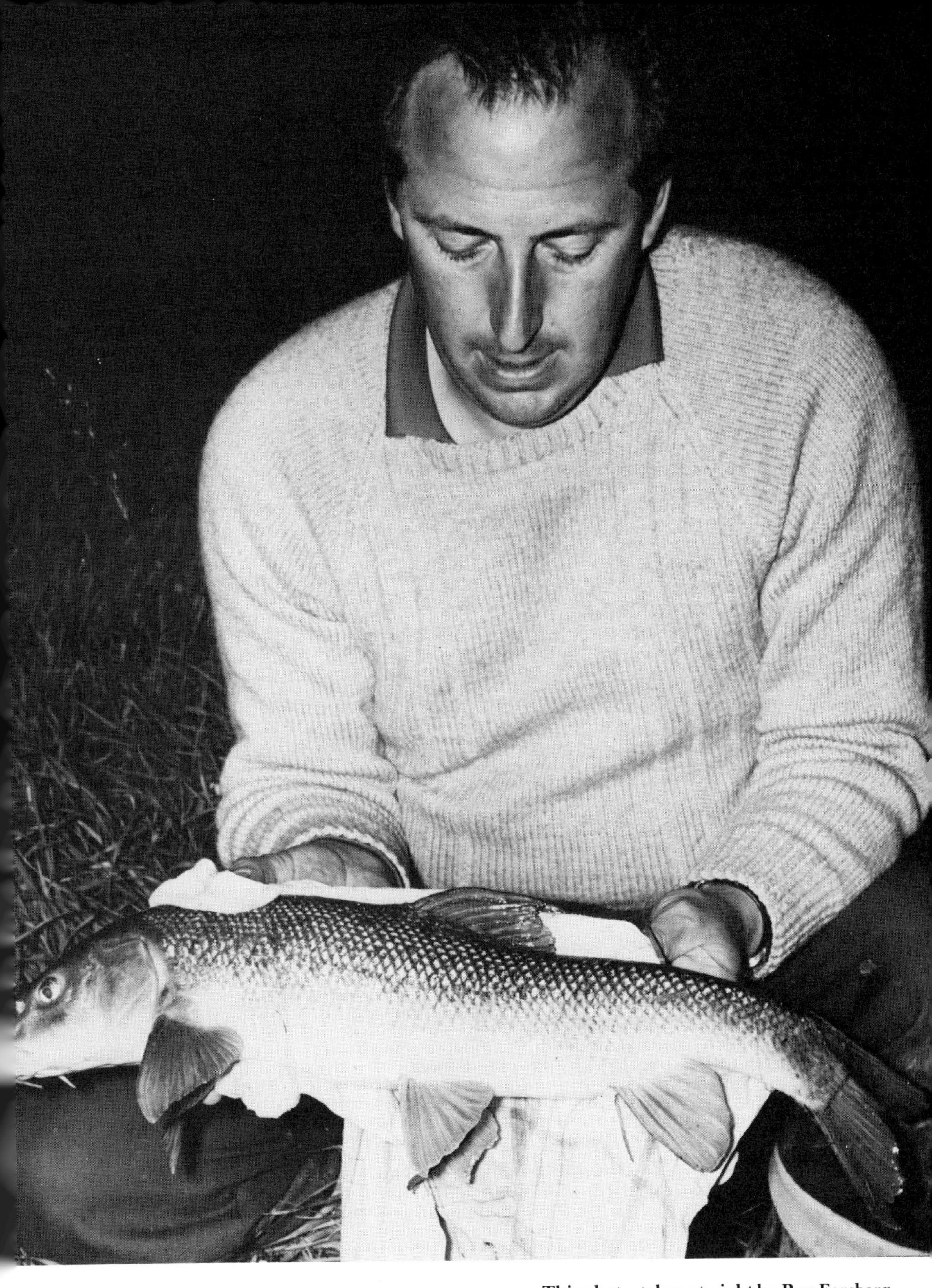

This shot – taken at night by Ray Forsberg – has sold to a number of angling publications, including *Angler's Mail*, *Angling* and *Coarse Angler*.

equipment; I have finally settled on the twin lens reflex camera as the most appropriate tool for this kind of exacting, rough and tumble photographic work. Frankly, I have always considered that the hardest part of all angling photography to be not the actual picture taking, but the careful keeping of the camera gear dry and free from damage so that it will function efficiently when the need arises.

As I always like to shoot in tandem (colour and B/W) so that I can obtain both 'big' enlargeable negatives and large transparencies which are saleable, the 2¼″ square format suits me admirably. Also, I consider that the 'thoroughbred', high precision construction of the top quality reflex cameras is a necessity where reliability is of paramount importance to the type of photography being done. At the risk of being branded a pessimistic doomwatcher, I will now divulge what I term my 'level of risk' formula and explain how it works so far as my cameras are concerned.

Very early on in my photographic career, when the only camera I possessed was a rather cheap 2¼″ square twin-lens reflex, I realised that some of the situations to which I subjected it were at most suicidal so far as sensible camera care was concerned. For instance, what photographer in his right mind would wade out on a rocky, slippery shoreline in breast waders, with his treasured camera slung around his neck, and with boiling surf and spray all around . . . just to take a shot of an angler fishing in the foam? Viewed from a purely common sense angle, the risks are too great. The chance of getting bowled over by a wave is always there, as is the possibility of stepping into a deep crevasse and floundering (camera and all) in the foaming brine!

Such risks, however, are all part and parcel of the angling photography game, so the obvious thing to do is to evolve some kind of high/low risk camera category to minimise financial loss should a camera get accidentally 'dunked'. My approach is novel, and I have yet to find it becoming popular as the initial expense is quite formidable, but it works well for me and that is all I am concerned about.

The Forsberg formula

Briefly, to explain what I mean, I will loosely bracket together a selection of four different 'camera danger' levels and give details of the value and type of camera I use for each separate situation. At the moment I have a collection of four twin lens reflex cameras and I rate them as follows:

High Risk camera: Microcord II (now obsolete but of sound, reliable construction and performance). Price second-hand, £15. This is literally my 'throw away' camera. I wade in fast flowing rivers with this one and take it out to sea in boats. Psychologically, this camera gives my photographic ego a tremendous boost. If I fall in and 'dunk' it — so what? All I have lost is a measly fifteen quid! If I stumble and fill it full of water or a rogue wave catches me and bowls me over, I'm laughing. I can even afford to swing this camera round by its strap and send it flying out to sea never to be seen again! To the owners of only one very expensive, cossetted camera, such a photographic approach may sound sheer lunacy. Far from it. It is good, sound common sense. You can't

Unhooking a trout. This picture, by Edwin Grant, has appeared in *Rod & Line*, *Angler's Mail*, *Angling Telegraph*, *Fishing* and *Angling Times Year Book*.

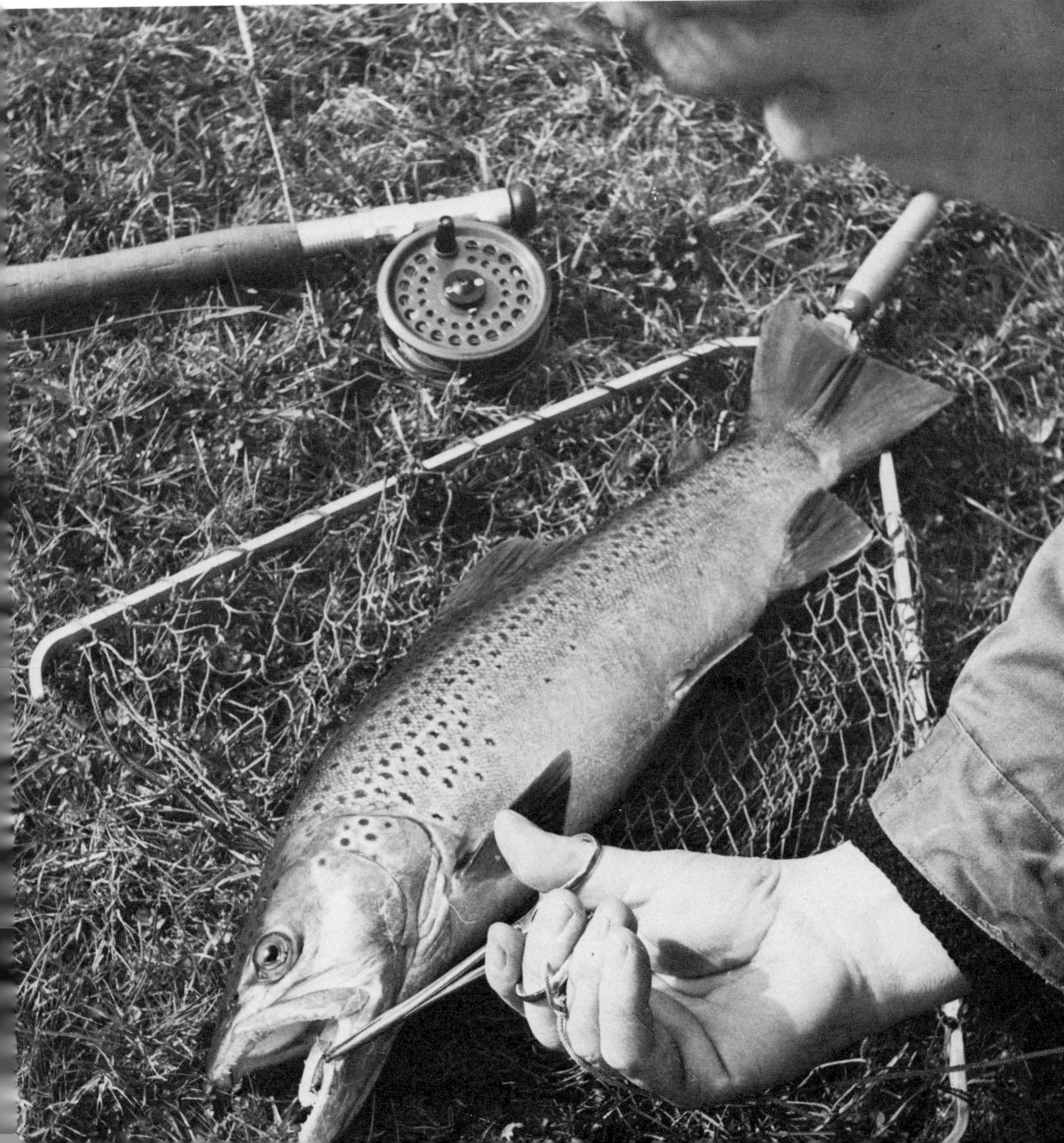

happily chance your arm in dodgy photographic situations and shoot extremely difficult pictures, if you are constantly worried by the thought of the three or four hundred pounds price tag on the camera which is at risk.

Moving up a little on the price scale and down slightly in the risk category comes number 2 camera. Another obsolete Micro Precision Products twin lens reflex job called the Microflex. Definitely a camera for hard work and long years of trouble free operating. Price second-hand about ten years ago: £25. This is another camera which I take on beaches, in boats and on rough rivers and shorelines. I don't subject it to the same risks as the other one, but nevertheless if it should come to grief and be irreparably damaged, I haven't suffered a great loss. I can scrap it, buy something else, and be more careful next time.

Camera number 3 is one for more or less safe jobs. It is a Rolleicord Va which has been with me for almost twenty years. I bought it brand new for £50, and until quite recently it was my 'best camera' which has earned itself the original purchase price many times over. I reserve this for my better class colour work and also do black and white with it. But in view of the fact that it would cost me about £150 to replace it, I treat it carefully and do only 'safe' jobs with it.

Last and most treasured, is my number 4 camera. A Rolleiflex 3.5F with 'the lot'. Coupled, built in light meter. Split-image, magnified critical focusing. Built in, coupled filter scale. Lever wind. New: a five hundred pound job – but obtained in 'mint' second-hand condition for £250 a couple of years ago. With this camera I shoot off many rolls of Agfa CT18 colour film at 'safe' locations and sell the transparencies through agencies and to angling magazines. Also with the aid of a full set of Rolleinars (close-up lenses) nos. 1, 2 and 3, I do lots of 'table top' tackle shots to be used as illustrations in my fishing articles and books. This is also my 'fish portraiture' camera with which I take close-up shots of fish – but remembering to use it only for dead safe jobs. If the camera is at risk, I don't use it, but revert to one of my 'cheaper' models according to how dangerous (camerawise) the job is.

Despite what the camera care experts say, if you do angling photography and carry your equipment in one of those large 'carve-out' custom built cases which cost the earth, your gear will not function efficiently for long. The drawback to such a sumptuous looking set-up, where everything is neatly housed in its own individual niche, is the ability of it all to collect sand, grit and salt-laden moisture every time the lid is opened. Far better to adopt my method and have each camera in its case, in a waterproof bag with a tight elastic band securing the top and every other single item of equipment protected in the same way. Then as an additional line of defence, all these separate items are stowed securely in a large, strong leather holdall, which again has an outsize plastic bag protecting it. That way, there are four lines of defence, and believe me, at times in an open boat in a rough sea they are all needed.

This picture proved to be a sure-fire seller for Edwin Grant. Although taken only recently, it has already appeared in *Angler's Mail, Angling Telegraph, Angling* and *Rod & Line*, and looks like chalking up many more sales in the future.

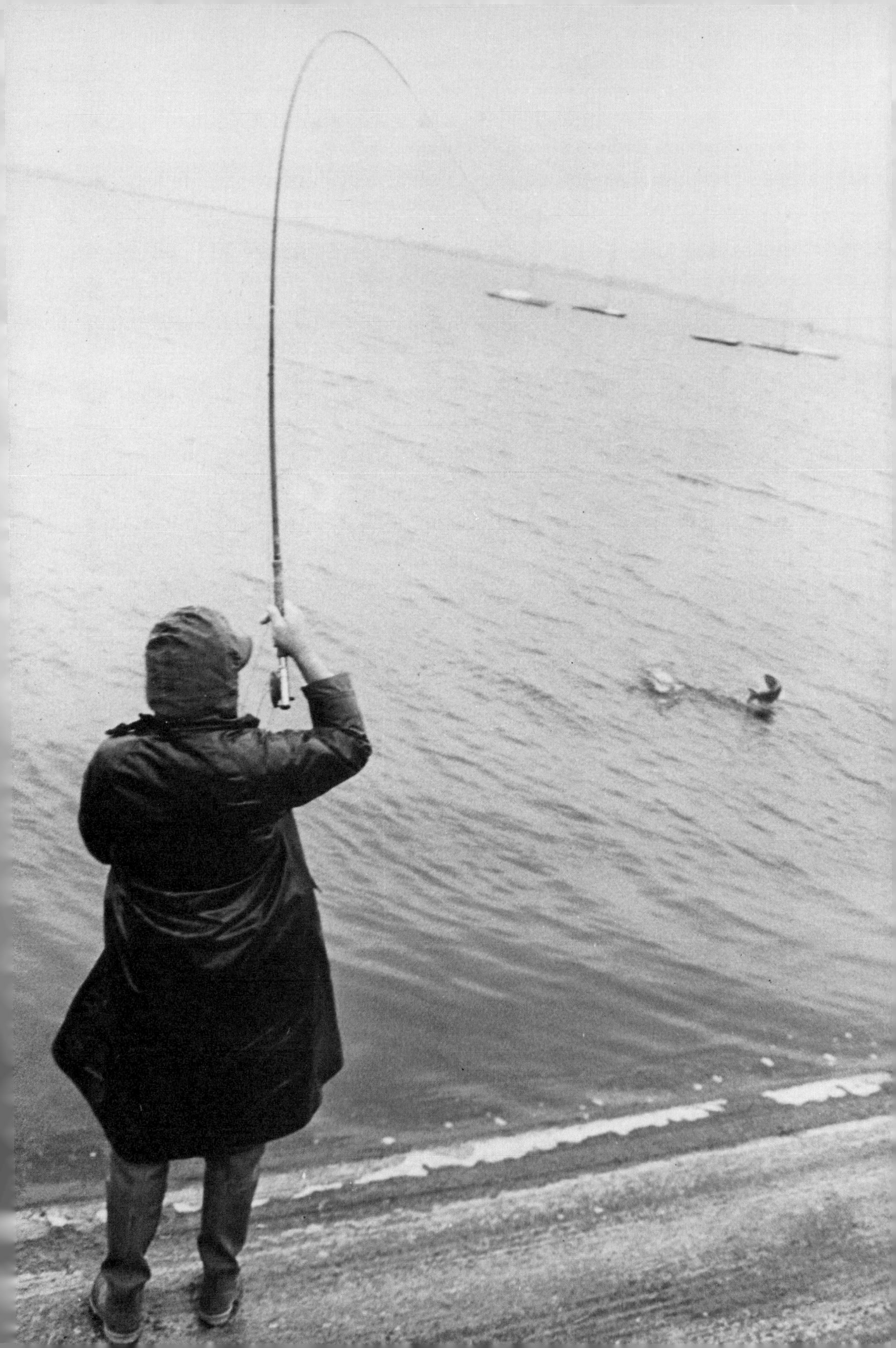

Fresh fish are photogenic

I will now approach the many and varied methods which I use to keep the cheques flowing through my letter box and my work appearing in all the fishing magazines.

First and foremost . . . Wet, live fish are most photogenic. Their fins stand erect and their eyes are bright. Photograph the same fish fresh from the water and again a few hours later when it is dead, with flaccid fins and glassy eyes, and there is no comparison. Of paramount importance when doing colour work is to remember that the colours of fish fade rapidly once they have been removed from their natural element.

While it is generally accepted that coarse fish are caught to be returned to the water, and game fish and sea fish are caught to be killed and eaten, the element of cruelty or the sight of flowing blood must as near as possible be absent from your pictures. Nothing is designed to activate the anger of 'antis' who oppose blood sports more than the sight of a shark being boated and then bashed over the head with a fourteen pound hammer! Keep your viewfinder off such subjects. They may happen occasionally in the heat of the moment aboard a fishing boat, but it is not good angling photography to have them paraded before the general public in a magazine or advert, even if the editors or art departments are prepared to overlook the gore and accept them for publication.

Critical focusing and high definition are two of the most important aspects to watch in angling photography. Where a fish is depicted, the scale pattern or skin texture must be clearly defined on the finished print or transparency. Also, if the shot is of an angler playing a fish on the riverbank with his rod well bent, it is essential that the line be shown. Should this be in the 3lbs. breaking strain category, then the thickness of the diameter amounts only to about .15 to .20mm. Therefore the resolving powers of both the camera and the enlarging lens must be equal to such a performance. It is foolish economy to indulge yourself in a high class camera with a superb lens performance if the quality of your enlarging lens is about equal to the bottom of a broken milk bottle!

Fishing in the dark

Flash photography at night, especially on remote riverbanks or shorelines, can present almost insurmountable problems, but these are precisely the type of difficult 'atmosphere' shots which editors love. During the daytime, I often resort to various dodges in order to get 'self-portrait' shots when I am all alone with no other human being within several miles. In daylight, by using a very firm 'studio type' tripod and either the self-timing device on the camera, or a long 20 ft 'bulb' air release, I am able to arrange all kinds of self-portraits. In the

An excellent picture shot against a natural background – and the type of illustration that angling publications find extremely useful. This one has been published in *Angler's Mail, Angling* and *Morning Telegraph* and has also appeared in a book on fishing, earning over £50 for Ray Forsberg.

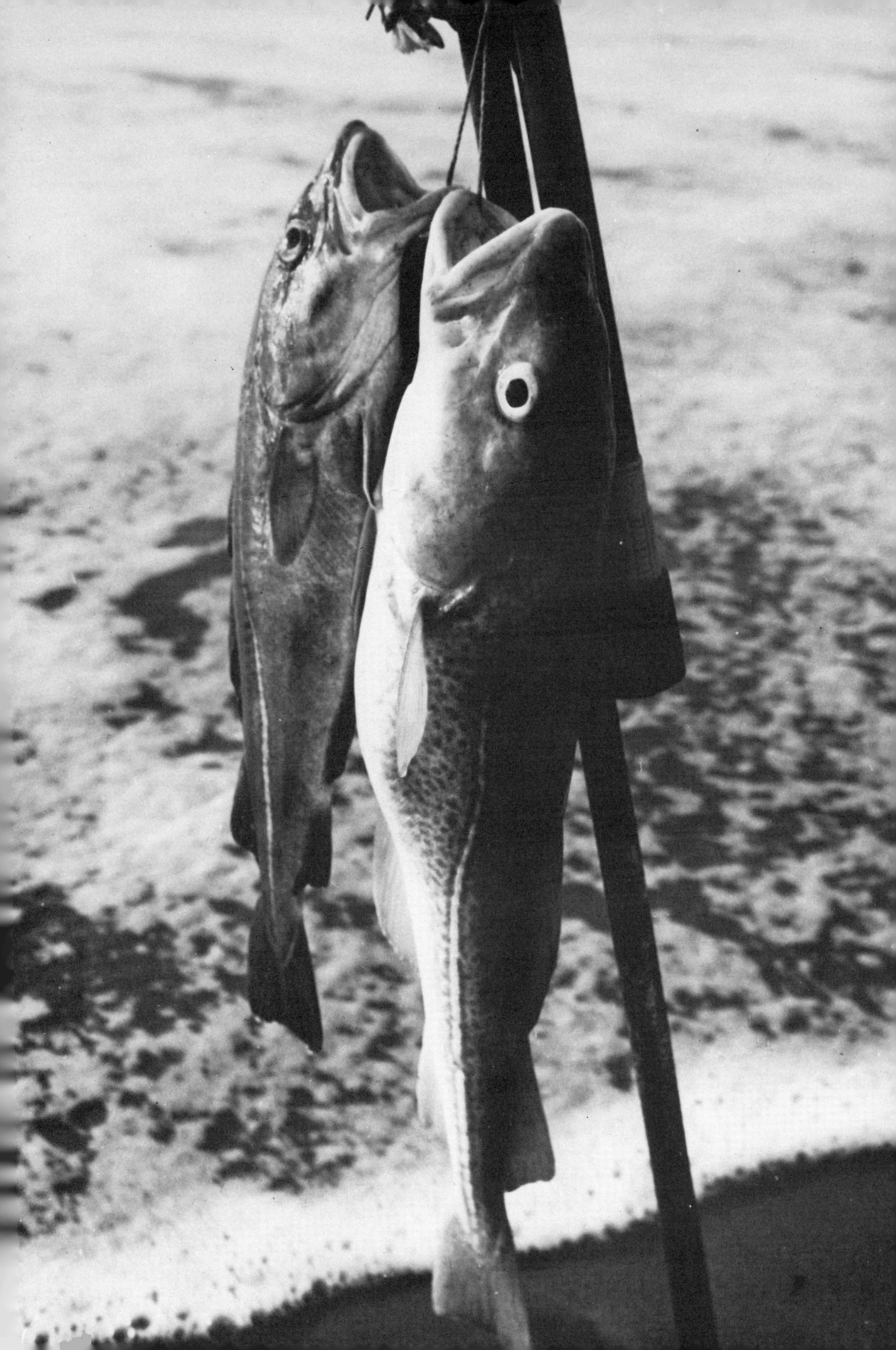

dark, however, the situation is fraught with many difficulties and often danger, if the river banks or rocks are slippery and the water deep and fast flowing.

For such hazardous picture making, a cool nerved, unflappable companion is a definite asset. Not to do the camera work, but merely to act as a fish holding 'stooge' or model. The problem with flash photography on pitch black riverbanks or shorelines is mainly one of focusing sharply on the subject and also getting your picture framed properly. To obviate such drawbacks, I have actually witnessed a budding angling photographer drive his car right down to the picture location, turn on the headlights, and then pose his subject (with fish) in the glaring beam, so that he could get the critical camera focusing he needed and also frame and compose the picture correctly in his viewfinder. Such methods are fraught with danger if the approach to the riverbank is steep or the shoreline is composed of soft, wheel trapping sand or mud. You could end up with your car stuck fast and the tide rising rapidly, or balanced precariously on an overhanging river bank, sinking slowly into the mud and threatening to slide down gracefully into the murky depths.

Far better to try my safe, no risk method and buy yourself a powerful torch with a good broad beam. With this held under one armpit and directed onto your subject you can focus at your leisure, with the fish or fisherman clearly illuminated, and fire off your flashgun in the secure knowledge that the picture will be pin sharp.

Remember the natural element

At this point I would like to approach the thorny subject of backgrounds. Please see that they are appropriate to the subject matter which is being shown. Since water is the fishes' natural element, do try to feature a little of it in the picture to produce a natural effect if it is at all possible. Nothing looks worse than to see the captor of an obviously long dead fish (pike are usually the favourite subject) displaying it proudly against the truly lamentable background of garage doors, garden sheds, lines of dangling washing or even rusty old motor bikes leaning against backgarden fences.

Piscatorial pitfalls

To conclude. Let me try to smooth the rocky pathway of any newcomer to the angling photographic scene by offering a few well proven tips which will save him from many piscatorial pitfalls.

If you have just bought yourself a very expensive camera and view with horror the thought of getting it wet, sandy, dusty or scratched – forget all about fishing photography and concentrate on dolly birds in comfortable, warm studio locations.

Never ever presume that large fish such as conger eels and sharks are dead, no matter how lifeless they may appear. If you carelessly put your foot in their mouth whilst stumbling on the deck of a heaving boat, you may later qualify for the title 'Most heroic, one-legged angling cameraman of the year'.

In a fishing boat, although the sea may appear as calm as a millpond, the very first time you leave your camera bag open on one of the thwarts (seats to landlubbers) with all the contents temptingly exposed, a naughty wave will just lap up gently over the gunwale and swamp it.

Never approach a fly fisher who is casting on his rod arm side from the rear. You could end up with a lobe full of Bloody Butcher and a visit to the local hospital for removal of such a novel ear ring.

When operating on a muddy, sploshy shoreline where there is no dry, safe place to rest your camera bag, always take along in the boot of your car a small, polythene baby bath. As a safe, dry container it has no equal. Should the rising tide sneak craftily up on you, whilst you are concentrating on picture making, your bag and gear will at least be dry and secure, as the whole lot will float like Moses in his wicker basket!

Ray Forsberg describes this picture as 'one of the biggest money-spinning shots I have ever taken'. It has appeared in most of the angling publications, as well as in a book on the subject. It has also won several photo competitions.

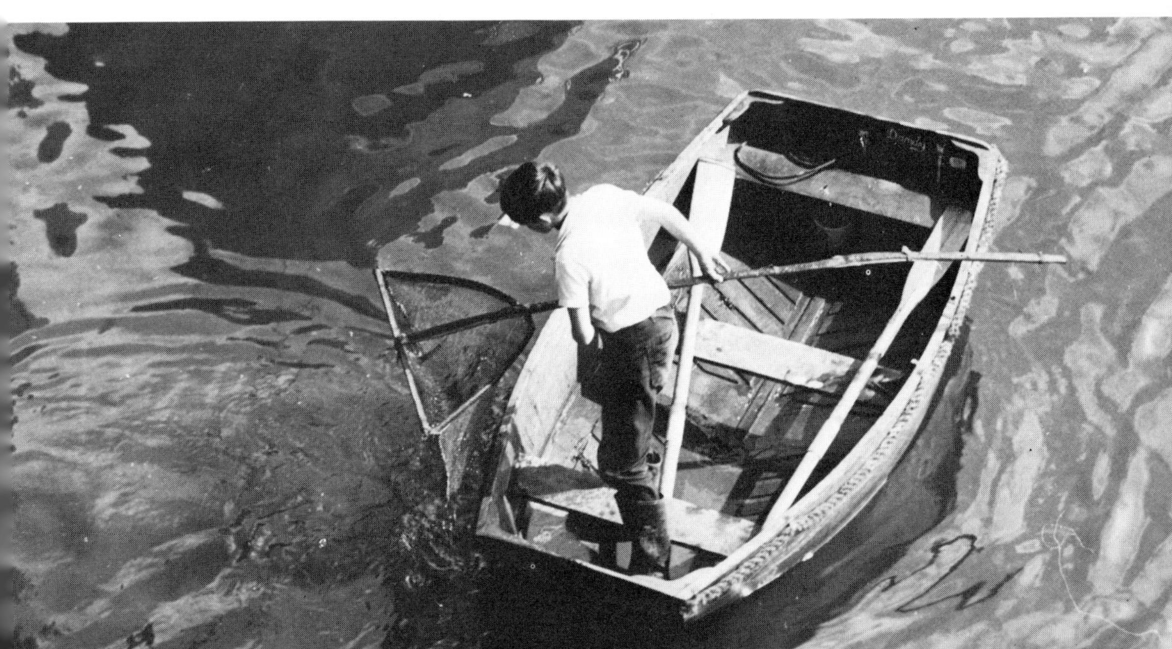

3,000 FEET UP!

by Lorna Minton   If you can't keep your feet on the ground, why not try your hand at aerial photography? The author sets out some of the problems you'll need to overcome – and the markets available if you're successful.

If you are not too happy when standing on the edge of a cliff looking down, then you would feel worse looking out of the open door of a light aircraft, so aerial photography would not be for you. But for those with a head for heights, this might be just the new branch of photography for which you are looking.

There are various branches of aerial photography of course, and for a speculative market some of these are not ideal for the freelance photographer. One such branch is air-to-ground work, for this is adequately catered for by commercial firms who cover vast areas and maintain libraries of pictures of towns, villages, stately homes and any interesting features on the ground which they feel might have a sales outlet one day. But there is plenty of scope for the freelance in air-to-air photography of light aircraft, gliders, and perhaps even hot air balloons.

The weather: your biggest problem

However there are quite a number of problems to overcome in air-to-air photography, and only a few of these are photographic ones. The biggest problem (in this country) is the weather. If the wind is too strong, formation flying is dangerous; if it is raining, any sort of club flying is dangerous because of the poor visibility; if the skies are grey, they will merge into the horizon producing a very nondescript background to the subject; and even if the day is sunny and bright the haze can be so thick at 2,000 or 3,000 feet that you are lumbered once again with a featureless background. Under the latter conditions, a yellow filter with monochrome photography helps slightly, but all thoughts of using a strong red haze cutting filter must be put out of your mind, because the exposure times would become unacceptably long, sitting as you would be within the confines of a vibrating cockpit.

After the weather comes the problem of the organisation of aircraft and pilots. The best type of aircraft from which to take photographs is a high wing machine like a Super Cub. The door of the Super Cub can be removed or tied open giving the photographer a fairly obstruction-free view. The wing's strut is the only thing likely to cause bother, but as a flat, side-on view of an aircraft or glider is rarely the best (because the near wing becomes foreshortened), this strut is not too troublesome. Shooting from a low-winged aeroplane, or one which cannot fly with the cockpit open in some way is hopeless, because of the problems of canopy reflection and the popular use of tinted perspex for cockpit covers.

Now find your pilot!

Once having located a suitable aircraft you then have to enlist the services of a pilot competent enough to fly in close formation with another machine, and if the subject is to be a glider, then your pilot must be happy to fly in close formation at a speed only just above stalling point, because if he flies any faster he will leave the glider behind. This is another point about the type of aircraft from which to photograph; it must be capable of flying at low speeds – around 50-60 knots. Gliders can of course fly much faster than this, in excess of 100 knots, but at these speeds their glide angle is considerably increased, and valuable height is soon lost. This might make you ask, 'Why not tow the glider up to say 5,000 feet, and start shooting from there?' but again, British weather is at fault, for it is very rare indeed for cloud base to be as high as 5,000 feet, and you cannot take pictures inside clouds!

The importance of the skill of the pilot flying the photographer's aircraft cannot be overstressed, for however brilliant you are as a photographer, you will get nothing worth having on film if the pilot cannot formation fly competently. Assuming now that you have an aircraft and a pilot to fly you; the weather is good, and you have a glider and pilot standing by keen to 'pose' in the air for you; the next thing is for the three of you to get together for a briefing. It is almost impossible to converse with your pilot once airborne because of the engine noise and wind whistling past the open door, and it is of course impossible to talk to the glider pilot. Most gliders are equipped with radio, but there is so little time for photography anyway, that you don't want to waste half of it chatting on the radio. Remember that unless a glider can circle in upcurrents, called thermals, it will all the time be coming down, and from 3,000 feet to the ground could be as short a time as ten minutes.

My own system before becoming airborne is to agree some hand signals with the glider pilot. Once I've given a hand signal, we both count to ten and then he does the manoeuvre asked for. This might be to bank to the left or right, or to peel away. The ten second pause is to allow me time to line up and focus the camera, and to give the glider pilot time to check on the proximity of any other aircraft or gliders before he makes any sudden direction change. Once the manoeuvre is completed, the photographer's pilot then has quickly to re-formate with the glider, and this sometimes means a very tight 360° turn with the wings almost vertically banked. A slightly unnerving experience if you are not prepared for it.

Know your subject

There is no doubt about it, photographers who succeed in photographing specialised subjects usually do so because they know a fair amount about that subject, and air-to-air photography is no exception to this rule. Therefore I would strongly recommend anyone keen to try their hand at air-to-air work to think about taking some sort of flying course first. This need not be very costly, for there is no necessity for you to reach the solo stage on the course (although this might be a secondary desire!). All you need do perhaps, is have half-a-dozen flying lessons in a light aircraft, or alternatively take a short gliding course. These are run at many clubs throughout Britain, and the current price for a gliding/holiday course for one week is between £45-£60. This fee includes accommodation, all food and, of course, the flying fees. Details about where these courses are held can be obtained from the British Gliding Association, Kimberley House, Vaughn Way, Leicester.

Having done this amount of flying with your hands on the controls, you will have learned a lot about flying techniques and the problems a pilot has to face. Thus when it comes to photography, you would not earn the disrespect of a pilot by asking him to do impossible or dangerous manoeuvres. You would also have made contact with the flying world in general, and this too is important. By talking to aeronautical enthusiasts, and letting them know that you are a freelance photographer, you will soon find aircraft and glider owners who would like photographs of their machines flying.

Choosing the right equipment

Many people ask me which is the best camera for air-to-air photography, which is rather like asking which is the best camera for wedding photography. There is no single answer, for so much depends on the type of camera you like to handle and what you want to do with the results. I can only answer by stating what equipment I use, and the reasons I use it, but in the long run you will just have to find out for yourself what is the best to use. Whatever type of aircraft you are in, the cockpit is always a very confined space, and your movements will be further restricted because of the necessity of wearing seat belts. Stowage space for extra cameras or equipment is usually lacking, and it is no good just putting things on the floor, because on the first occasion when the aircraft banks steeply, your equipment will go hurtling across the cockpit and may end up jamming the rudder pedal. So all equipment has to be carried on one's person, and two cameras are the maximum you will be able to cope with round your neck. Accessories are best housed in anorak pockets, but before taking off, make sure these pockets are not clamped shut by the seat belts. In addition to a coat with pockets, you will need to wear gloves, because however warm it is on the ground, there is always a dramatic drop in temperature by the time you reach 3,000 feet. So whatever camera you use on an aeronautical assignment, you must feel competent to use it whilst wearing gloves (something that can be practised on the ground).

For most air-to-air assignments I take two 2¼'' square Mamiyaflexes, each

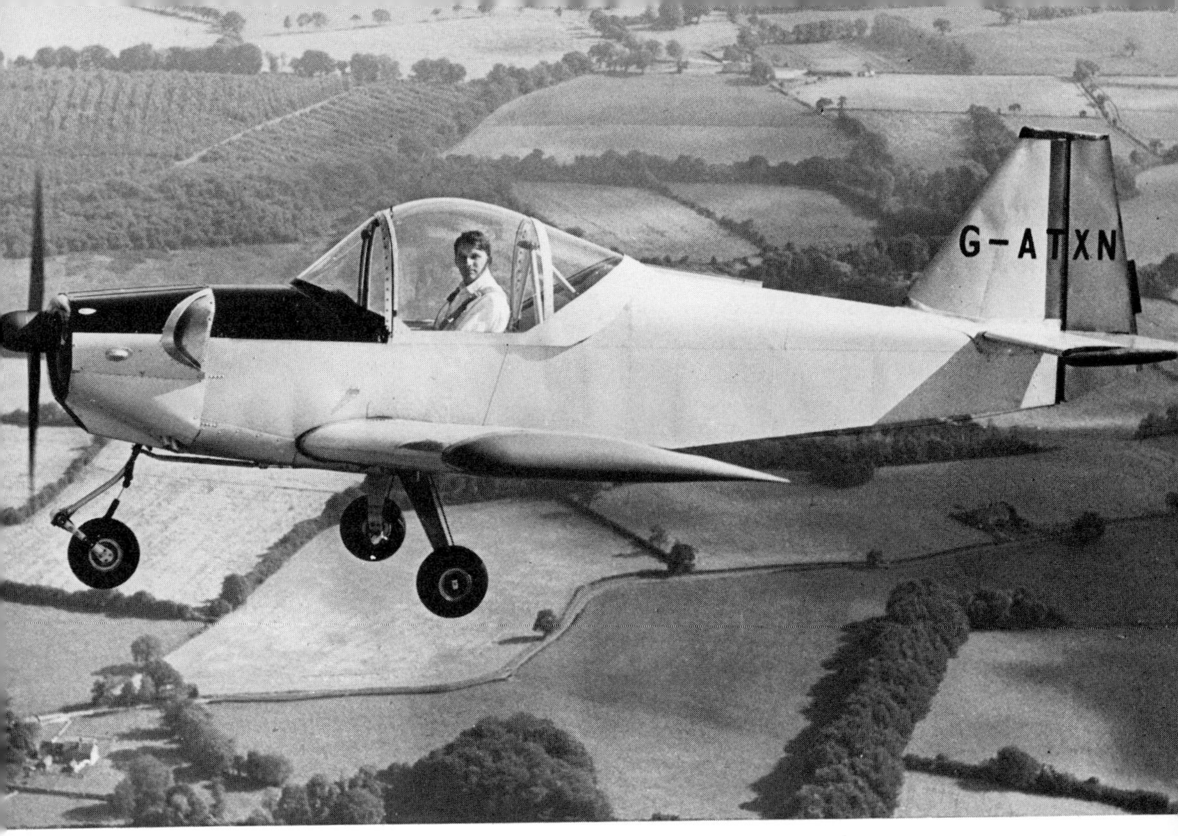

Lorna Minton's superb picture of a Kittiwake light aircraft in flight, has appeared in *Air Pictorial, Sport Aviation* and *Cranfield Magazine*, as well as in several books on aviation.

fitted with a 135mm lens. One camera will usually be loaded with Ektachrome, and the other with a colour negative film of the same speed. Having calculated the exposure time, I can set identical controls on both cameras, and fire away with either camera at will. The reason for the two types of colour film is perhaps obvious. The client usually wants colour prints, but for publication purposes I need colour transparencies in my stock library. If required I can also make black and white prints from the colour negatives, using Kodak's Panalure printing paper. However, if the client requires black and white only, and also needs a wide selection of shots, I would choose to use a Leica camera loaded with a 36 exposure cassette of Panatomic X – and fitted with a 90mm Elmar lens. Many of you single lens reflex readers may wonder why I choose to use a rangefinder camera. The reason is simple. Once airborne on a good day with blue sky and white clouds everywhere, the aeroplane to be photographed is forever popping in and out of cloud shadow, and when viewing this through a single lens reflex camera fitted with a yellow filter, it is extremely difficult to judge whether the aeroplane is in or out of shadow at any given moment. For the photographer's aeroplane will also be popping in and out of cloud shadows, but *not* under the same clouds or at the same time, so you very soon find yourself wondering whether it is your own or the other aeroplane in shadow, and by the time you have taken your eye away from the yellow tinted viewfinder to make sure, the situation has changed again. But with a rangefinder camera, no such problems occur and shooting is made simpler. The 90mm lens has proved over the years to be the best focal length to use, for a shorter lens would necessitate even closer formation flying which would be unsafe. As for longer focal lengths, they run too much risk of camera shake, as they are being used in a vibrating cockpit with a strong slipstream rushing by the open door just where you would be holding the camera. Longer focal lengths also have the disadvantage of perspective errors occurring, in particular, the foreshortening of the near wing.

My reason for choosing such a slow film as Panatomic X is because I'm rather a fine grain fanatic. With so much sky in the pictures, any slight intrusion of grain would become very obvious. Since air-to-air photography is only really possible in good weather, I do not find the slow film speed a hindrance. Using this film, the exposure time is usually in the region of 500th sec at f5.6 (with a X2 yellow filter).

Avoiding copyright problems

Earlier on in this chapter, I mentioned shooting one type of film for the client and another type of film for my stock library, but perhaps I should clarify this situation from a copyright point of view. If a client commissions you to take some air-to-air shots, then the copyright of anything which you take on that mission is the client's. This is fine and as it should be, but if you also wish to run a picture library and need to be free to sell the pictures anywhere, then you will have to be more wary about the terms and conditions of doing the job. My own system is to explain openly that I wish to retain copyright of the pictures, and that therefore I will not charge a fee for doing the work. The client is then under no obligation, and can buy prints at my usual rates if he wants to afterwards. For my part, I am of course taking a gamble, for I am involved in a fair amount of expense in hiring aircraft and so on, but in the long run I can usually more than repay myself from reproduction fees. In any event, it happens to be a system which suits my purposes perfectly. It also pleases the clients!

Speculative markets

Having made a start on a collection of good air-to-air pictures, your most pressing need will be to find sales outlets. Magazines are obviously an outlet, and the aeronautical press is quite an extensive one these days, and many photographs are used with every issue. But like all other freelancing activities,

As well as being reproduced in *Book of Air Sports*, this picture of an Eagle glider, taken by the author, also made the cover of *The Lady*.

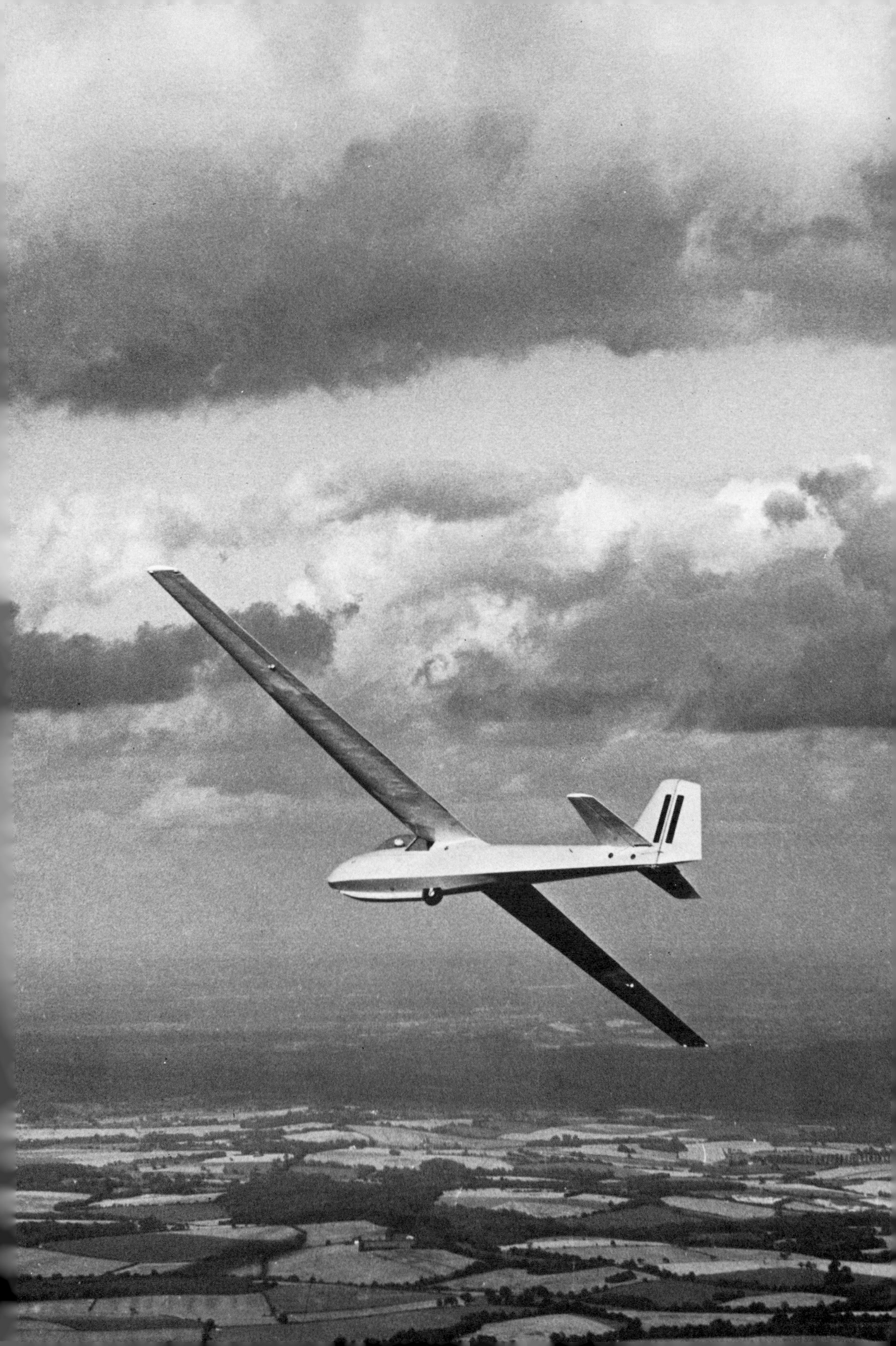

always agree a fee *before* publication, for there are still a few periodicals in this field which do not pay at all for contributions. Other magazines only pay low reproduction fees if they think they can get away with it. So you have to be business-like in your negotiations, for it seems that not even the aeronautical press knows what it costs to hire aeroplanes for photographic work.

On the whole book publishers are a better outlet, for there is a steady output of books on aeronautical matters, and the number of titles published each year appears to be on the increase. These publishers need to be informed of your existence though, and the best way to do this is to organize a mail shot to all publishers who have issued aeronautical titles in the past, and let them have a list of the aeroplane/glider types which you have on file. For a start, a study of aeronautical books in the library and local book shops will supply you with the names of several publishers, and others can be obtained by reading the advertisements in the aeronautical magazines.

Another excellent outlet for aeronautical pictures is the greetings card market – but they will of course only be interested in colour transparencies. On the whole, greetings card publishers have difficulty finding pictures for their male interest range, so they are usually pleased to see aeronautical subjects. For this market, the pictures do not necessarily have to be air-to-air, for some very dramatic ground-to-air pictures can be obtained, and general flying club ground scenes are also used occasionally. The two most important aspects for this market are that the aeroplane or glider is colourful, and that the sky is really blue. Most greetings cards are upright in format, because they show up better on the racks in the shops, so there must be a large area of clear blue sky at the top of the picture where the publisher can overprint the greeting in black or gold. Technical details about the aircraft are of no interest to this market, and neither does it matter if the outline of a particular machine is not very true; all that matters is that it is a colourful, striking picture.

However for the other markets mentioned, it is *very* important that you know precisely what type of aircraft you are photographing, who owns it, where you are flying, and as many other relevant details as you can collect. The attitude of the machine you are photographing is also important, and ideally it should be positioned to show off its lines to perfection. Forget the dramatic angles, or dramatic lighting, and concentrate on obtaining perfect pictures which could be used in aircraft recognition books. These are the shots which sell best.

Start with your feet on the ground!

If you feel inspired to try aeronautical photography having read this far, I suggest that you first go along to your local flying club and ask the C.F.I. (Chief Flying Instructor) if he minds you taking a few ground-to-air shots of launches and landings. Check with him where it is safe to do your photography, and then start to perfect the art of panning, focusing and shooting aircraft all at the same time. After some experience from the ground, and a collection of excellent shots to prove it, you will be ready to start the more expensive, but more exciting task of shooting from the air.

by Raymond Lea　This chapter may come as something of a surprise to those who have been brought up to believe that the bigger the format, the better. While there's still more than a grain of truth in that dictum, the author has successfully sold pictures produced with a 110 camera which he bought mainly for fun. Provided you recognise the limitations, 110 freelancing does offer possibilities.

It is obvious that no-one should try freelancing with only a 110 camera, neither should anyone try who does not have a sound technique and an idea of the markets which might be available to pictures taken on this format. There is also the question, why should anyone bother with tiny 110 negatives, especially since so many people find difficulty in obtaining good quality results from the much bigger 35mm size?

Easy to 'carry a camera'!

The answer to this last point must be sheer portability. In other words, it is better to carry a small 110 camera in your pocket than no camera at all. True, there are several very small fixed lens 35mm cameras now available, but they still tend to be heavier and less pocketable than the smaller 110 cameras, and many people may not wish to pay their usually high price for a camera they feel will not be particularly useful in their freelancing. There is also the fact that the photographic press is taking an increasing interest in 110 photography and therefore there exists a requirement for pictures from this format.

A new challenge

It was these factors, along with a strong desire to discover just what I could do with 110 (as a challenging change from my 35mm work) that led to my acquiring a 110 camera. Obviously it had to have a first-class lens if there was to be any hope of selling its pictures. It must also be truly small but have some form of exposure control. The camera I settled for was a Voigtlander Vitoret 110 which literally clips into my inside jacket pocket or slips comfortably into a trouser pocket. I had read good reports of its lens performance and found these to be fully justified. Its maximum aperture of f5.6 was reasonable since no-one would seriously try to get good results from this format in really poor lighting, and it closed down to f8-11 and f16. Its two shutter speeds were 1/50th sec and 1/125th sec.

This is a pretty basic but realistic specification, given the films available, for 110. Because the film is cartridge loaded it cannot be held dead flat by a pressure plate (as in 35mm), thus depth of field at apertures larger than f5.6

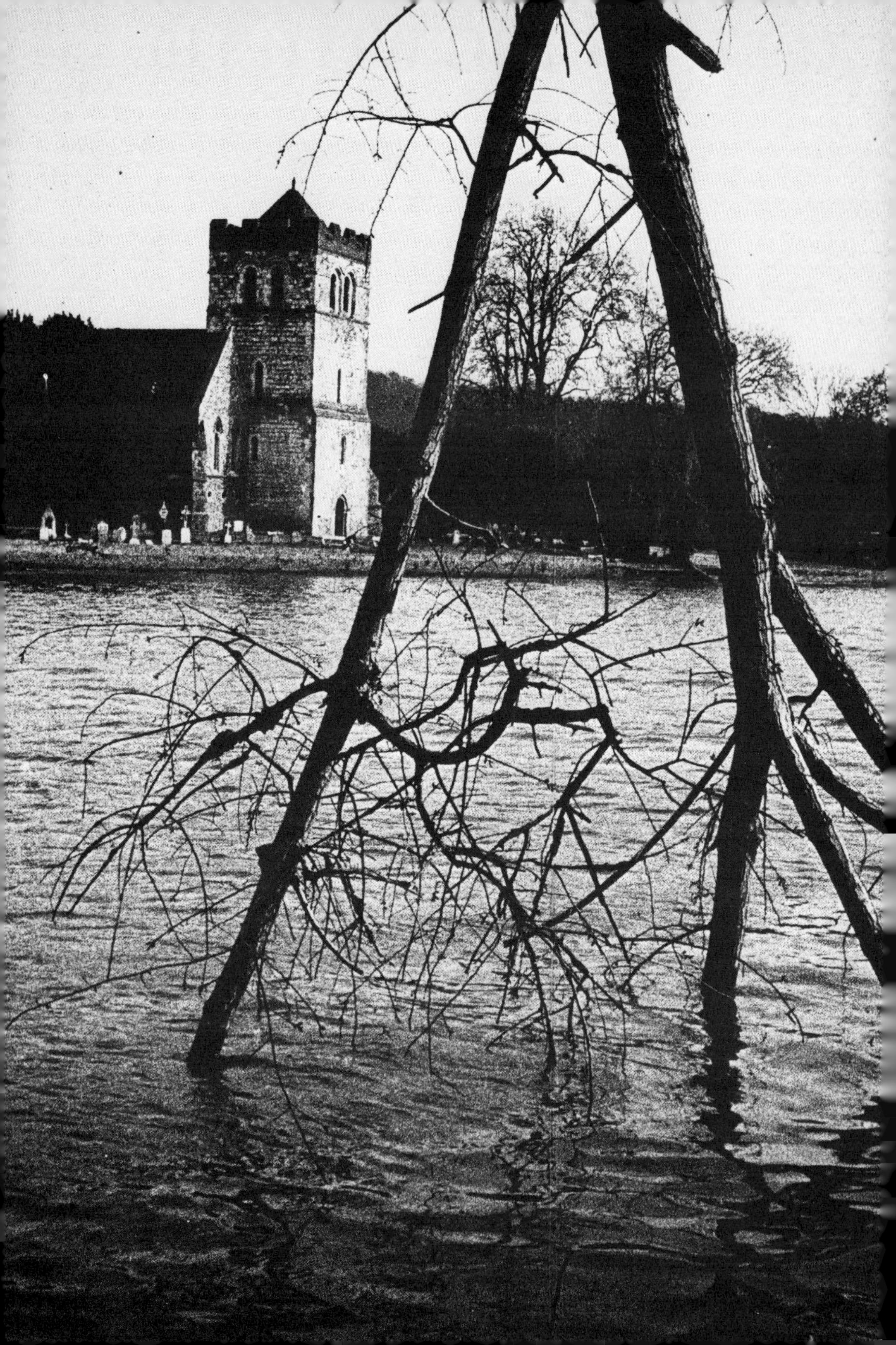

may not be sufficient to compensate for less than perfect film flatness. There are several good quality, small 110 cameras on the market which provide suitable specification and performance without too much cost, and they include one or two with built-in telephoto lens or zoom lens. Also, of course, there are (at present) two SLRs, the Minolta and the Asahi Pentax. The latter in particular suggests that 110 may have much greater scope for serious quality photography in the future since it has a range of lenses, motor-wind and other tailor-made equipment.

110 must be considered as being primarily of interest to a freelance in the field of black and white. True, photographic magazines occasionally use 110 colour transparencies, so there is also an outlet here, but it is unlikely that any other type of publication will use 110 colour in the forseeable future. The only black and white film currently available is Kodak's venerable Verichrome Pan which has been around a long time. Obviously, for use in 110 cameras Kodak improved the emulsion and it can give remarkably good results in the right developer, but 110 does need a modern high performance black and white film.

First results were encouraging . . .

In the meantime one must use Verichrome Pan. When I first tried 110 I expected very little. I had my first film processed commercially as I did not own a 110 tank, and then did my own printing. If you take up 110 you must know what you are doing in the darkroom and own a really good enlarger lens. I found that with my enlarger head at the very top of its column I could get a whole-plate print from the entire area of a 110 negative. I focused using a micro focus finder and measured the required exposure with a CdS enlarger meter. Obviously, with the lens set to f5.6, exposure times were considerably longer than for 35mm printing, being anything between 20-60 seconds depending upon negative density, and one must make sure that the enlarger will remain rock steady during the exposure if sharpness is not to be affected. The first prints I made were decidedly encouraging; somewhat grainy but sharp and well detailed.

From this happy start I went on to doing my own developing as well as printing. The most promising developer seemed to be Kodak's Microdol X, on which I have standardized for nearly 20 years. I always use it diluted 1-3 and find it gives unbeatable sharpness, fine grain and good tonal range with the opposition's (!) FP4, and with Kodak's Tri-X. I had to guess development time with my first 110 film and tried 10 minutes at the usual 75°F, agitating for 5 secs every 30 secs. This produced negatives which printed easily on soft and normal grades of Kodak and Ilford bromide papers, quite the best grades for such tiny negatives because they keep the effect of graininess at a minimum. Hard grades emphasise grain in 35mm photography and this is accentuated with pictorial 110 pictures.

**This unusual shot, taken by the Thames at
Marlow, has illustrated articles in** *Amateur
Photographer* **and** *Practical Photography*.
Taken by the author with a 110 camera.

. . . And they sold!

I also managed to extend my enlarger so that I could make approximately 10 x 8 in. prints from the tiny negatives. The upshot of all this was to discover that Verichrome Pan in Microdol X, exposed in a 110 camera with a really good lens, was quite capable of producing results of a standard high enough to be saleable to a variety of magazines and other publications. Apart from the photo press I realised that these would include country and county magazines, some women's magazines, *The Lady*, *This England*, boating journals, etc., etc. I contribute articles to a number of journals and there was no doubt that when suitable these could be accompanied by 110 pictures.

But be realistic

Now common sense must come into all this. It is still much easier and more practical to use 35mm for professional quality results and the use of my 110 camera has not made my 35mm equipment redundant! But 110 does have its own specialised markets in the photo press and on some occasions helps to obtain pictures when carrying a 35mm camera would not be so convenient. As I wrote earlier, better to carry a 110 camera, in case a good subject presents itself, than to have no camera at all.

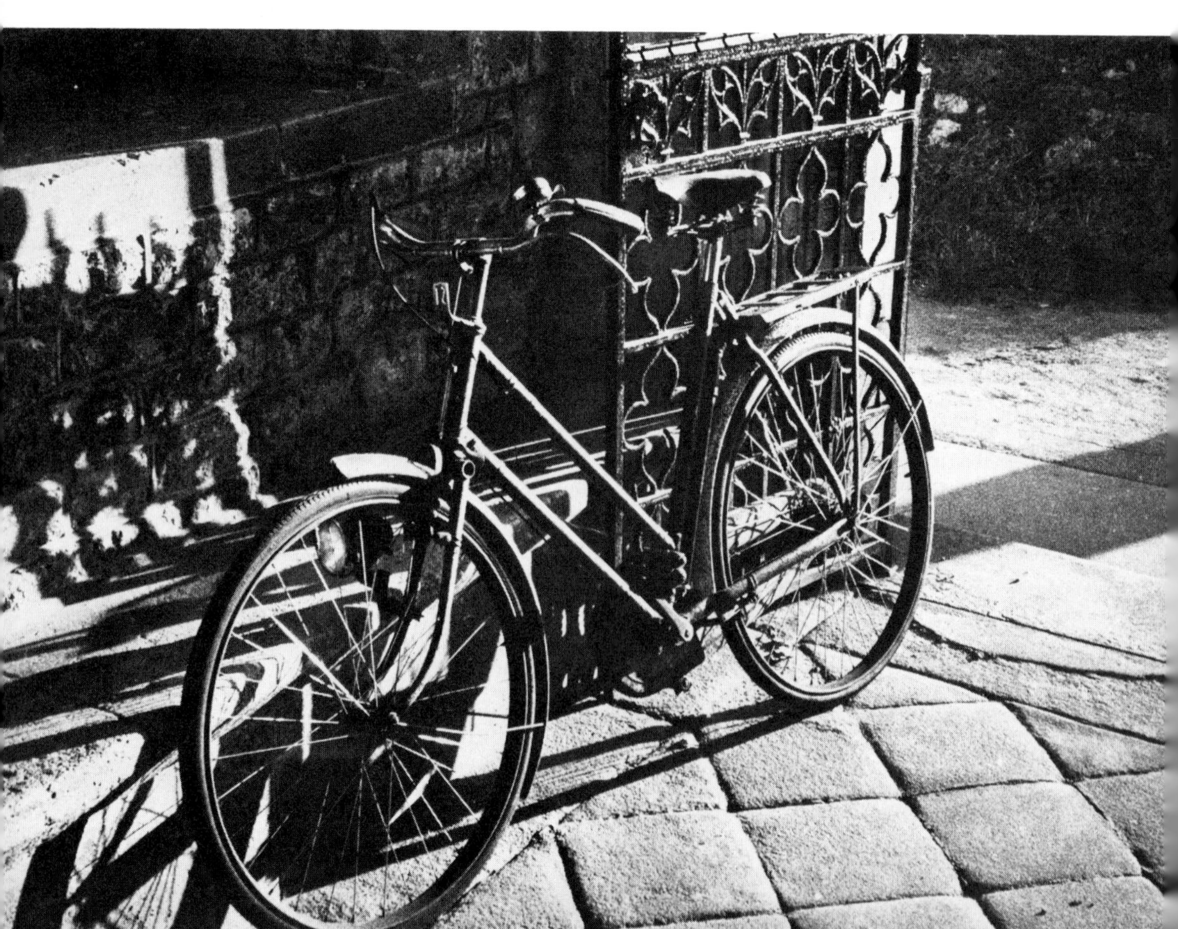

In order for results to be viable, considerable care must be taken over the subjects you photograph and the way you go about it. With such a small negative the frame should be filled as much as possible – there is little scope for enlarging just a part as with a sharp 35mm negative. So subjects must be suitable for this. For example, in the case of animals you could hope to get a good shot of a horse but cats and most dogs, taken singly, would prove too small since most 110 cameras do not focus closer than about 6 feet. It is because of this that some 110 models have a built-in telephoto lens to enable you to get a large image without having to approach your subject any closer. Obviously an SLR will be much more flexible but always the frame must be 'all lean meat with no fat'. Remember that even with my enlarger head extended I can only just get a 10 x 8 in. print (the usual freelance size) using the entire area of a 110 negative. This is with the standard 50mm enlarger lens. A lens of 40mm would be more suitable for this format but a good one is a really costly item.

Best results on sunny days

I have taken black and white 110 pictures in dull lighting but the best results come on days of sunshine, and all the usual considerations of shooting in angled lighting to produce textures and an impression of depth within a scene apply. I was surprised to discover how well 110 can cope with back-lit subjects, so long as the lens is shaded by either holding one's hand out over the lens (tricky, this, for the hand can intrude on the image), or else by shooting from the shade of a tree trunk, wall, blind, etc.

A wide range of subjects

The subjects I look out for with my 110 vary considerably, always bearing in mind the markets to which they might sell. For the photo press you can, of course, take a wide range of subjects and the more you can show the potential of 110, the better. I have also taken shots with a much 'humbler' 110 camera, and this too has proved capable of producing quite sharp 10 x 8 in. prints of interest to the hobby magazines. For country, county and other usual freelance markets I take any subject which might prove to be of interest, whether it be an interesting building (perhaps undergoing a conversion), an attractive landscape scene, a subject suited to one of the correspondence pages of magazines such as *Country Life* or *The Field*, a human interest picture, and so on. The scope is very wide, given that you keep your eyes open at all times and use your imagination.

A shot which shows how well 110 can cope with a tricky, unusual subject. This is one of a series of pictures taken by the author and published as a portfolio in *Practical Photography*.

My constant companion!

Above all I regard my little 110, carried so easily in my pocket, as a constant companion ever-ready, if the light is good enough, to capture pictures which otherwise I might miss. I also find it useful to take along on those occasions when I primarily concentrate on shooting colour. It's always there if a subject crops up.

The author succeeded in placing this 110 picture with *Buckinghamshire Countryside* and *Amateur Photographer*.

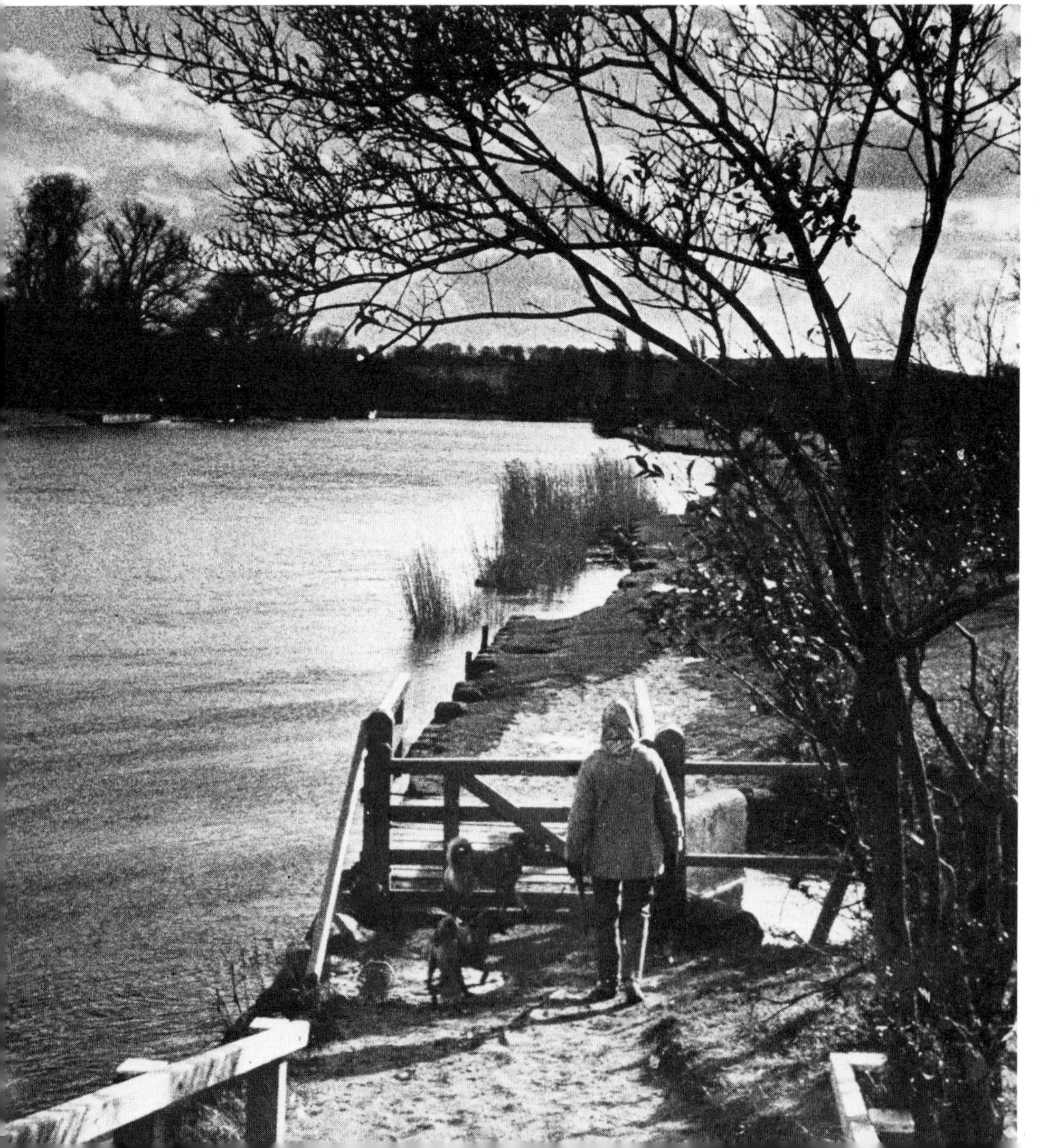

13

CASH FROM HOUSE MAGAZINES

by Willie Pereira House magazines are frequently overlooked by the freelance photographer, yet they do present a potentially lucrative market. The author has achieved considerable success in this area and reckons that the field is wide open to the competent contributor who can supply the somewhat undemanding needs of house journals.

Look at the rather ordinary picture shown here of a contestant proudly displaying a floral arrangement which won her first prize in a horticultural show. This is just one example of the type of photograph which has earned me hundreds of pounds from publications which are very often ignored by the freelance photographer.

I refer, of course, to the numerous house magazines produced by firms and organisations all over the country. They are aimed at the staffs and/or the clients of the companies concerned.

I stumbled across two of these house magazines some years ago when I moved to work in Oxfordshire and my patch included the atomic research establishment at Harwell, and the Didcot Power Station.

I sent off my first story and picture about a Harwell employee to *Atom News* – the Atomic Energy Authority's staff newspaper. The material was accepted and I was pleasantly surprised when I received payment for the effort: *Atom News*, which is London based, pays near Fleet Street rates.

Finding stories and markets

With this under my belt I began looking around for other similar markets and soon I was submitting material to publications like *South Western Power* (the newspaper for the Central Electricity Generating Board's staff working in the south western region); and *Watney's West* and *Wales News*.

For some time I was quite fortunate in that the stories and pictures I sold to these publications emanated through my work as a reporter with a local newspaper. But I always scrutinised other local newspapers as well as the one I worked for to pick out likely picture stories covered by other reporters.

All I did then was to look up the people in the stories, take the pictures, and I was home.

Now that I run my own business I follow this same procedure for, invariably, the stories in newspapers tell you what a person does for a living or where he works. It is then not difficult to find out if the firm where the person works publishes a house magazine.

However, before setting out I find it useful to ring up the editor of the publication to enquire if he is interested in the story.

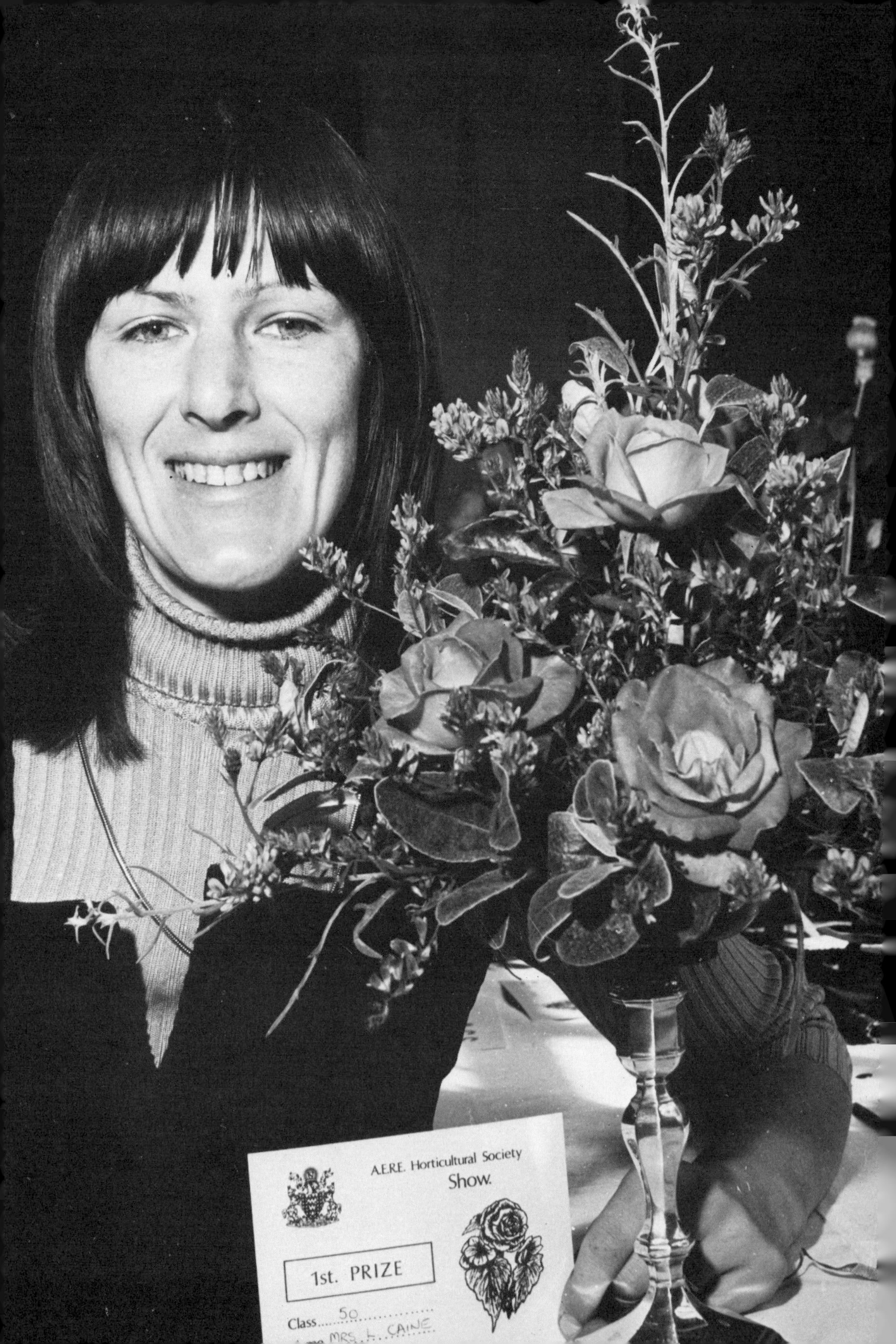
A.E.R.E. Horticultural Society
Show.
1st. PRIZE
Class 50
Name MRS L CAINE

But my involvement with house magazines over the years has given me a sixth sense which has not yet failed me. When I pick up a story from a local newspaper I can usually tell whether it is likely house magazine material.

If I believe it has a good chance of selling, I do the story regardless and submit it on spec; for there is always another local newspaper which could be interested in an updated story and picture on the same subject.

House mags use wedding pictures!

Another avenue which I have exploited successfully is wedding pictures.

Whenever I cover a wedding I usually submit a few prints to the local newspapers – provided, of course, that the couple do not object.

Here, again, I question the couple and find out where they work and invariably there is a house magazine which will be interested in a picture of the happy couple!

The same goes for any function you care to name, from sports meetings to stamp collecting. If you are there for some reason or other it is always worth having a quick word with prize winners to find out where they work.

The picture reproduced here was taken after I did a general story for the newspaper I then worked for. There were numerous potential pictures I could have taken for *Atom News*, but the lady happened to be near her prize-winning exhibit and she was more than pleased to pose for me.

I am usually able to provide copy with any pictures I take but if, for some reason, I am not able to do so I always make sure the editor of the house magazine concerned gets the name, address and telephone number of the person I have photographed so that he can follow up the story.

'Hold the front page!'

There is one final point I wish to make. This is that I always endeavour to find out the deadline of a house magazine, and should I have a picture story which is running very close to it, I always ring the editor to inform him of what I am doing. In that way he can decide whether to hold a space for the story or leave it over for the next edition.

This picture, taken by the author and depicting a Harwell employee, sold to *Atom News*, the Atomic Energy Authority's house journal.

14

ADDING WORDS FOR ADDED PROFITS

by Roger Ashford The contributor who can not only offer an editor top quality photography, but who can also provide well-written copy, is something of a rarity. The author, who has written and illustrated articles for many different types of publications, explains how to set about producing a complete package of words and pictures.

Undoubtedly the sale of single photographs can be quite profitable, but sooner or later every ambitious freelance will want to find ways of increasing his income. There are two ways to do this. Either one must increase one's output of photographs or one can start to offer a complete package, in the form of illustrated articles. Of the two courses open the latter is by far the more profitable and, in many ways, easier, for there comes a point in the sale of photographs alone when one physically cannot produce a greater volume of work – after all, there are only twenty-four hours in a day and even the most creative have to admit that they sometimes run short of ideas. The latter course has the added advantage that, whilst it is relatively easy for publishers to find good writers or photographers, the person who successfully combines the two crafts is a rarity.

That is not to say, however, that producing a concise, well written article, illustrated with one's own photographs, is difficult. Looked at from an editor's viewpoint, it is far more logical to buy an illustrated article from a single source where the illustrations and text will complement each other, than to attempt to match photographs from the publication's files to a particular article. By producing illustrated articles you are, therefore, creating a market for your own photographs, rather than relying upon other writers to do this for you, and hence are increasing your sales.

You will also find that your choice of subjects will be increased when you can produce the complete package. This puts you very much in command of your own destiny as far as sales are concerned. No longer are you limited to basically visual or newsworthy topics where the photograph tells the story. By adding words you are able to explore areas previously only open to the writer – you, however, have the advantage in that your writing is illustrated. In terms of sales the difference, once one begins to add words, can be phenomenal. But the approach to producing saleable illustrated articles is slightly different from that required to sell single photographs. The adoption of a truly professional and systematic approach, however, will more than repay the extra effort involved.

Getting started

But how does one start selling illustrated articles? The answer to this question really depends upon one's preferred method of working. Some writer-photographers attempt to match an article idea to a market, whilst others prefer to select a specific market and then tailor their articles accordingly. But whichever way one likes to work, market research, as in all branches of freelancing, is of the essence. If you do not know the requirements of a cross-section of the magazine publishing industry you will never attain significant sales. If you are already selling single photographs you should be fairly conversant with the needs of a fairly wide variety of magazines. Newcomers should, however, research several issues of any publication to which they hope to contribute.

The choice of magazines is entirely up to the individual concerned. Obviously if one has interests outside photography then any publications dealing with that topic would make a good starting point. If photography is your all-consuming passion then it may seem that an article for the photographic press would be a good bet. Alternatively, you could start by concentrating upon the 'countryside' or county publications. Nearly every county in the country has its own magazine, and an article sold to one of these has started more than one successful photojournalist on the road to fortune. It will be found that this type of market does not pay very well – but that first acceptance slip is worth its weight in gold. It convinces you, if you needed convincing, that what you have to say is worth publishing.

First get the facts

When researching a magazine it is not enough simply to browse through the pages stopping when something catches one's attention. This aspect of freelancing is the most important, for it is the basis upon which all your future sales are founded. It must, therefore, be tackled in a businesslike fashion. Personally, I like to build up a 'fact sheet' on each magazine for which I intend to work. The first item on this sheet is the name and editorial address of the magazine. Also, if possible, I add to this the name of the editor or the contact within the magazine to whom the work is sent.

When researching a magazine the first task is to try to establish how many articles in a particular issue have been produced by outside contributors. This is done by comparing the names of the authors with the list of the magazine's editorial staff which usually appears on or near the contents page. Then, by reading a representative sample of the articles published, one must get a clear idea of the writing style used. For instance, is it a light, 'chatty' style as used in many women's magazines or is it a heavier, more formal style reminiscent of that used in some professional journals. Next, and perhaps most obviously, one must look at the type of subject matter which the articles deal with and what, if any, bias they have – for instance is the magazine conservation minded, or does it lean towards one particular political group.

All of these details, along with any peculiarities or idiosyncrasies which you notice about the magazine, should go down on your fact sheet. In the course of time this sheet is added to or amended as your knowledge of the publication grows. A word of warning – never rely on your memory here, as in time you will find that you are producing work for so many magazines that sooner or later you will forget a vital point. All of the information which you glean about a particular magazine must go on the fact sheet. In addition to this your fact sheet should also contain details of the type of photographs which illustrate each article – whether they are colour or monochrome; whether they are predominantly upright or view; whether they contain human interest; and so on.

Now – what to write about?

Having built up a fact sheet on about six magazines you will now have a good idea of the type of subject matter with which they concern themselves. Now comes your greatest problem, and one which is likely to beset you for the rest of your freelance life – what to write about. Even assuming that your chosen publications are in one of the specialist fields you are still spoiled for choice as far as subject matter is concerned. To be successful then, you have to become an 'ideas machine'. You must look at everything with an eye to a possible future publication.

For a start your articles will, no doubt, be of a fairly straightforward nature. If you are writing for a county magazine the article may be about a place of interest in your locality; or if your article is for a specialist publication – a hobbies magazine for instance – it may be about an aspect of that subject with which you are particularly familiar. Nevertheless you must still be on the look-out for new subjects upon which to produce articles. Careful study of your local newspapers will often yield ideas. But, again, your reading must be purposeful. In fact you must approach everything which you read in a rather mercenary frame of mind – trying all the time to think whether what you are reading can be, in some way, incorporated in, or developed into, an illustrated article.

In some instances you may find that seemingly trivial local matters have some bearing upon a far larger national issue – it is then up to you to exploit the connections between the two. A case in point occurred in my locality recently. The local water authority were involved in trying to get a Bill through Parliament giving them controlling rights over recreational use of the waterways in its area. Had this Bill been passed it would have had far-reaching consequences nationally. The issues raised enabled me to sell five different illustrated articles on the topic for a total of several hundred pounds. And my initial information came from a ten line paragraph in the local paper.

The successful freelance soon develops a habit of thinking of everything he reads, hears or sees in terms of a possible article. A process which, incidentally, becomes almost subconscious after a time. Again, however, you must not be tempted to rely on your memory. If an idea comes to you make a note of it immediately.

Other great sources of ideas are your local societies. Try to get to know people in all of your important local groups such as conservation societies, natural history groups etc. It is surprising how often their activities can yield a profitable article. I have also found that browsing through back numbers of the BFP *Market Newsletter* can often spark off ideas.

Make the most of your ideas

Once you have taken the first steps in producing illustrated articles, you may find that you are in the position where you have several ideas but you are not sure which to concentrate on. It is always wise in this instance to try to assess the market potential of each idea. Remember that once the article has been published it is not necessarily dead. It can often be re-written and sold to other publications. Indeed, this resale potential should be one of your major considerations when assessing the potential of all non-topical subjects. The only time that you should even consider spending valuable time on the preparation of an article which can only possibly be sold once is if that sale is for a high fee.

When the idea is one which is connected with a topical issue then it is usually worth considering how many different articles can be written on various aspects of the theme. If the subject can be approached from several angles to yield more than one article then these can safely be sold to non-competing magazines at the same time. It is important to be sure, in this case, that the publications in question are not competitors in the same field, for if you ignore this rule you will lose many friends and influence no-one.

Once you become known . . .

Initially you will, no doubt, be producing articles 'on spec' and submitting them to your chosen markets in the hope that they will be accepted. Once your name becomes known within those markets, however, you can change your tactics. If you have an idea which you think may appeal to a market which has already accepted some of your work, a short letter to the editor giving brief details of that idea is a far better initial course of action than actually producing the article on spec. If, for some reason, the editor does not like the idea, you will know without having to go to the trouble and expense of actually producing the article. Your time can then be spent more profitably in other directions. You may find it best, if you have a lot of ideas, to send out these letters a few at a time. In this way you can be working on the ideas which have already aroused some interest while you are awaiting replies from other editors. Obviously the number of ideas which you send out, and at what intervals, depends upon how long it takes you to produce an article.

Finally, a word of warning on the theme of writing to editors. Never send them a list of ideas and ask them to pick the ones which they would like you to produce for them. Each letter should contain one or, at most, two ideas – a list of five or six will usually find its way straight into the waste bin.

The time to broaden your horizons

Once having successfully sold articles to a small group of magazines it is time to widen your repertoire of prospective markets. Your initial choice of five or six magazines will probably have covered basically the same field. It is now, having got your name known in this field, that you must broaden your horizons in order that you become familiar with the requirements of a far greater variety of publications. In this way you will be able to tailor all of your ideas to a market and none will be wasted.

Obviously, buying copies of every magazine which you could ever conceivably work for would be prohibitively expensive. The answer to this problem is to make use of the reading room in your local library. Here you should find a fairly wide variety of publications – many of which can be included in your market research. Additionally, a browse through the titles to be found on the shelves of any large booksellers will often yield further new markets.

The aspiring freelance should also never overlook the opportunities offered by new publications. When a magazine first appears on the bookstalls its payment to outside contributors is often quite low. This tends to discourage many of the more experienced freelances from approaching this market – but when considered in a businesslike way this attitude can prove wrong. Although the fees offered initially may be low, these are likely to be increased as the circulation of the magazine grows – and, invariably, the editors of these magazines look more favourably upon the work of their earlier contributors. Additionally, a new magazine may be so short of material in its first few months that one may have several different articles published in a single issue. In fact one magazine to which I contribute regularly did just this when it first appeared – aside from the regular columns in the magazine, all except one of the feature articles in one particular issue were mine; and although the fees paid for each were relatively small, the total on the cheque at the end of the month ran into three figures.

Overseas markets

Sooner or later in the career of every freelance, whether he be full or part-time, the question of overseas markets arises. In most cases they represent a rather thorny problem, for they are almost impossible to research in the same thorough manner as those published nearer home. However, if one is basically a specialist producing work for one particular type of publication then the problem is not quite so great. Titles and addresses of the overseas magazines in one's field of specialisation may be found in most of the major 'Press Guides'.

Once having established the existence of a particular magazine it is then really a question of submit and see what happens. If, however, one's work has already been widely published, then a letter to the editor of your chosen overseas market may bring results – sometimes even in the form of sample copies of the magazine.

Overseas marketing must be considered as a long term issue for, whichever way one tackles the problem, knowledge of a wide variety of publications will take a considerable time to build up. The only alternative to this is, of course, the use of an agent. But if one is to adopt this course of action one must keep up a high output of new material to justify the added expense.

Producing the goods

Knowing the markets is only one aspect of freelancing. It is no use knowing where to sell if one cannot produce the goods – and this is the real 'nuts and bolts' side of the job. Not only must one be able to produce the illustrated article but this must be in a form which the prospective market will accept.

You must thoroughly research your subject to ensure accuracy. If the subject is one which is familiar to you this should not present any problems, but if, as must eventually happen, you are venturing into pastures new you must be sure of your facts. If you are not an expert in the subject about which you are writing then you must have enough facts at your fingertips so that you at least appear to be one. Failing this you must seek the help of an expert in the particular field.

You will soon learn, however, that every magazine has amongst its readers a fair smattering of amateur critics who will be only too eager, given the chance, to air their expertise, at your expense, through the magazine's correspondence columns. Too much of this type of criticism can damage your credibility with other readers and, equally important, the editor. On a more heartening note and, in effect, the other side of the same coin is the fact that if your articles are really interesting and informative you will get more than your fair share of mail from readers – many seeking advice or guidance – and these should always be answered.

As to how one goes about researching an article – it really depends upon the subject. If the article is purely factual and of a non-topical nature then the local reference library is a good place to start, but if the article is of a topical, or human interest, type this usually means interviewing those involved. There is no special technique involved in interviewing the subjects of an article. Most people are only too pleased to talk about themselves – but do respect anything which you are told in confidence. It is often a good idea before an interview to make a few notes as to how you wish the story to unfold. You then have a logical pattern for your questions to follow – but, needless to say, do not be too rigid in your adherence to these notes as this can often lead to your missing an important point.

These pictures, by Raymond Balfour, are part of a series which were used to illustrate an article about 'John Christmas Thomas, Coracle Maker'.

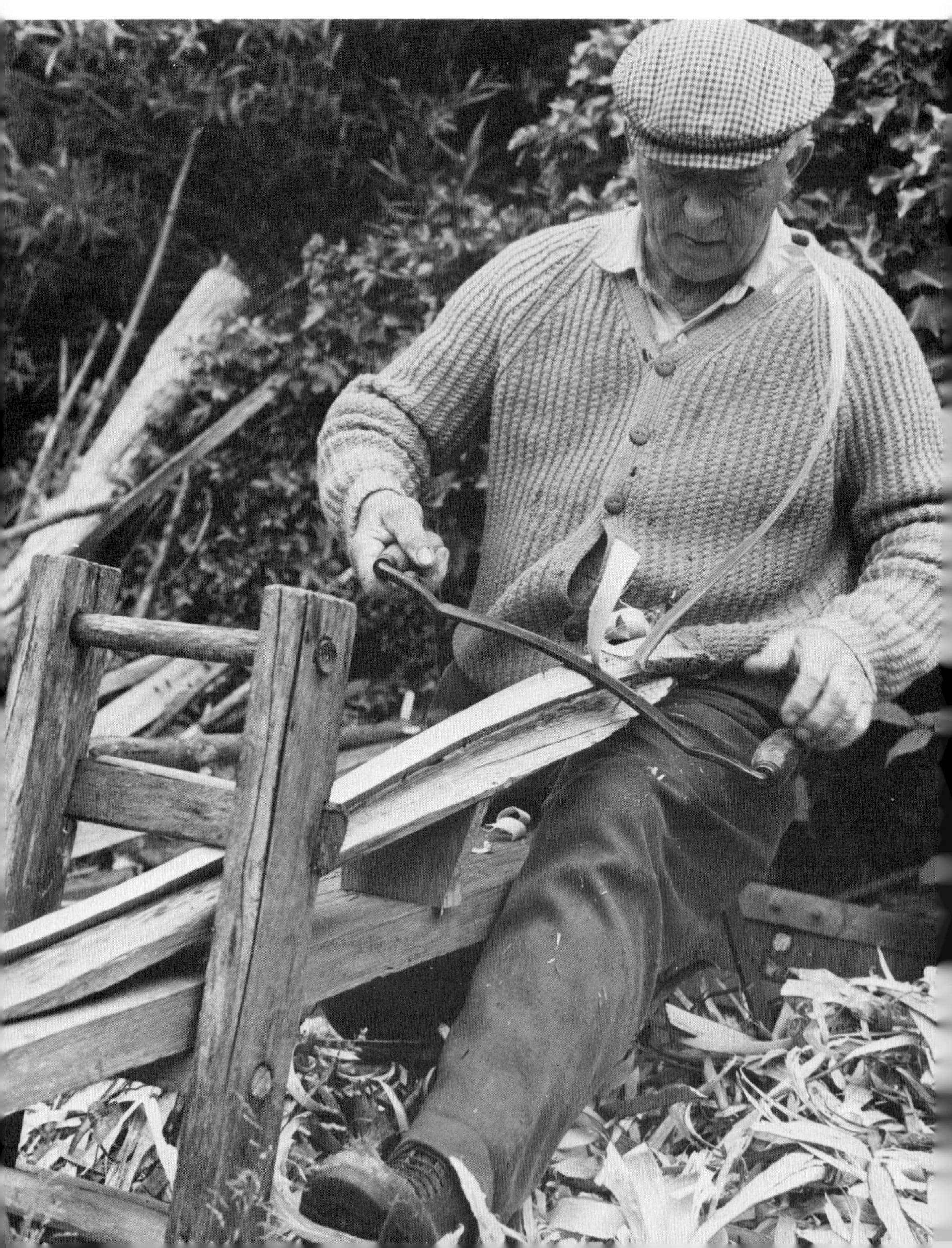

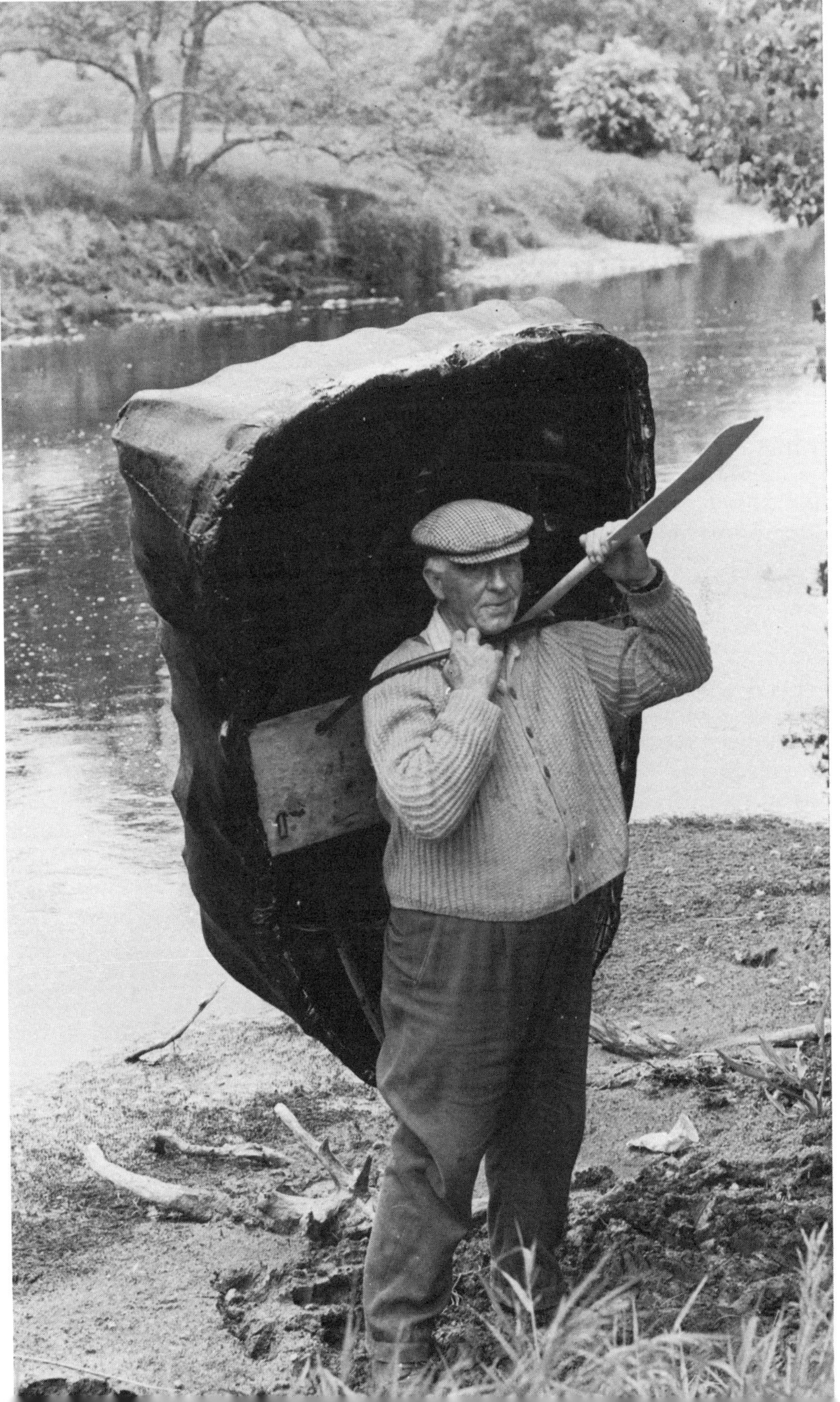

How many words?

Once having established the facts which you intend to use in the article you are ready to begin writing. You must first, however, set yourself a target as far as the length of the article is concerned. In some cases, where the pictures tell the story, the article may be no more than an extended caption of a few hundred words. 'Fillers' of up to about 800 words also sell quite well but the average illustrated article runs to between 1,000 and 3,000 words depending on the market and, of course, the subject; a few magazines will use articles of 5,000 words and even longer.

Your first step in actually getting something down on paper should be to assemble all of the facts which you have gathered into some sort of logical sequence. You can then use this as the outline of the article. Initially you may find that you have to write out the entire piece in longhand before you commit it, irrevocably, to a typewritten manuscript; but after some practice you will find that it is quite easy to produce the finished article from your rough outline. But as previously indicated, whichever way you work, you must always bear in mind the style of the magazine for which you are writing. It is no earthly use writing a light-hearted, chatty article for a publication which uses a formal style – or vice versa. You must conform to the style of your market: do not think that they will change it just so that they can use your article – no matter how interesting it may be.

Grab the editor's attention

It is as well to give careful consideration to the title and opening paragraph of your article, since they can have a profound effect on its sales potential. An inappropriate title or an opening paragraph that fails to grab the reader's attention can destroy the saleability of an otherwise well-written piece. Remember that magazine editors are busy people and are unlikely to wade through an article that doesn't immediately grab their interest.

If an article has an interesting title this will attract the editor's attention and make him want to know more. This will, naturally, lead him to read the opening paragraph and this, in turn, should make him want to read more. It is for this reason that you should give a great deal of attention to those first few lines. They should contain just enough facts, presented in such a manner, to motivate him to read on.

Many writers find it advantageous to write out this entire paragraph as a part of their outline before going on to produce the article. This has the advantage that it may then be altered or amended until the balance is just right. With a little practice you will find that once having perfected your opening the rest of the article flows quite naturally, moving easily from one to another of the salient points which you wish to make.

Finally, never let the article ramble. All of the most successful articles are clear, accurate and concise, dwelling only upon those points which demand extra attention.

Needless to say all manuscripts submitted for possible publication should be neatly typed – and double-spaced. When finished it should have a cover sheet bearing the title, approximate length, author's name and address, the number of illustrations included and a declaration of the copyright being offered e.g. First British Rights, First North American Rights, etc.

Make sure the pictures are right, too!

Having written the article our attention must now be turned to the production of the illustrations. The number of prints accompanying a particular piece of writing is really dictated by the subject of the article. If possible every point discussed in the article should be illustrated – if, of course, it is capable of being expressed visually. You can rarely give an editor too many illustrations from which to choose, but every one submitted should be included for a good reason and not just as a 'make weight'. It is only on rare occasions, however, that every print which you submit will be used and for this reason you should never make direct reference to any particular illustration in the text.

You should know the type of illustrations preferred by a particular market from your research and your findings in this context must be followed. As you will probably, over the course of time, sell articles on the same subject many times, your negatives must be filed in such a way that they are easily accessible. Every time that you sell such an article you will have to produce a new batch of prints to illustrate it, and in order that you can find the required negatives easily some form of referencing is essential.

Personally I prefer the card index system whereby each film exposed is given a reference number and this is recorded on cards under subject headings. As each of my negatives is printed many times over the years I also make notes as to enlarging exposures – something which, incidentally, you can only do if your technique is standardised. In my darkroom I have a set of charts made from large sheets of squared paper. On these each negative is allocated a square and on that square I note, when the negative is printed, details of the height of the enlarger head above the baseboard and the exposure time required. By reference to this I can then produce the identical print at a later date without having to resort to the time- and material-wasting business of making test strips.

Keep adequate records

The really successful writer-photographer must be able to spend as much of his time as possible on the production of the illustrated articles which provide his income. Nevertheless, a certain amount of time must be spent on seemingly unproductive administration. Most freelances find this an extremely tiresome task and therefore many do not bother to keep adequate records – but such an attitude is entirely counter-productive. If you are to benefit to the full from any freelance activities you must have an efficient filing system. Obviously, the more streamlined this is, the less time it will take you to keep it up-to-date and, more important, the easier it will be to find information when it is needed.

In addition to the negative filing system already mentioned you should keep records of all the articles which you produce. In my case this is again based on a card index system. Each article written is given a separate card on which are noted the title, length, reference number and the references of all the negatives used to illustrate it. Below this I then list the markets to which it is sent and the date posted. If the article is accepted I put in the date upon which I was notified and then when it is published I put in the publication date and the fee paid. If, on the other hand, the article is returned, I simply insert an 'R' against the entry and submit it to another outlet – usually after some rewriting to suit the new market. By a close study of the file cards over a period of time it is possible to build up a very clear idea of the working methods of many of your regular markets.

Needless to say I also file carbon copies of every article which I produce and these are stored in numerical order – the number being that given to each in the card index. Freelances who base much of their work upon local issues may also find it advantageous to keep on file details of these in the form of cuttings from local newspapers. These are best filed under subject headings and it will be found that over a period of time the knowledge gained from them will be invaluable.

It's worth the effort

There is no doubt that the time and effort spent in acquiring the extra skills involved in supplying a complete package of words and pictures can be most rewarding, both financially and in terms of added interest. So why not try it and reap even greater rewards from your freelancing?

by Ted Schwarz The United States offers a vast market for freelance material, and most American publications are more than pleased to consider contributions from Britain. A top American freelance, whose work appears regularly in many U.S. publications, explains how the British contributor should approach the market.

Many freelances fail to realise that distance and desirability often go hand-in-hand when selling to a publisher. What gives an editor the 'I've-seen-it-all-before' blues in one country is excitingly 'exotic' to an editor of a similar publication in another country.

For example, I live in the American Southwest, in Tucson, Arizona, a growing community which is seldom featured in American magazines. It is true that the desert region around the state is regularly photographed, but I am speaking of pictures taken within the city itself, images which could be taken in any cosmopolitan area anywhere in the country. There is little market for them unless they are truly unique, and this seldom occurs. However, because of my location more than 2,500 miles from the New York publishing centre, my photographs are in great demand. Photo stories about a black dress designer working in Tucson, a girl who recovered from severe brain damage, a barber who runs a club where you can get your hair cut while watching a belly dancer, and numerous others, all sell regularly. I also have work appear internationally in Germany, Australia and elsewhere. As one editor explained, 'We don't want to be in the position of taking only the work of photographers in New York or Los Angeles. We want to show our readers what is going on in lesser known parts of the country.'

How does all this relate to you, a photographer who lives in a different country? Well, the demand for your work is even greater than mine if you address it to the right publications. Once you have an understanding of the vast, seemingly insatiable American publishing market, you will discover that your photographs on file can bring you a far larger return than you ever thought possible.

Basically there are three types of magazines published within the United States — trade journals, special interest publications and general interest periodicals. These three categories account for several thousand different magazines, the majority of them constantly 'hungry' for pictures such as yours, if you know how to market them.

Trade journals

Trade journals are publications which relate to a particular business or industry. In the field of photography, for example, American trade journals include *The Rangefinder Magazine,* the *Journal of the Professional Photographers of America, Studio Photography, Functional Photography* and *Technical Photography.* In the hotel and restaurant field there are such publications as *Managing The Leisure Facility, Motel/Motor Inn Journal, Resort & Motel Magazine, Innkeeping World* and others. There are publications relating to doctors and hospitals, law, leather goods, education, journalism, groceries, government employees and numerous others. Each is concerned with a specialised business as well as with jobs within the field. For example, there will be a magazine for the director of a hospital, others for the doctors, still different ones for nurses and numerous publications for each job skill within the institution.

The pay offered by trade journals ranges from a low of perhaps £10, to a high which can be £300 or more. If you are able to supply an article with your photo submission and not just caption material, your pay will increase. Some publications also raise their rates when they can count on regular, usable submissions from you.

In order to break into the trade journal field, you need to think about stories which will be of interest to the American reader. For example, take the case of fire fighting. *Fire Times* is the trade journal of volunteer firemen and is published by the American Fire Fighters Association. Volunteer fire fighters work in sparsely populated areas outside major cities, either providing total protection or supplementing an undermanned force of full time fire fighters.

If you wanted to sell photographs to *Fire Times,* you would want to start with images which relate to the rural fire fighting techniques in your area or other parts of Britain. These might show specialised techniques, unusual equipment or similar visual information. Talk with the people in charge of rural fire fighting to give you insight into the potential picture stories. Ideally you will ride with the firemen when they answer calls so that you can record as much action as possible.

Another American trade journal relating to fire fighting is a potential market for the freelance who has access to more sophisticated areas. *Fire Engineering* would be interested in unusual ways fire prevention information is presented to the public, techniques of fire fighting, new equipment that might not have been introduced into the United States (the heads of the departments and equipment manufacturers can guide you) and similar information. You might also consider a photo feature which shows fire fighting in several areas. This would be sold as an illustrated piece on fire fighting abroad. Remember, to Americans, your local scenes represent 'abroad'.

Presentation

The types of photographs you take must be consistent with every publication. The first consideration is film. Most magazines buy more black-and-white than colour work because of reproduction costs. It is cheaper to use black-and-white prints than to publish colour. Thus black-and-white images should be your primary concern. As in Britain, editors normally prefer 10 x 8 in. glossy prints.

For colour, slides are the only acceptable medium. Some U.S. publications will reproduce from glossy colour prints, but they are rare. Transparencies are considered the professional way to submit, and almost all American magazines will use 35mm slides. Just be certain to stay with the finest grained film you can use for the lighting conditions with which you will be working.

Plan your photographs so both horizontal and vertical images of similar subjects are included. A magazine's picture space is determined by the room taken by advertisements first, then articles. If there is a horizontal hole for the picture and you send images which are only effective as verticals, either the work will be rejected or the picture will be cropped in such a way as to lose impact.

The best approach is to include both horizontal and vertical images of the same situations. This way the editor can pick pictures which have the greatest impact.

One photograph should be included which can stand alone; an image which has all the elements needed to tell the story. With a trade journal, your picture series might show a new product in use under a dozen different circumstances. However, one photograph – and there should be both a horizontal and a vertical image – will be a clear representation of the product in use, the equipment itself being the focal point. This varies with the subject of course, but the basic concept is the same.

Roll film photographers taking 2¼'' square images should frame their work so that there is room to crop to a vertical or a horizontal. Most of us have been trained to fill the frame, and this is still a good idea. However, when filling the frame, constantly keep in mind that a certain amount of material should be removable in order to alter the format without hurting the impact of the image.

The wider markets

The second type of American magazine is the special interest publication. Special interest publications are among the most numerous sold. They are the ones available on news stands throughout the country, and include a range as broad as *Family Circle, Playboy, Popular Photography, Modern Bride, Parents, Motorboat Magazine, Over 50* and others. Each appeals to a particular hobby, lifestyle (*Apartment Living, Better Homes and Gardens*) or even an age group (*Seventeen, Over 50*). Some are meant for single men and women. Others are meant for people with growing families. Where they cross over into each other's fields, they do so with a particular point of view that remains constant.

For example, suppose you wanted to sell an illustrated article on photographing people. A highly technical article on the subject might be ideal for *Modern Photography,* but of no interest to *Woman's Day* which sells mostly to housewives and family oriented women. *Woman's Day* might be interested in an

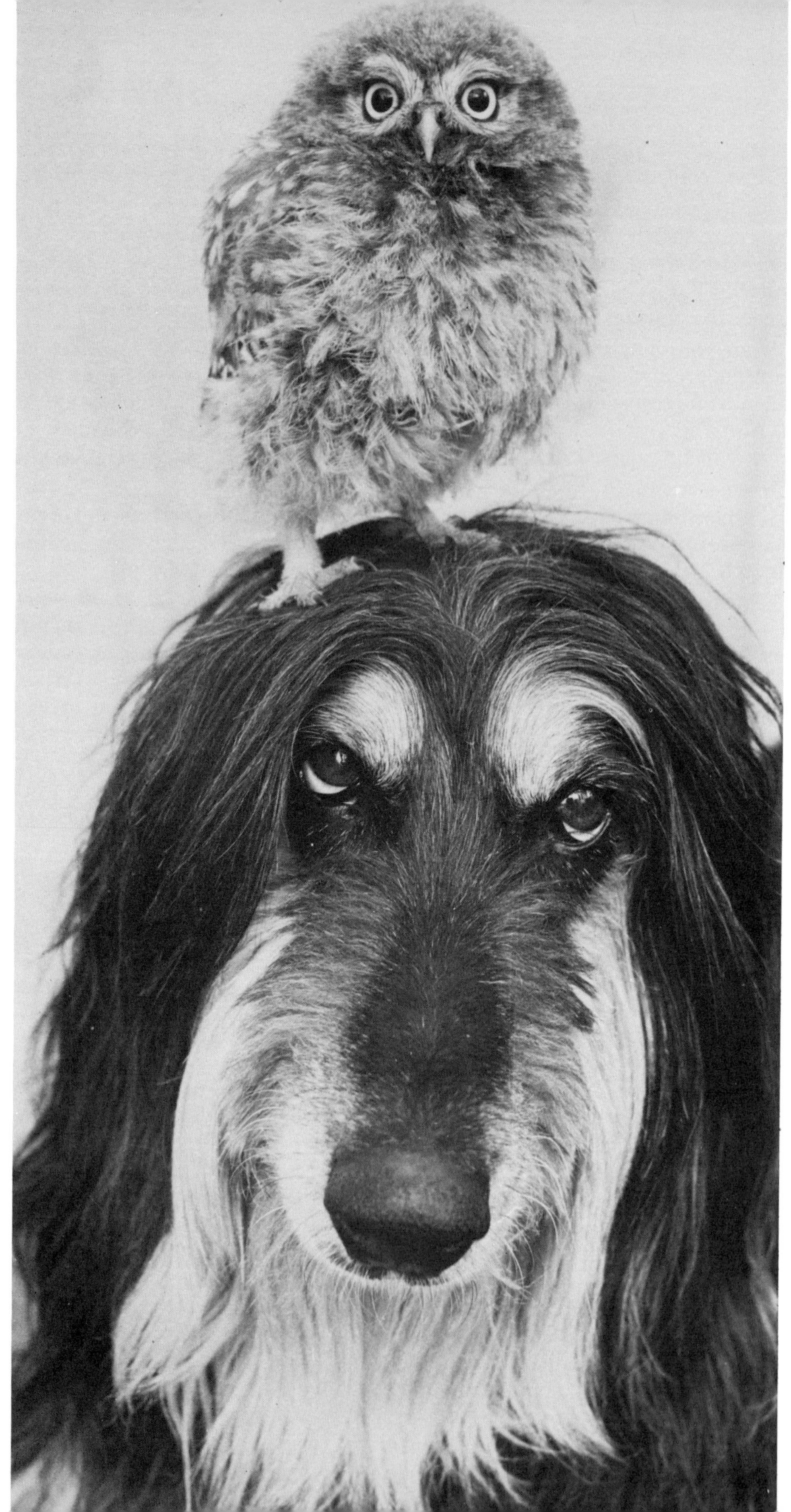

illustrated piece along the lines of '10 Steps To Better Family Photos'. The material is slanted for the market to ensure a sale.

The third type of American publication is the general interest journal, of which few remain today. The weekly *Life* fell into this category and the monthly *Life* is still a good market, but the reduced frequency means fewer sales can be made. *Saturday Evening Post*, also a former weekly publication which now exists as a monthly, fits this category but does not use pictures by themselves for the most part. Weekly tabloid newspapers are actually the strongest markets for your pictures in the general interest field.

Of special importance to freelances interested in general publications is the weekly tabloid *Grit*. This is a newspaper meant for a rural audience, though its distribution is national. Human interest stories are strong in this market. For example, among the photo stories I have sold *Grit* are one about a woman in her 90's who is blind and sews, and a feature on a woman who has a rare blood pressure problem. The latter woman is confined to a wheel chair, unable to sit erect for more than a few minutes, yet teaches gymnastics.

The *National Enquirer* is the largest circulation weekly newspaper in the United States and a major tabloid photo market. There are also such publications as the *National Star*, the *National Insider* and *Midnight/Globe*, among others.

Human interest images sell well to all these publications. *Grit* might be considered the broadest of the markets because of its rural readership. A story on rural England which visually shows a way of life to which the American reader can relate, if only by contrast, may sell, for example. So would a photo feature on an elderly individual following an unusual lifestyle.

Breaking in

There are several ways to break into the American markets. The simplest is to sell pictures from file. However, this will take a certain amount of planning and knowledge of the markets.

There are two American market guides, updated annually, which offer the most value to the freelance photographer. These are *Writer's Market* and the companion *Photographer's Market*. They are published by Writer's Digest Books, Alliance Road, Cincinnati, Ohio, 45242, United States of America. The books list several thousand markets as well as in-depth information concerning pay scales, needs, type of readership, and all other aspects of the business with which you need to be familiar to make a sale. Although there is some cross referencing, the books are so different in scope and content that you should purchase both.

Study the market guides to see which publications buy photographs sold

This picture, by Peter Hoare, has been published in the *National Enquirer*, one of America's highest paying markets and a big consumer of freelance material – much of it from Britain.

singly and not based around a photo story. Then submit appropriate material in both black-and-white and colour.

Illustrated articles should be proposed before mailing. Send a letter addressed 'Dear Editor,' regardless of the market to which you are sending it. The market guides mentioned include the names of editors, but editors are notorious for changing jobs. In one six month period, I worked with six different editors for the same magazine. As a result, I developed the attitude that if I was not absolutely positive the editor was there, I would use the 'Dear Editor' appelation. It is non-sexist and avoids any problems.

Be professional

The letter should open with a paragraph describing the photo story or illustrated article you are offering. The opening should arouse interest and give the editor an understanding of exactly what you are offering. For example, suppose you want to sell a photo story on a circus act involving an elderly high wire artist. Your opening might read something such as:

'The circus high wire artist is traditionally young and supple, fearless as much from the naïvety of youth as because of the skill she has developed. Letitia Bainbridge is a high wire artist with the London-based Jumbo Elephant Circus where she has been dazzling audiences for more than 50 years. The 67 year old Ms. Bainbridge skips rope, turns cartwheels and partakes of a 7-course meal while balancing herself 50 feet above the ground.

'Would you be interested in seeing, on speculation, a picture story about Ms. Bainbridge, her act and the way she lives? I am a professional photographer and can supply both colour and black-and-white photographs.

'Thank you for your consideration. I hope to hear from you at your earliest convenience.'

Notice how the first paragraph arouses the editor's interest and describes what you wish to sell. In the second paragraph you establish your professionalism, not only by mentioning that you are a professional but also by saying that you will send material 'on speculation'.

Many amateurs think that if an editor asks to see his or her work, the editor has become obligated to buy it. The amateur doesn't realise that an editor asks to see work because the description sounds interesting. However, if what is sent is not good, does not fit the editorial needs or duplicates recently published material, it will be rejected. As a result, some editors automatically refuse to look at work when the term 'on speculation' is not mentioned. Thus the addition of the words indicates you understand the editorial problems and will not have unrealistic expectations.

Always say that you are a 'professional' photographer even if you are trying to sell for the first time. I have experienced an editor who said, 'Normally we don't pay for pictures but since you are a professional, we can offer you a token fee.' That 'token fee' proved to be far more than I normally received from better paying markets. Since you never know how a magazine editor will respond, always mention that you are a professional.

The finishing touches

Should you say anything about yourself other than what I have mentioned? My feeling is that you should not. The only time I add any additional information is when it relates. If you made £10,000 taking glamour photographs last year, that doesn't matter to the person buying architectural photographs. However, stating that you are an experienced glamour photographer will make a difference when selling to a men's magazine.

Protect your work carefully. Use two pieces of corrugated cardboard to protect your prints and/or slides. A self addressed return envelope with International Reply Coupons totalling enough money to pay for the postage should be included. The envelope must be large enough to hold everything and may have to be folded in half for inclusion.

Be certain that you can supply adequate caption material. If an article must accompany your pictures and you feel you cannot handle the text, you might team up with a reporter from your area newspaper. Many reporters like to supplement their incomes with freelance assignments of this type.

Try to study the magazines in advance of querying about specific picture stories. There was a time when the majority of magazine publishers had sample copies available for free. However, the rising cost of publications has led the majority to demand a fee for sample copies. If you want sample issues, explain to the editor that you are a professional with possible images for the magazine. Say that you want to study the market before trying to sell the work and ask for the price of a recent copy. Enclose a self-addressed envelope with proper International Reply Coupons so the editor can bill you. The magazine will be sent separately, though you will find that usually there is no charge. When someone writes, says he or she is 'professional' and wants to study the magazine before submission, most editors assume the person is who he or she says and will send samples at no charge. It is an arbitrary judgement that will almost always work in your favour.

The wide open spaces

The American magazine market is wide open for your pictures and the pay rates are generally high. By studying the market guides and following the procedures outlined here, you should be able to make extra money through the sale of both file images and stories you take on assignments.

THE TOOLS OF THE TRADE

by Brian Durrant In freelancing, it's the picture that counts: it matters not whether i
was taken on a Hasselblad or a Zorki. In this chapter the BFP's resident technical exper
considers the suitability of different formats and equipment for different subjects and
markets.

If you are expecting this chapter to tell you that Nikon is better than Canon, or
that Sekors are not as good as Zenzanons, then I am afraid you will be
disappointed. Naturally, the equipment you use must be capable of producing
pictures of a good technical quality, but this can be achieved nowadays by a
wide range of equipment, in an equally wide price range. The main purpose of
this chapter, then, is to consider the choice of formats in relation to the available
markets for particular subjects.

Black & white or colour?

There has been a general acceptance of 35mm in recent years, resulting in the
majority of publications using it without question. Of course, with black and
white work, 35mm is at no disadvantage, since the fine-grain properties of the
modern film, coupled with fine-grain developers and high resolution lenses, can
result in a print which is difficult to identify as having originated from a
miniature format. As far as the average publication is concerned then, black
and white and 35mm are perfectly compatible. However, for those jobs where
the end result is a picture for advertising or publicity use, or perhaps for
enlargement for exhibition purposes, the 35mm may start showing its limitations; for industrial, architectural and much publicity work in black and white,
a larger format is still preferable.

We should consider the relative sizes of the black and white and colour
markets. If you look at a selection of magazines, you will see that there is still a
considerable predominance of black and white pictures. This tells us that not
only is black and white the biggest market to aim for, but also that the demand
for this medium is very much greater. This is compounded by the fact that this
vast market can only be supplied by the relatively small number of people who
are in a position to produce their own prints, while the smaller colour market
can theoretically be approached by anybody who owns a reasonable camera. Of
course, in practice the majority of amateur pictures would never stand a chance
of being used – even if they were submitted – but I have made the point to press
home the differences between these two very dissimilar markets.

Formats for colour

It is with colour work that we have to consider the choice of equipment more carefully. Although playing no part in photography for publication, colour print material is used for social photography by many freelances. The inherently coarse grain of these emulsions does rule out the 35mm for anything which is likely to require much enlargement, though Vericolor II is a fine-grain colour print film which is capable of producing acceptable 10 x 8 in. enlargements from good negatives, and for much of this type of work – weddings, portraits, babies and so on – larger prints are rarely ordered. A 2¼'' square should really be considered for the best results in these fields however.

It is the colour slide field which interests us most from a freelancing point of view, and here there is a choice to be made between the two major formats.

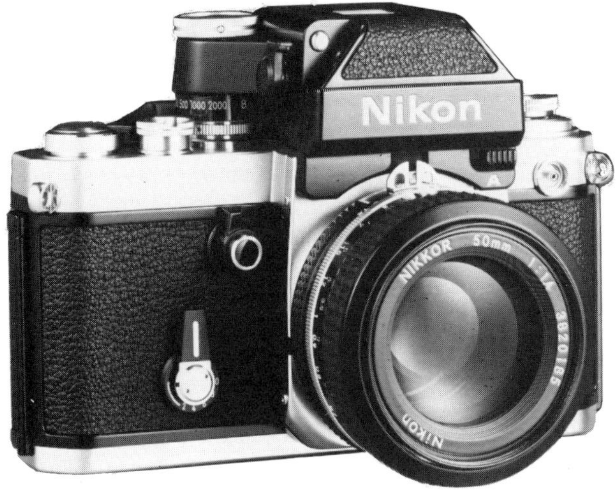

Pentax and Nikon – both have their adherents amongst amateurs and professionals alike.

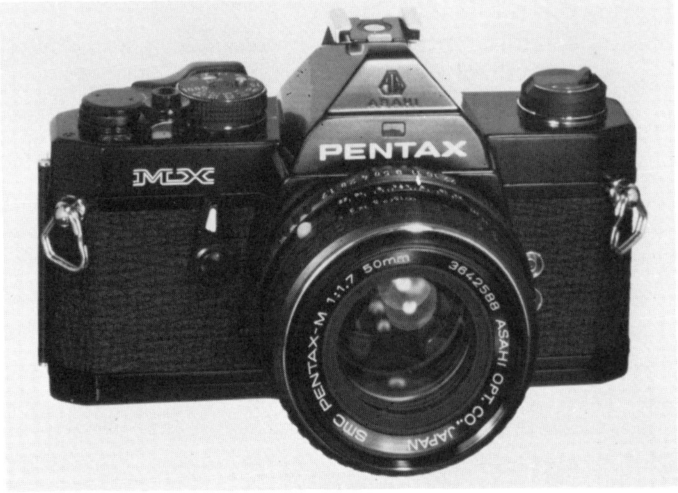

35mm slides are accepted by the majority of publications now, though it is still probably safe to say that an editor will prefer to use something larger if he has it available. It is worth mentioning here that in view of the degree of enlargement required by a 35mm slide for publication, grain has to be kept to a minimum, thus Kodachrome – the finest grain slide film available – is preferred by many editors; indeed, demanded by some. In certain fields the 35mm slide does reign supreme, and those are where the extra versatility and portability of the smaller equipment is necessary for the subject and the techniques involved. In particular, subjects which demand speed of use or extremes of lens focal length need this format – wild-life, sport, climbing and mountaineering, yachting, exploration, close-ups, candids, under-water and so on.

At the other end of the pictorial scale however, we come to well-lit, static and readily-available subjects such as landscapes and other scenics. We have to remember that the market for this type of picture is likely to produce a high quality product – a calendar, greetings card, record sleeve and so on – and will demand a format capable of defining the wealth of detail that the subject has. In many cases, a 35mm slide will not even be considered. The repeatability of these subjects means that there will always be many similar pictures available, and some of these will have been taken on a medium format, so the editor's choice will be quite easy. A 35mm scenic slide may well look crisp and sharp, but bear in mind that if it is a popular view, then it is likely that the same picture is taken many hundreds of times in the season – mainly on 35mm – so competition is intense, and only the very best will ever stand a chance of use.

35mm Cameras

After considering all these factors, we have to try to equip ourself for our own spheres of activity. Few freelances specialise to the extent that they can positively state that they would never need more than one format, so ideally the freelance outfit should contain a medium, as well as a 35mm camera. However, 35mm is still the most versatile, convenient, and reasonably-priced format to use, so we shall have a look at this first.

The 35mm camera market is so vast and rapidly changing that it would be pointless to try to make comparisons between makes and features, but it is pretty safe to say that there are no bad cameras nowadays, and that there are few 35mms that are not capable of producing saleable pictures. Of the many reflex cameras available, there really is little to choose between any of the well-known brand names. Nikon, Minolta, Olympus, Canon, Pentax, Contax, are all used by professional and amateur alike, and there is a considerable number of photographers regularly selling work taken on Zeniths, Prakticas, and practically every other brand. Again I should make the point that it is the photographer who takes the picture – the camera only records it – and I doubt if there exists a 35mm camera which is not capable of doing that well enough for reproduction, provided the user has thought enough about the picture. Nonreflex cameras do have certain limitations with viewing, interchangeable lenses and parallax, but the great accuracy of their rangefinders, and the quietness of their shutters, can be very useful. There are few interchangeable-lens cameras of this type, though of course the Leica is known to all. The Zorki is another camera of this type which is particularly good value for money.

Automatic cameras have been condemned by many people as being too restrictive, though in fact they can relieve the photographer of some of the technical decisions, and let him get on with the business in hand – that of seeing and taking the picture. The ideal situation to achieve with any camera is to know it so well that you do not have to think about its operation, and the automatic camera can hasten this familiarity. Compact 35mm cameras have also gained respectability in the last few years; their optics are as good as many reflexes, so there is no reason why they should not produce perfectly saleable pictures.

Lenses for 35mm

I do not intend to dictate what lenses the freelance should buy for his 35mm use, since this is entirely a matter of personal choice, techniques, and specialisation. Although the 135mm lens seems to be the automatic choice for a first additional lens, I personally consider that wide angles are of wider and more general use. At this stage it is also worth considering whether we really need a 'standard' lens at all. Some makers are now offering their cameras as bodies only, and many users have taken advantage of this to change to a slightly wider lens for normal use. The 35mm is rather closer to our angle of view, even though the perspective is slightly different, so it has become increasingly chosen for standard use. The 28mm has now become the most popular wide-angle lens, and indeed, is my own favourite focal length. Wider lenses – 20 and 24mm – can find a use with the pictorial, scenic and architectural photographer, though for the latter care must be taken to keep the back of the camera vertical to the ground, to avoid problems with converging verticals. The average freelance may not think that he would have very much use for a lens in the 85mm to 100mm range, but in fact this can be a very useful length – especially if you have opted for a 35mm standard – as well as being the ideal portrait lens and useful for near-distance sports and candids. The 135mm can also be suitable for this, though perhaps a 200mm would be rather better. If you have an interest in wild-life, then a 200mm could be too short, and you should perhaps consider a 300mm.

There is a great divergence of prices for different makes of lenses, and this can be confusing, especially where 'name' brands are often twice the price of similar lenses from independent makers. A higher-priced lens is probably better than its cheaper counterpart, but the difference can be small – especially with telephoto lenses, where the optics are relatively simple. A cheaper telephoto lens is quite likely to be a good buy, whereas a cheap wide angle – with its complicated optics – may be noticeably inferior. At this end of the range then, it is best to buy quality lenses; which usually means those sold under the camera brand-name.

A few words about converters is relevant here, since they are so cheap and convenient that many will already own one. Converters have rather a bad name, but in fact they can be very serviceable if used carefully. The 3X converter seems to be taking the laws of optics a little too far, but quality from a 2X can be good. They are generally computed to operate on lenses of 100mm and above, though the central area of a 50mm + 2X converter combination can be quite usable for portraiture, where edge definition is not of the utmost importance. If both the converter and lens are good, definition loss should be small provided the aperture of the lens is closed a couple of stops; what loss there is should occur only on the edges and corners, so this should be remembered when choosing the subject. The obvious disadvantage is, of course, the loss in light throughput – reduced to a quarter that of the lens, or two stops less – so this has to be borne in mind when considering its application with longer telephoto lenses with their small apertures.

Moving into larger formats

There is no need for the 35mm photographer to think that he is going to have to

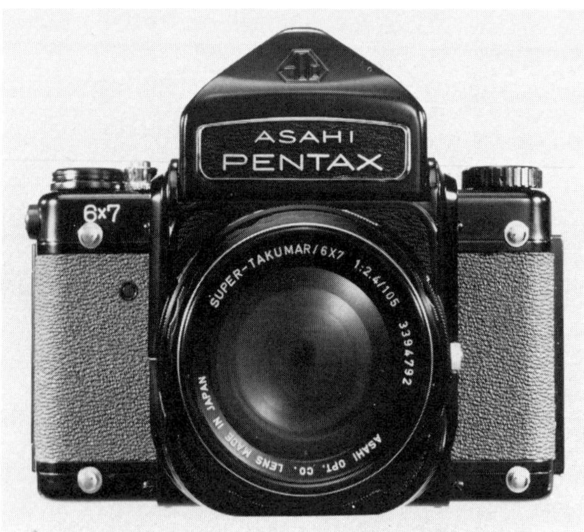

The Pentax 6x7. In many respects, 6x7 cm is the ideal format for editorial colour work, although it hasn't proved as popular with freelances as might have been expected.

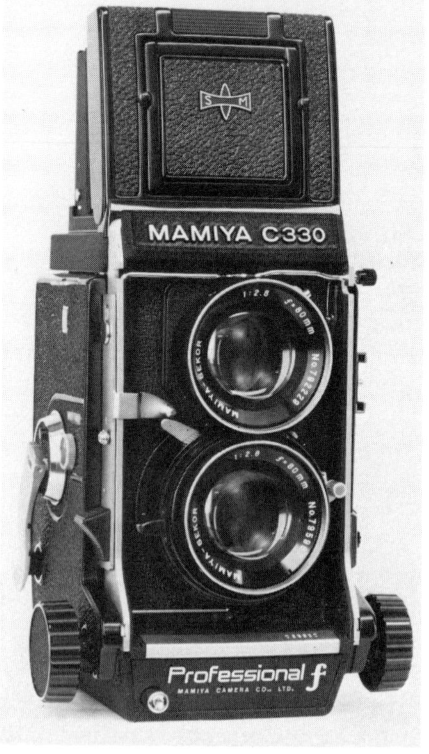

The Mamiya C330F. A very versatile piece of equipment.

spend a fortune to move into a larger format. Even a modestly priced 2¼″ square should produce better results than the very best 35mm; a second-hand Yashicamat for example, need not cost more than around £40 – less than the price of a medium quality additional lens for a 35mm camera – yet it will produce very high-quality pictures, which will be acceptable to a very much larger market.

2¼″ square camera choice is more limited than 35mm, though the 6x4.5cm format can also be considered in this group. The major advantage of the 6x4.5cm format is the extra three exposures which are gained on every film, though of course the equipment is also smaller and more portable than a 2¼″ square slr. As the format is oblong, like the 35mm camera the 6x4.5cm does require turning onto its side for upright pictures – unlike the 2¼″ squares, where the camera is used the same way for both picture shapes. This can produce slight handling difficulties, and makes a viewing prism an essential accessory. Although the usable area is little smaller than that of a 2¼″ square, there is a slight psychological disadvantage with the smaller format, since a mounted transparency tends to look rather like an oversized 35mm, and rather less impressive than the apparently much larger 2¼″ square. While the reproduced results would be indistinguishable, it is worth bearing this point in mind.

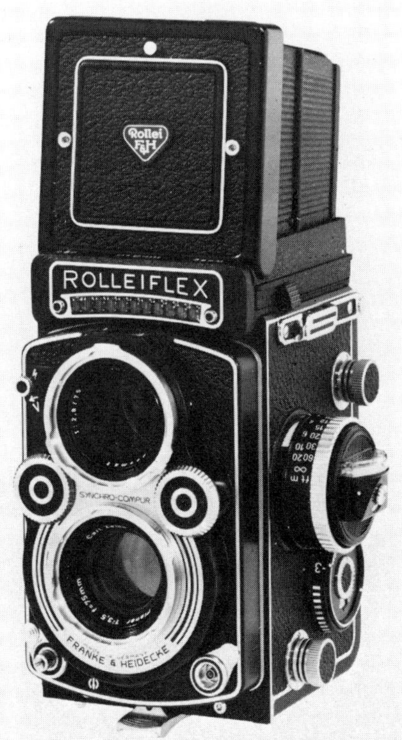

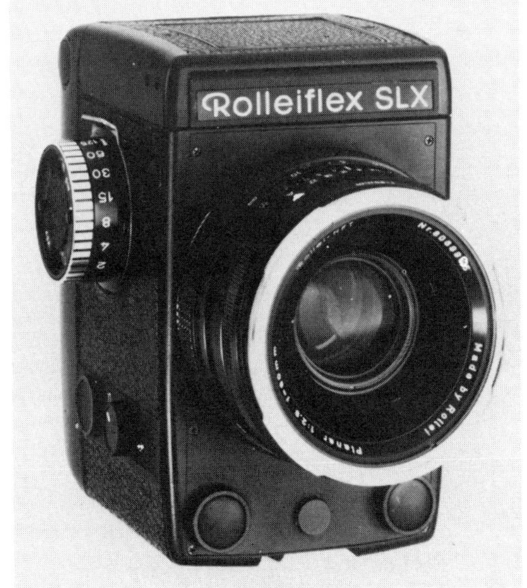

The Rolleiflex 3.5F and the latest model – the superb SLX 2¼″ square single lens reflex. Rollei have a long-deserved reputation for top performance and reliability.

When considering anything other than a fixed-lens 2¼'' square twin-lens reflex, costs can become frighteningly high. However, there are many tlr cameras to be found on the second-hand market, and these will cope with the majority of subjects. Used Yashicamats, Microcords, Rolleicords, Autocords and others, can be picked up at very reasonable prices, and it is unlikely that such a purchase would ever be regretted. The disadvantage is, of course, that the lens is fixed, which does impose certain limitations, though in practice these are not great. The one tlr which does feature interchangeable lenses is the Mamiya C series camera, also often seen at bargain prices, second-hand. The Mamiya is very well built and reliable, and has excellent optics, and with its choice of focal lengths could be the cheapest and most versatile entry into medium format photography for the 35mm worker.

It is a little surprising that the 6x7cm format was not taken up by other makers after the almost simultaneous entry into this size by Pentax and Mamiya, since to all intents and purposes it is an ideal size – particularly for colour transparency work. The Pentax is an extremely usable camera considering the size of the format, though its 35mm camera-shape has meant that it does lack the film-back changeability which seems to be a necessary feature for a camera of this format. The Mamiya does have this, though the unavoidable increase in size and weight has resulted in a camera which is better suited to the studio tripod than the hand.

The 5'' x 4'' may seem to be an antiquated contraption to the modern photographer with his miniature electronic marvel, but in fact, with transparency work in particular, it is very likely to result in vastly increased sales to markets such as greetings card and calendar publishers. In spite of the extreme simplicity of these cameras, they do seem to be exorbitantly expensive, though again, the second-hand market can often produce the odd MPP or Speed Graphic at a good price. These cameras are expensive to run, but perhaps this is all to the good, since it encourages greater thought and care with every exposure. The best quality industrial, architectural and product photography demands 5'' x 4''.

Finally, one frequently overlooked item is the very case that all our treasures are kept and carried in; but this is important. It must be sturdy enough to withstand knocks; it should keep the individual items secure – preferably in separate compartments – and, if at all possible, it should be strong enough to stand on. The suitcase types may well keep equipment snug and safe in their little foam cut-outs, but they are not very convenient to use. In order to change a lens, filter or film, they have to be put down flat somewhere, and very often that is impossible. They seem to attract a lot of dust as well. The shoulder case which opens at the front – Vivitar make a very good one for a 35mm outfit – or some of the top opening cases, are probably the most convenient in use, but few are sturdy enough to stand on. The big aluminium boxes are best for that, though they are rather cumbersome.

by Dave Saunders To reach the top, learn from those already there. The former production editor of *Amateur Photographer*, now himself a successful freelance, talks to a number of top photographers about how they became involved in freelancing and what motivates them to succeed.

For many, the thrill of having their material published is the driving force which inspires them to freelance. But, as you've probably discovered, the going is not always easy. Just like any other challenge, there are setbacks and disappointments – usually in the form of rejection slips or closed doors. In order to take these in your stride, you will need two things: a goal, and determination to reach it.

Your goal may be to become a regular contributor to one of the hobby magazines, a full-time freelance contributing to a large number of national and international publications, or a staff photographer working on a big national newspaper. *Someone* has to fill these posts, and if you have the ability there's no reason why that 'someone' shouldn't be you.

Once you have set your goal, there's the question of how to reach it. What steps should you take? What's the best plan of campaign?

If you have set your target high – and why not? – getting there may seem rather daunting. Yet there's no need to feel overpowered by this; you are not the first to embark on such a venture. All successful people started *somewhere*, and few of them began at the top.

Reading how others turned their dreams into realities can be a great inspiration. Why do you think biographies of famous people are so popular? Not only because it is fascinating to pry into the private lives of public figures, but also because readers can associate with the person and identify with the worries and problems he or she has to face. Seeing how other photographers have forged a name for themselves can help you approach freelancing with a determined attitude. After all, these people are human – they eat, sleep, buy cameras, create pictures and try to sell them – just like the rest of us. They do this successfully because they know what they want and have the drive to achieve it.

A bit on the side

Many successful photographers began by taking pictures as a hobby or to earn a little pin money. Michael Joseph was accepting commissions by the time he was 14, photographing children and animals. He says 'This gave me a lot of confidence and taught me never to be embarrassed.'

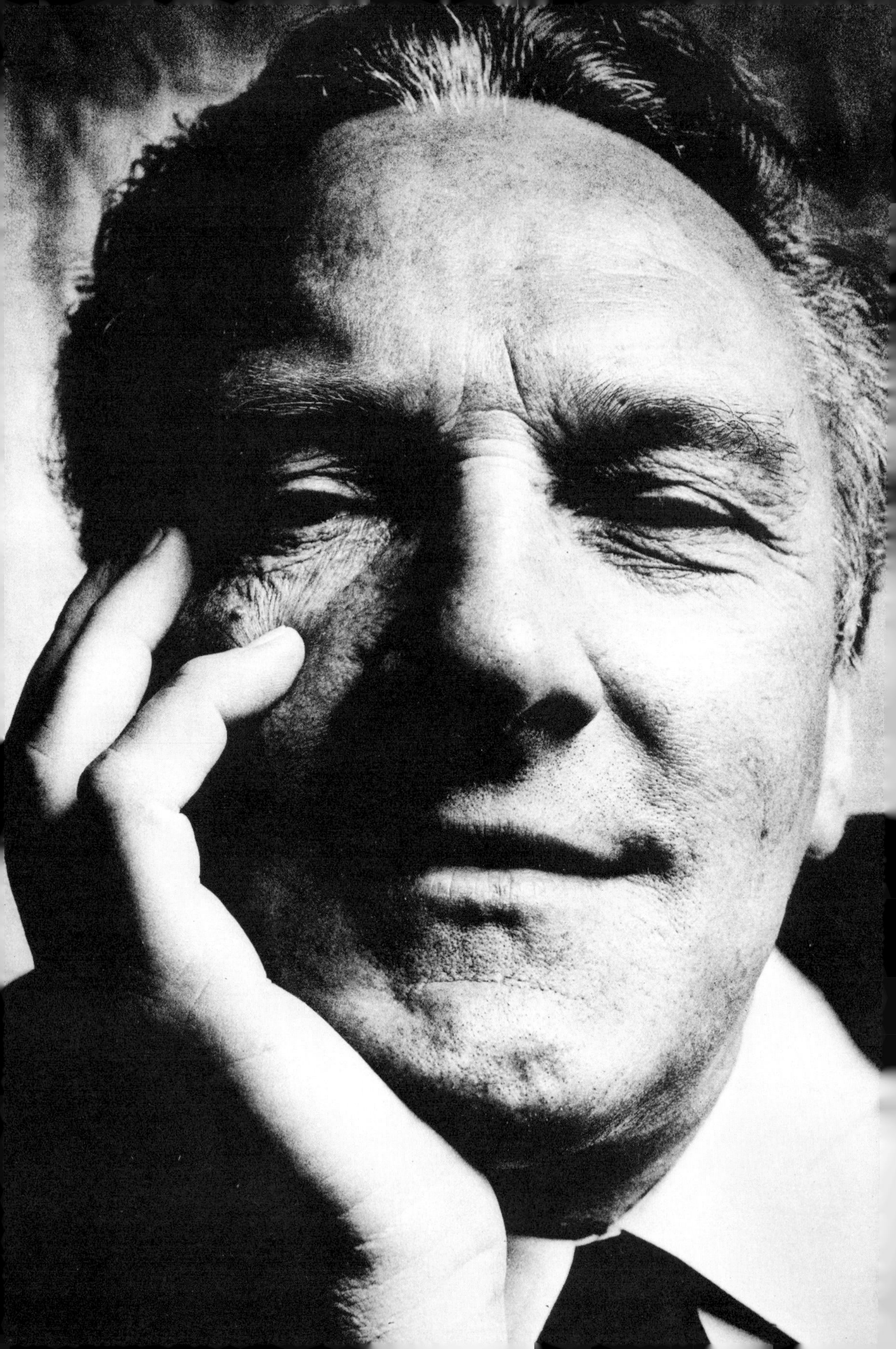

It is a sense of achievement, even in small things, which spurs you on. Don't shun the minor jobs, as they can help by giving you experience not only in taking photographs but in organising subjects and handling clients. Then, by keeping your wits about you and taking note of market demands, you can build on these early experiences. Eric Crichton has found there's a lot of trial and error at first, finding out how your shots are received. He says, 'Where possible try to get a reaction from people who see your pictures. It's like a ball going down a tube, bouncing off the sides until it goes straight. You soon learn what sells and what doesn't.' Crichton has found 'Publishers demand certain types of pictures. There's no point offering them arty shots for books on animals and plants, they want record shots. And remember, a front cover may earn £150 or so, but then it's killed stone-dead. There's only one cover shot on a book, but perhaps 250 inside. Therefore, you should concentrate on pictures inside.'

In the early years of his photography Derek Berwin developed an eye for pictures that would sell. At 15 he worked in a darkroom in Fleet Street and took photographs on spec in his spare time. 'I found what I thought were good press stories, local interest things. That gave me an early insight into what the media wanted. And it gave me my first ego kick from getting my work published – that was what really got me going.'

Berwin built on this success and became a full-time photographer in Fleet Street. 'I soon moved on to royal assignments, and was attached to the Royal Family. Again it started on a freelance basis: I realised there was a marketing potential in taking pictures of the Royals. I used to study court circulars and if there was, say, a theatre visit, I used to turn up, take a picture and give it to the agency as a freelance story.'

Submitting work on spec can be a depressing and gruelling business if you are not fairly sure of supplying what the market wants. It involves investing time and money in what is essentially a hunch. Berwin continues: 'I went to Florida for two weeks and spent three grand of my own money. I had to be absolutely determined my pictures were going to turn out. But I get a kick out of taking the risk; that makes it more exciting.'

Mike Portelly goes to even greater lengths to get his pictures, which he takes for photographic competitions and also sells on spec. His most impressive work is shot underwater where equipment and travel costs run much higher than for ordinary land photography. 'To make sure I'm not let down by equipment I take 10 back-up flash units with me, and, at £500 a time it's rather expensive. But if I've gone 5,000 miles to take a picture, I make sure I get it.' Some of Portelly's shots are quite elaborate; if you're taking an air balloon down to a coral cliff 40 feet beneath the waves and putting a model in the basket, you've got to be pretty confident that something will come of it.

Hugh Cudlip photographed for
Management Today by **John Claridge**.

Only the best

The mark of successful photographers is their absolute dedication to picture quality. If they accepted second best of themselves then editors wouldn't accept them. To rise above small-time dabbling you must be your own most stringent critic, and make sure you know your subject. This doesn't necessarily mean taking a college photography course, as Anthony Blake points out: 'Too many people in colleges have no knowledge of commercialism. I think that to pretend that photography is not a business is the big mistake of the '60s that is still with us. In fact it's very serious; if you are going to make a profit you have to watch your costs.'

Eric Crichton gained much of his early experience working for a variety of studio photographers. Unlike many college courses, it gave him a good grounding in the commercial side of photography – how to sell pictures. 'You need a taste for a photograph that someone will buy; by watching, talking and listening you soon pick it up.' Crichton adapted techniques he learned from his

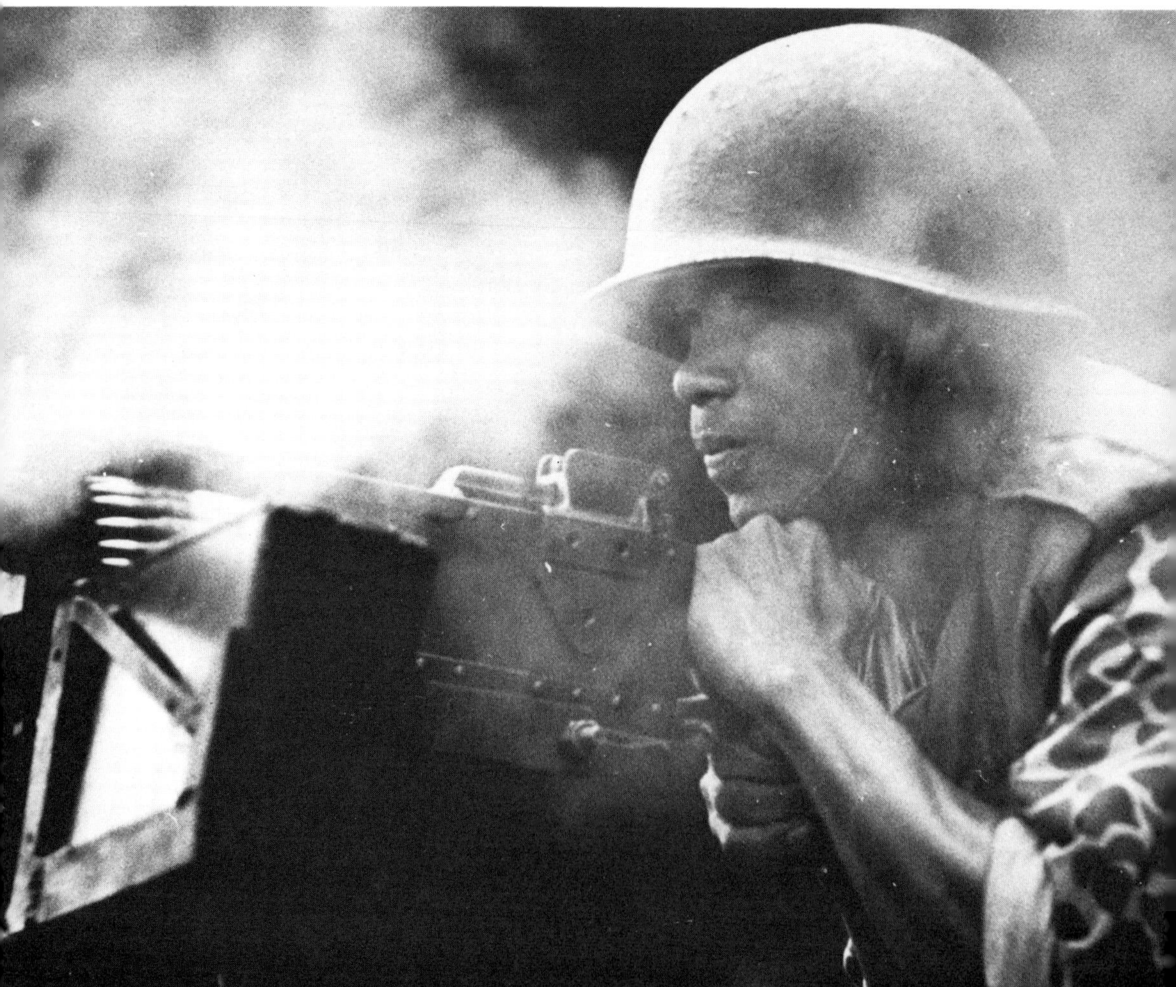

Michael Joseph is an advertising photographer whose pictures have been used to promote numerous products, including wool, watches, cigarettes, cars, chocolates and whisky.

Eric Crichton provides book illustrations and specialises in plants and animals. He is noted for his macro photography.

Derek Berwin's advertising and editorial work takes him all over the world, and many of his pictures are syndicated worldwide.

Mike Portelly is a part-time photographer whose imagination in conceiving underwater photographs has won him great acclaim.

Anthony Blake has explored many avenues in photography. He has taken promotional shots for industrial companies, has been deeply involved with food photography, both in advertising and for book illustrations, and he runs a photographic gallery, studio and stock photo library.

John Cleare is a mountaineering photographer who has illustrated and written several books and many magazine articles. He has helped in the making of television outside broadcasts and assisted in the making of 'The Eiger Sanction' starring Clint Eastwood.

Heather Angel has a large library of natural history photographs which she operates as a photographic agency. Her pictures have appeared in over 700 books, 28 of which she wrote herself, countless magazines, calendars and greetings cards.

John Claridge earns his living from advertising photography and has many prestigious campaigns to his name, including Benson and Hedges, Smirnoff, Miss Selfridge, Levi, Range Rover and the Indian Tourist Board.

John Thornton has made a great impact on the photographic press with his bizarre and erotic photographs which also appear in his book 'Pipe Dreams', yet he too makes his money from advertising, notably Winston cigarettes and Smirnoff.

Arnold Newman is a portrait photographer, best known in this country for his series on 'The Great British' which was featured in the *Sunday Times Magazine* and exhibited at the National Portrait Gallery in London.

A Cambodian mercenary with South Vietnam forces photographed in 1965 by Michael Joseph.

employers to photographing animals and plants. 'I used exactly the same lighting techniques as the photographers used for their fashion models: one, two or sometimes three flash heads, bouncing the light off reflectors. I built a hood which fits over the light source and worked out the optimum angles to bounce the flash to get rid of the shadows.'

John Cleare received his basic grounding at Guildford School of Photography, and as assistant to John Hedgecoe for two years before going it alone. The academic course gave him the techniques and working for Hedgecoe gave him an opportunity to put the techniques to commercial use.

When confronted with the prospect of becoming a housewife at the age of 25, Heather Angel turned to nature photography as an interest and way of making an income. She built up her enterprise based on picture quality and business sense. 'I learned not only how to take, but also how to sell pictures. Personal contact with both picture researchers and editors provided me with feedback on which subjects and regions they have difficulty in obtaining shots.'

John Claridge received some of his training working in the photographic department of the advertising agency McCann Erickson. He then worked for photographer David Montgomery, and was ready to launch himself on a freelance career at the age of 19. 'David Montgomery was a great teacher and I met some great people, but what you can *do* is more important than who you know.'

Claridge enjoyed his early years drumming up business. 'I had already got a portfolio together, and took this around to various Art Directors. I'd advise someone wanting to take up full-time freelancing to work for a photographer first. But to be accepted you'll probably need to keep on and on 'phoning people. There's no easy way.'

Although Berwin never had the opportunity, he advises: 'You can't beat being assistant to a known photographer to learn the way he approaches jobs. It's better to make cups of tea for good photographers than to go through college photographic education. That way you learn the names of the right people, how to cut corners and get jobs done quickly.'

Yet both Heather Angel and Mike Portelly were essentially self-taught. Says Portelly, 'I learned very quickly that the standard of your equipment dictated the technical quality you can achieve. I bought the best system I could afford, and with an expensive camera I felt committed to taking good pictures. I studied photographic techniques and soon realised that, for the sort of images I wanted to create, the techniques just didn't exist. For some shots I had to redesign some of the equipment.'

Knowing how to use your cameras and understanding the subjects you are photographing is most important if you are going to achieve any measure of success. Says Crichton, 'A knowledge of the subject is important in many fields of photography, natural history perhaps more than most. I read a lot and

In this picture by John Cleare, climbers are dwarfed by the huge fluted northern flank of Nuptse, in the Himalayas.

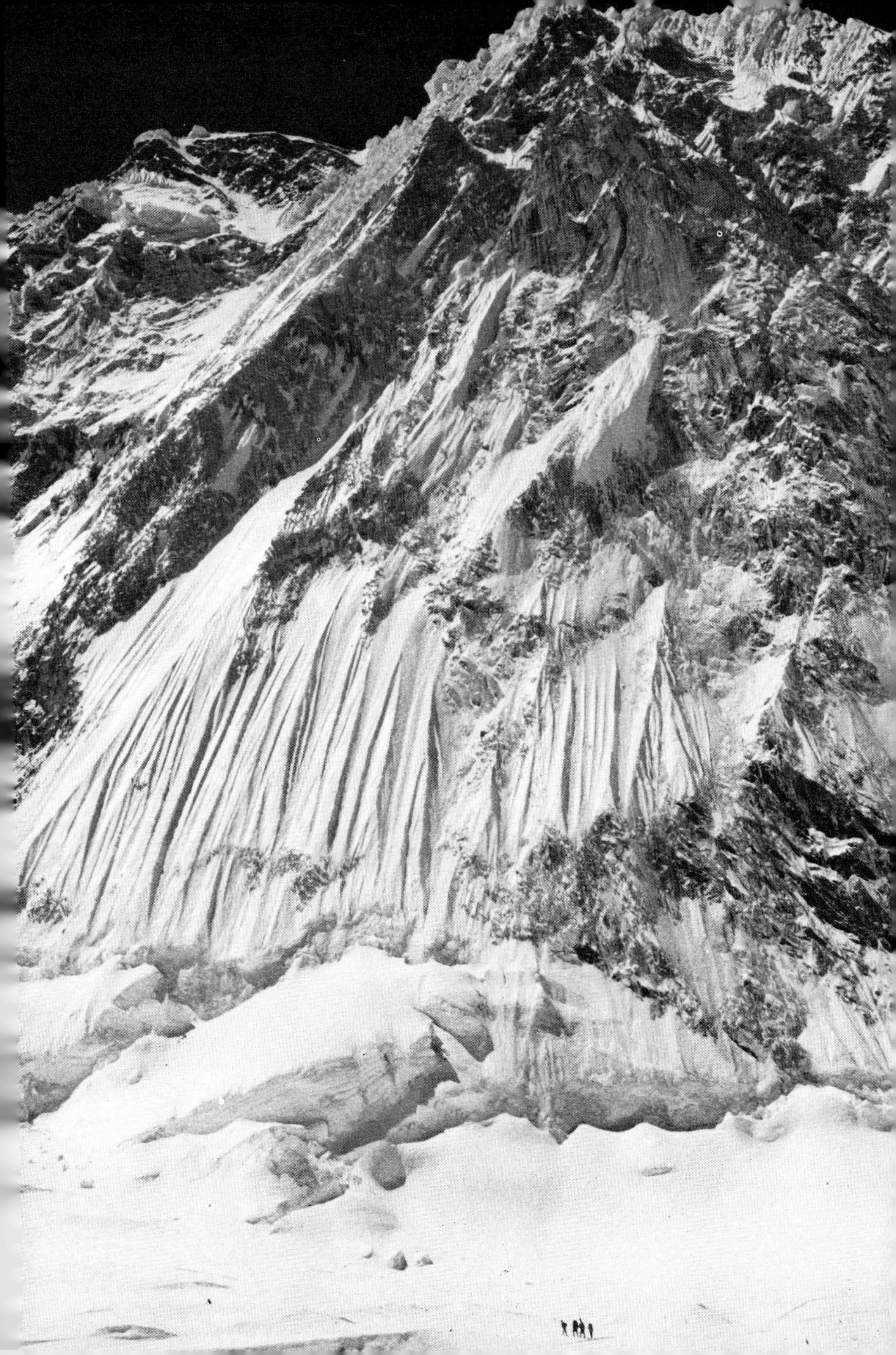

researched the subject thoroughly – both photographic techniques and biology. Knowing why a plant flowers, for example, will help in getting the best pictures of it. A plant flowers when it is under stress because it doesn't have any water. The photographer could recreate that situation, so the plant thinks "I'm going to die." Then it goes into flower to produce the next generation, and you can take a beautiful photograph.'

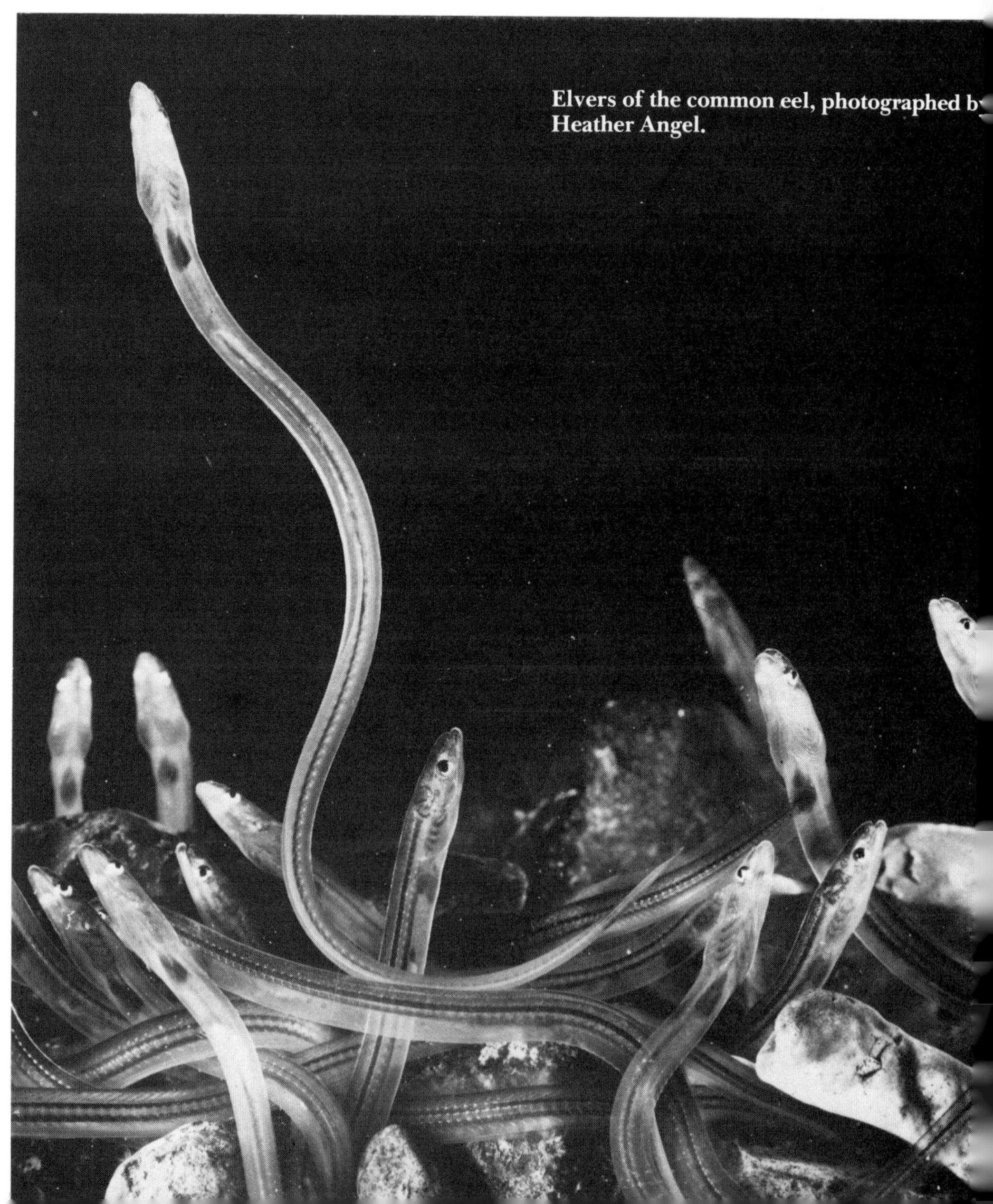
Elvers of the common eel, photographed by Heather Angel.

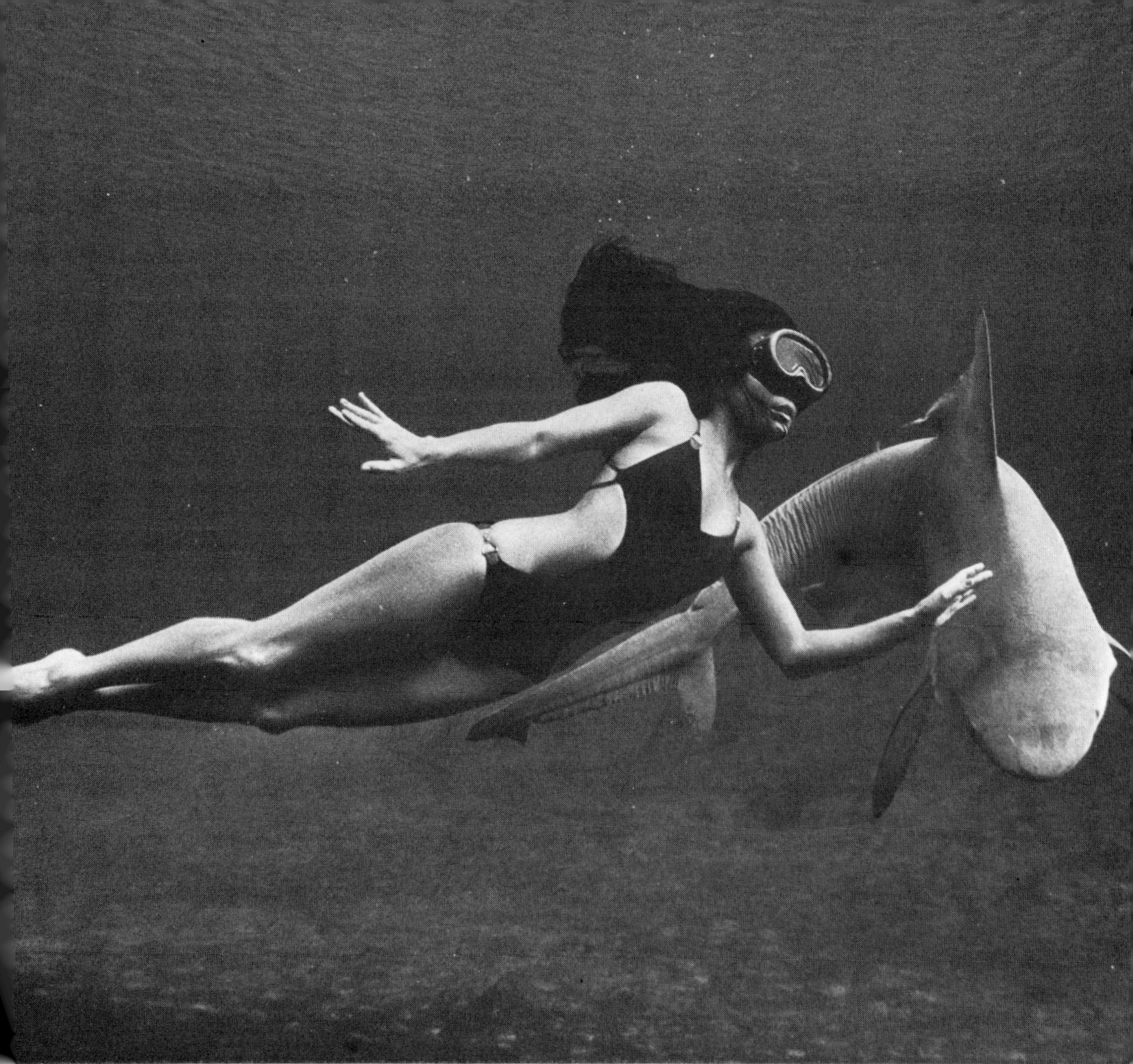

The lady and the shark, photographed by David Berwin.

So you think you've got problems?

If you're put off by bad weather or a touch of indigestion, then you'll never make the Big Time. Those who really break through have the determination to combat setback after setback.

When John Thornton came to London he got together his portfolio; the photographs were good and he had faith in them, yet he still had to convince clients to share his enthusiasm. 'Money was always low. After the first 18 months or so I started to approach advertising agencies with my book of work. Reception varied from being thrown out to being really liked. When someone tells you they hate your work, it's more than disheartening. I must have gone bankrupt in theory again and again because there were actually times when I couldn't pay for the processing.'

Big returns usually demand great commitment. Arnold Newman is another example: 'When I began serious photography I devoted all my spare time to it, giving up any kind of private life, using all my money for photography. At the time I literally lived from hand to mouth. I moved in with friends and paid the rent when I got the money.'

One of Newman's first assignments for *Harpers Bazaar* was to photograph Stravinsky. He produced that classic shot of the composer at the grand piano, leaning on his elbow – the shot was rejected!

If you feel despondent about the problems which face you, take comfort from what the pros have to contend with. John Claridge went to India during the monsoon to shoot a series of advertising pictures. 'It's difficult to promote a place in a monsoon because it's all black and raining continually. To overcome this we started very early in the morning before the rain broke. We were going to photograph elephants in their full regalia – gold, braid and so on. We had been told that everything was set up and we'd have no problems, but when we arrived at the site it was all marshland and we could hardly do anything. We wanted to get three elephants across the marsh and into position. On the horizon the monsoon was gathering rapidly. We had to get everything together before this thing hit. The elephants were getting in a mess, legs crossed, grabbing each other's tails and starting to sink in the mud. If the monsoon hit that would be the end. By the time everything was ready I had about five minutes to shoot. Then the clouds broke and there was total chaos; elephants stumbling about and the whole place was like one big river.

'But I had the shot.'

When Michael Joseph photographed the cover for the Rolling Stones' album *Beggars' Banquet*, he found that having control over the subject proved a little tricky: 'They were a bit boisterous when they arrived at the studio. They had their own ideas about how they wanted to look and I had to manipulate them to do things that would make the shot work.

'Being a photographer is like being a tightrope walker-cum-magician. You go on a trip to, say, the Caribbean, and usually you get to the last day before everyone is looking good, and you almost have to do three or four days' work in one afternoon.'

Yet, despite all the frustrations and setbacks, not one of the photographers interviewed even considered another line of work. The enjoyment and satisfaction they get from freelancing makes it all more than worthwhile. Anthony Blake summed it up best when he said: 'You meet so many different people in this business; there's always something new and exciting to keep up your enthusiasm.'

Navaho Indians photographed for Shlit Posters about Classic America by Joh Claridge.

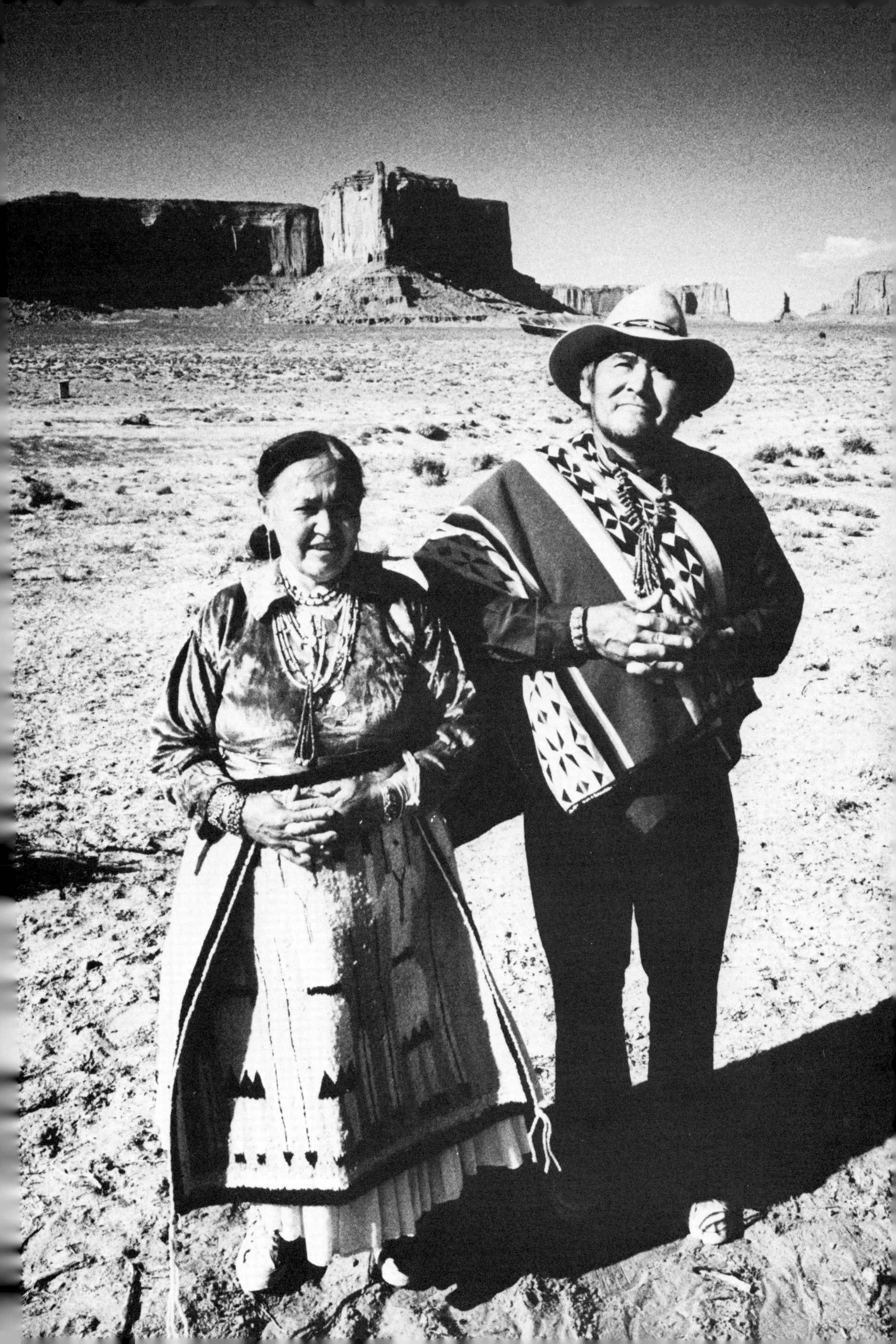

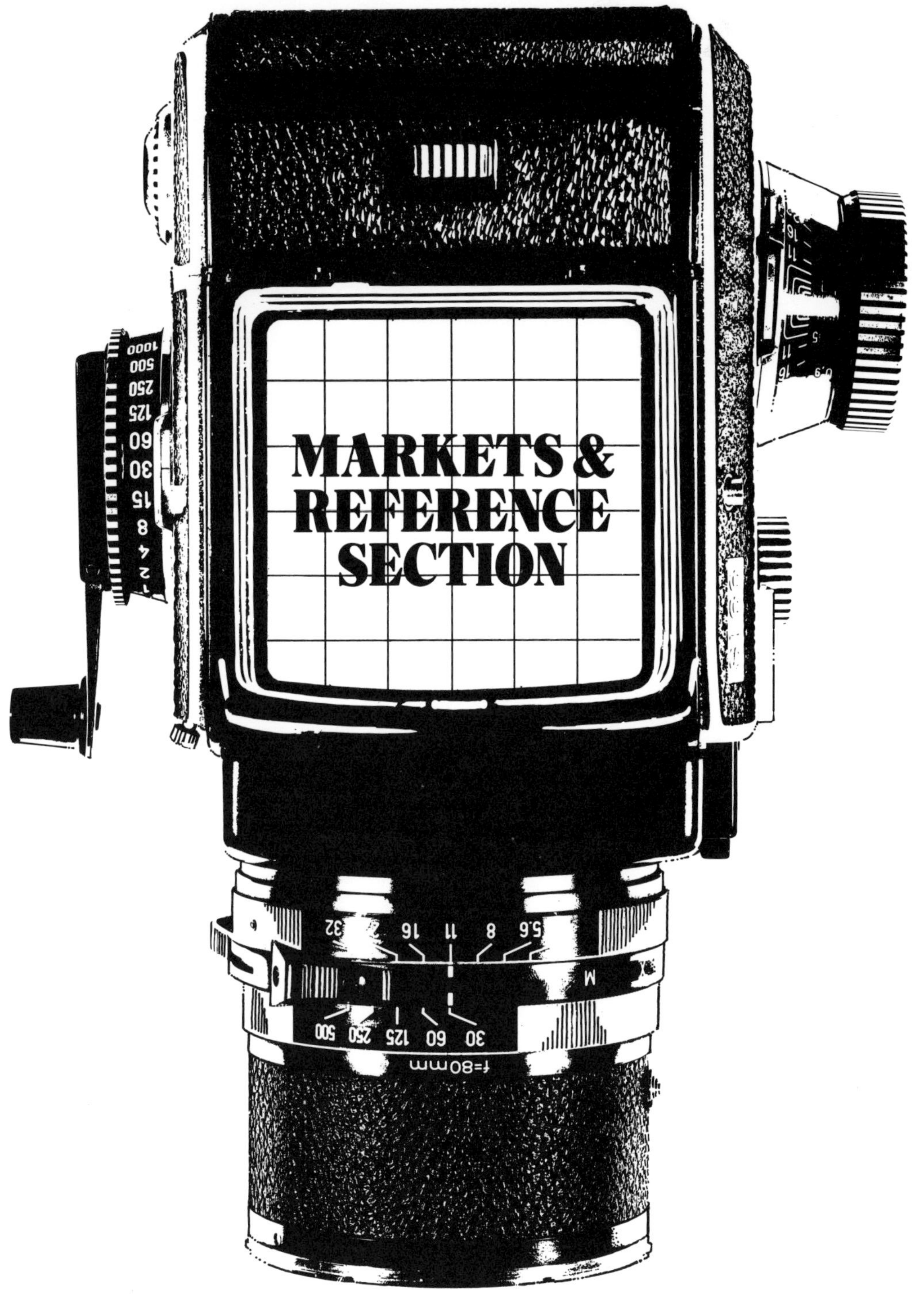
MARKETS &
REFERENCE
SECTION

The information published in this section was correct at the time of going to press. However, since editorial requirements are subject to change, the market information should be treated as a general guide rather than a definite indication of current needs. Readers should query the publication or company concerned before actually submitting material. Additionally, as advised elsewhere in this book, readers should always carefully study an up-to-date issue of any publication to which they hope to contribute. Members of the Bureau of Freelance Photographers are kept up-to-date with market trends and picture requirements through the BFP monthly *Market Newsletter*.

Markets-1
USING AN AGENT

Is an agent likely to be able to sell your pictures better than you can yourself? There is no easy answer to this question; much must depend upon the individual photographer, the type of subjects he shoots, how much time and energy he can himself devote to selling pictures, what expectations he has of an agency, and other personal factors.

While the use of an agency can in many cases be worthwhile, it must not be thought of as an automatic formula for success. One obvious advantage of using an agent is that he is invariably on the receiving end of a constant stream of requests for pictures of particular subjects. Whereas most freelances must be continually circulating their photographs – or, at least, lists of their subjects – in order to achieve sales, once an agent becomes known to picture buyers, he can simply sit back and wait for them to approach him. Of course, a good agent does much more than this; he ensures that all potential markets are aware of the pictures he has available and is in constant touch with changing requirements and trends.

But if you do decide to use an agent to market your pictures, you should think of it as a long-term investment. Indeed, many agents now stipulate that contributors lodge their pictures for a certain minimum period – which can be anything from two to five years, with three months to one year's notice being required for their return. While most agents are fairly flexible in their application of this rule, its purpose is to avoid a situation whereby the agent must be constantly asking prospective users to return pictures which they are holding for consideration, because the photographer has suddenly decided that he wants them back. Most agents also now insist on a minimum initial contribution from a new contributor – which can be anything from 100–500 transparencies. This is to cut-out the non-serious contributor; once again, although most agents do not stick rigidly to this rule, it is not usually worth their while taking on a new contributor who thinks he has produced half-a-dozen earth-shattering pictures with which he expects to make his fortune.

Most agents also expect their contributors to regularly submit new material. Indeed, only when you have several hundred pictures lodged with an agent can you hope for regular sales – and regular cheques. Even then, it must be remembered that no agent can guarantee sales; and your pictures might prove to be slow sellers!

Although agents will sometimes negotiate a special rate with their more prized contributors, 50 per cent is the usual rate of commission charged. This may seem high, but it is unlikely that any agent could operate economically on a much lower rate of commission. After all, an agent must cover all his overheads – which includes office rent, staff, the production and distribution of catalogues and other advertising literature to picture buyers, etc. However, agents say, with some justification, that they are frequently able to obtain higher fees than those obtained by individual freelances. But perhaps one of the most important reasons why many freelances decide to use an agent is simply because picture buyers invariably approach a library first when looking for a particular stock picture.

There are points to be made both for and against using an agency. Some freelances reckon they achieve better results through their own exclusive marketing efforts, while others like to use an agent so that they can concentrate exclusively on the thing they like doing best – taking pictures. It is up to the individual freelance to decide what suits him best. If you are already familiar with the markets for your particular subject, you may see little point in using an agent. In any event, you should certainly try to gain some experience of marketing your own work before considering an agent. And whether or not you use an agent, you should certainly continue to study the market, keeping up-to-date with requirements and trends.

Many agents have an 'exclusive' clause in their agreements, aimed at preventing the photographer from using another agent. This is simply to avoid a situation whereby similar photographs are being submitted to the same markets by difference sources. But provided you are sensible about it, and avoid submitting similar material to another agency or direct to markets, you should experience few problems.

Making an approach

Right. You've decided to use an agency. You have a sizeable number of pictures which you think are saleable, and you fully appreciate that the use of an agency must be considered a long-term investment. The first thing you should do is carefully read through the listings that follow . Select the agent or agents likely to be interested in your material; the information under 'Specialist Subjects/ Requirements' will help here.

Having decided upon a particular agent or agents, you should write to them in the first instance with details of the material you have available.

Finally, don't expect to make a fortune by using an agent. And don't think that his job is to handle the rejects you haven't been able to sell yourself: most agents will only handle top quality material. On the other hand, if you can team up with the right agent, you could well be on the way to increased profits from your pictures.

AEROFILMS LTD
Gate Studios, Station Road, Boreham Wood, Herts, WD 6 1EJ.
Telephone: 01-207 0666.
Principal: W. H. Brooker.
Specialist Subjects/Requirements: Air to ground and air to air only. 'We are prepared to consider for inclusion in our Library, any aerial photography that may be submitted if not already included from the work of our own photographers.'
Stock: B&W and Colour. Minimum 2¼″ square colour transparencies.
Usual Terms of Business: Negotiable: 'Our prime business is not that of an agency.'
Commission charged on Sales: Negotiable.
Additional Information and/or Advice for Intending Contributors: 'The exact location of every photograph must be specified. We will not look at 35mm transparencies nor any photography that has been taken through the windows of an aircraft.'

ALL-SPORT PHOTOGRAPHIC LTD
All-Sport House, 55-57 Martin Way, Morden, Surrey, SM4 4AH.
Telephone: 01-543 0988/9.
Principals: Tony Duffy (Managing Director), Don Morley, Steve Powell, John Starr.
Specialist Subjects/Requirements: All Sports. Most material is supplied by All-Sport's staff photographers, but will consider top quality generic colour shots of the following sports: Lacrosse, trampolining, professional boxing – 'and children playing any sports except athletics'.
Markets Supplied: Prestige publications at home and abroad, advertising markets, etc.
Stock: Colour only. 35mm transparencies.
Usual Terms of Business: Negotiable.
Commission: 'By negotiation but usually 50 per cent.'
Additional Information: 'We do not accept much work from outside photographers except in areas in which we are light (see above). We do insist that anything we accept is of the highest quality.'

ANCIENT ART & ARCHITECTURE PHOTO LIBRARY*
6 Kenton Road, Harrow, Middx.
Telephone: 01-422 1214.
Principal: Ronald Sheridan.
Specialist Subjects/Requirements: All historical material, including buildings of every period from archaeological pre-history up to 16th or 17th century but little after that. Historical art and artefacts mainly from pre-history up to the Middle Ages; everything which can illustrate the civilisations of the ancient world, its cultures and technologies, religions, ideas, beliefs and development. Also warfare, weapons, fortifications and military historical movements. Statues, portraits and contemporary illustrations of historically important people, kings and other rulers. Areas covered: mainly Europe and the Mediterranean including the Middle East.
Markets Supplied: Mainly book publishers, but including magazines and TV.
Stock: Colour. 2¼″ square preferred. 'Only the rarest items accepted in 35mm and then only if most critical technical standards are met.'
Usual Terms of Business: 3 years minimum retention of material; 12 months notice of return. 'Because books can take up to 2 years in production and seldom less than 1 year our time-scale for all activities must be geared to this.'
Commission: 50 per cent.
Additional Information: 'All submissions must be accompanied by return s.a.e. Only material of the highest quality can be considered. Verticals must be vertical always. Historical buildings or sites must not include cars or brightly clothed tourists whose presence would destroy the illusion of the period which the author works hard to recreate. Normally no people should be visible but occasionally one person (not obviously posed) where necessary to show scale and never brightly dressed unless in local costume (e.g. an Arab). All material must be fully and historically accurately captioned with names, dates, places, etc.'

AQUILA PHOTOGRAPHICS
P.O. Box 1, Studley, Warwickshire, B80 7JG.
Telephone: Studley 2357.
Principals: Alan J. Richards, Jennifer M. Richards.
Specialist Subjects/Requirements: All natural history subjects. Birds a speciality.
Markets Supplied: Book and magazine publishers.
Stock: B&W and Colour. 2¼″ square transparencies preferred but 35mm acceptable.
Usual Terms of Business: Minimum initial submission of 100 transparencies and/or 100 b&w prints.
Commission: 45 per cent.

A-Z BOTANICAL COLLECTION LTD*
Holmwood House, Mid Holmwood, Dorking, Surrey, RH5 4HE.
Telephone: 0306 888130.
Principals: M. H. MacAndrew, J. Finlay.
Specialist Subjects/Requirements: All aspects of botany (not just flowers).
Markets Supplied: Publishers and advertising agencies.
Stock: Colour only. Minimum 2¼″ square.
Usual Terms of Business: 'No minimum initial submission, but must continually supply pictures. Minimum period for retaining material: 3 years.'
Commission: 50 per cent.
Additional Information: 'We do not want U.K. subject matter except outstanding garden scenes. We are always prepared to consider overseas material, but it must be captioned with Latin botanic name.'

BIPS-BERNSEN'S INTERNATIONAL PRESS SERVICE LTD
9 Paradise Close, Eastbourne, E. Sussex, BN20 5BT.
Telephone: 0323 28760.
Principals: Theo C. Bernsen (Managing Director), M. E. de Vries.
Specialist Subjects/Requirements: General interest feature material; popular science; technology; medicine; education; inventions; animal situations; material suitable for women's magazines; etc.
Markets Supplied: 'Magazines at home and abroad in most cases via our own branches in New York, Stockholm, Helsinki, Hamburg, Amsterdam (for Benelux), Paris, Milan; elsewhere via agents.'
Stock: Colour and B&W. Colour transparencies, 35mm and 2¼″ square.
Usual Terms of Business: Negotiable.
Commission: 'Depends upon material. We also buy rights.'
Additional Information: Specialises primarily in photo-features and general feature material. 'We prefer to get story ideas which we can assign.' Send for leaflet 'Some Guidelines for Photographers'.

CAMERA PRESS LTD*
Russell Court, Coram Street, London, WC1.
Telephone: 01-837 4488/1300/9393/0606.
Principal: John Blau (Managing Director).
Specialist Subjects/Requirements: Mainly photo-reportage material. Also, portraits of personalities and others in the news; Beauty (women's magazine material).
Stock: Colour & B&W. All formats.
Usual Terms of Business: 'By mutual agreement.'
Commission: 50 per cent.
Additional Information: 'Only submit material that is very good artistically and technically; ideally, also journalistically.'

J. ALLAN CASH LTD
74 South Ealing Road, London W5 4QB.
Telephone: 01-840 4141.
Principals: Alan Greeley, Rick Strange.
Specialist Subjects/Requirements: 'All types of technically good and interesting subjects reflecting the world and its people.'
Markets Supplied: General and educational publishing, travel, advertising, design.
Stock: B&W and Colour. 35mm transparencies acceptable if top quality. Prefers roll-film and 5'' x 4''.
Usual Terms of Business: Initial submission about 100 pictures. Minimum 2 years retention; 3 months notice of withdrawal.
Commission: 50 per cent.
Additional Information: 'Write in for details first!'

BRUCE COLEMAN LTD*
17 Windsor Street, Uxbridge, Middx. UB8 1AB.
Telephone: Uxbridge 57094.
Principals: B. Coleman, G. Coleman, P. D. James.
Specialist Subjects/Requirements: Natural History; Geographical; Travel; Scenics; Archaeology; Medical; Science; Anthropology; Geological.
Markets Supplied: Book publishers, Advertising agencies, Calendar publishers.
Stock: Colour only. 35mm, 2¼'' square and 5'' x 4''.
Usual Terms of Business: Minimum submission: 500 transparencies; Minimum 5 years retention.
Commission: 50 per cent.
Additional Information: Contributors should write for literature first.

COLORIFIC PHOTO LIBRARY LTD*
Garden Offices, Gilray House – Rear, Gloucester Terrace, London, W.2.
Telephone: 01-723 5031; 01-402 9595.
Principals: Terence and Shirley Le Goubin.
Specialist Subjects/Requirements: General top quality, mainly photojournalistic material. Industry; Agriculture; Beaches; Couples; Sunsets.
Markets Supplied: Advertising, Books, Brochures, Calendars.
Stock: Mainly colour. 35mm.
Usual Terms of Business: First submission, 500. Minimum 3 years retention.
Commission: 50 per cent.
Additional Information: 'Material must be fully captioned and carry photographer's name.'

DAILY TELEGRAPH COLOUR LIBRARY*
135 Fleet Street, London EC4A 4BL.
Telephone: 01-353 4242 extension 3686/7/8.
Specialist Subjects/Requirements: Agriculture, Animals, Architecture, Catering, Commerce (Offices, etc), Ecology, Education, Entertainment, Fashion, Health, Horticulture, Industry, Landscape, Military, Occupations, People, Personalities, Religion, Technology, Transport, Sport.
Markets Supplied: Advertising and Publishing.
Stock: Colour only. 35mm and 2¼'' square.
Usual Terms of Business: Minimum initial submission – 50 followed up with regular additional submissions. Minimum retention: one year. Prefers exclusive representation.
Commission: 50 per cent.
Additional Information: 'We're always seeking new top quality material on a variety of subjects, particularly action animals and sports, natural and man-made disasters, bad weather (including electrical storms), people (especially crowds, children and families), industry and technology.'

GEOSLIDES (PHOTOGRAPHY)
4 Christian Fields, London SW16 3JZ.
Telephone: 01-764 6292.
Principal: John Douglas.
Specialist Subjects /Requirements: Africa (S. of Sahara); Asia; Antarctic; Arctic; sub-Arctic
(including Scandinavia, N. Canada, Alaska). Subjects of general and educational interest.
Markets Supplied: Book & Magazine Publishers, Advertising and TV.
Stock: Mainly colour. 35mm.
Usual Terms of Business: 500 pictures normal initial submission. Write first.
Commission: 50 per cent (UK sales); 60 per cent (overseas sales).
Additional Information: Send s.a.e. for leaflet before making any other inquiry.

THE ROBERT HARDING PICTURE LIBRARY*
17a Newman Street, London W1P 3HD.
Telephone: 01-637 8969.
Principal: Robert Harding.
Specialist Subjects/Requirements: 'People, places and objects from more than 180 countries.' A
general library covering all subjects, world-wide.
Markets Supplied: Publishers, Advertising Agents, Design Groups, Calendar Publishers, etc.
Stock: B&W and Colour. 35mm transparencies.
Usual Terms of Business: An initial sample of 100 transparencies 'to enable us to judge quality and
saleability'. Minimum retention: 36 months; 12 months notice of withdrawal.
Commission: 50 per cent.

MONITOR INTERNATIONAL
17 Old Street, London EC1V 9HL.
Telephone: 01-253 7071/2 and 01-253 6281/2.
Principal: S. R. White (Managing Director).
Specialist Subjects/Requirements: Portraits of personalities from Sport, Commerce, Politics,
Showbusiness. Travel library. General subjects.
Markets Supplied: National and international press, television, advertising agents, publishers, etc.
Stock: Colour only for travel and general subjects (2¼'' square or larger). B&W and colour
(35mm) for portraits.
Usual Terms of Business: No minimum submission or minimum retention period.
Commission: 50 per cent.

THE NORTHERN PICTURE LIBRARY*
Unit 2, Bentinck Street Industrial Estate, Ellesmere Street, Manchester M15 4LN
Telephone: 061-834 1255.
Principals: Roy Conchie, Janet Conchie.
Specialist Subjects/Requirements: UK and World views, Industrial Archaeology, Glamour, Sport,
Industrial Scenery, Tourist Views, Natural History, People at Work.
Markets Supplied: Advertising, Packaging, Calendars, Greetings Cards.
Stock: Mainly colour. Minimum 35mm, prefers 6 x 7cm or 5'' x 4''.
Usual Terms of Business: Minimum retention 3 years 'but not obligatory'. No minimum
submission: 'We want quality rather than quantity'.
Commission: 50 per cent.

PHOTO LIBRARY INTERNATIONAL*
St Michaels Hall, Bennett Road, Leeds LS6 3HN.
Telephone: Leeds (0532) 789321.
Principal: Kevin Horgan (Managing Director).
Specialist Subjects/Requirements: General world-wide subjects including Agriculture, Animals, Beach Scenes, Botany, Children, Fairs, Fishing, Girls, Sunsets, etc.
Markets Supplied: Advertising, Travel Brochures, Greetings Cards, Publishers, etc.
Stock: Colour only. From 35mm up.
Usual Terms of Business: Minimum first submission: 200. Minimum period: 36 months with 12 months notice of withdrawal.
Commission: 50 per cent.

PICTORIAL PRESS LTD
30 Aylesbury Street, London EC1R 0BL.
Telephone: 01-253 4023.
Principal: Anthony F. Gale.
Specialist Subjects/Requirements: Feature stories; Glamour sets (as seen in *Mayfair*, etc.); Girl portraits; Historical war pictures; Vintage transport (cars, bikes, buses).
Stock: Mostly colour. 35mm Kodachrome.
Usual Terms of Business: By individual arrangement. No minimum submission.
Commission: By individual arrangement.
Additional Information: Suitable s.a.e. must be sent or material will not be returned. 'Ask yourself: Is it sharp, is the colour balance good, does it tell a story, would I buy it if I was the editor?'

PICTUREPOINT LTD
Hurst House, 157/169 Walton Road, East Molesey, Surrey KT8 0DX.
Telephone: 01-941 4520.
Principals: G. W. Constantine; K. Gibson.
Specialist Subjects/Requirements: World Economic Geography; Sports; Pastimes; Industry; Agriculture; Travel.
Markets Supplied: Books; Travel; Advertising; etc.
Stock: Colour only. 2¼″ square or larger preferred, but top quality 35mm acceptable.
Usual Terms of Business: Minimum initial submission must produce at least 100 retained transparencies. Minimum retention period: 3 years.
Commission: 50 per cent.
Additional Information: This agency handles work only of the highest professional quality.

REX FEATURES LTD*
18 Vine Hill, London, EC1R 5DX.
Telephone: 01-278 7294.
Principals: F. Selby, E. Selby, A. G. Day.
Specialist Subjects/Requirements: Human interest and general interest features; Personalities; Animals (singles and series); Humour; High class glamour; Library stock material; Current affairs.
Markets Supplied: U.K. national newspapers and magazines and international press.
Stock: B&W and colour. Any formats.
Usual Terms of Business: No minimum submission, 'though not really interested in the one-off'. Preferred minimum retention: 2 years.
Commission: 50 per cent.

SPECTRUM COLOUR LIBRARY
146 Oxford Street, London, W.1
Telephone: 01-637 3681.
Principals: Keith Jones, Ann Jones.
Specialist Subjects/Requirements: Travel, Natural History, People, General.
Markets Supplied: Advertising, Publishing, Travel Brochures, etc. etc.
Stock: B&W and Colour. Minimum 35mm transparencies, but prefers larger formats.
Usual Terms of Business: Minimum initial submission: 300 transparencies; Minimum retention period: 5 years.
Commission: 50 per cent.
Additional Information: 'We require only top quality material – the buying market is at present so competitive that only the best will do! We can only view photographers' work *by prior appointment*.'

TRAVEL TRADE PHOTOGRAPHY
18 Princedale Road, London, W11 4NJ.
Telephone: 01-727 5471.
Principal: Teddy Schwarz.
Specialist Subjects/Requirements: Holiday destinations worldwide and activities of tourists (games on beaches, shopping, markets, excursions to places of historic interest, displays of fruit and food, national dances, surfing, boating, eating in the open and in restaurants, etc.). Ethnographical, Archaeological, Ancient Monuments, Folkloristic.
Markets Supplied: Travel Brochures, Guide Books, etc.
Stock: Colour only. 2¼'' square only.
Usual Terms of Business: No minimum submission. Minimum period: 1 year.
Commission: 50 per cent.
Additional Information: Shots must have been taken under sunny conditions, be of excellent quality 'and have deep saturated colour'.

UNITED PRESS INTERNATIONAL (U.K.) LTD
8 Bouverie Street, London EC4Y 8BB.
Telephone: 01-353 2282.
Principal: Julius B. Humi, Vice President & General Manager.
Specialist Subjects/Requirements: World newspicture service. News and feature material.
Markets Supplied: European and North American press.
Stock: B&W and colour.
Usual Terms of Business: Direct purchase of material only.

(*Agencies marked with an asterisk are members of the British Association of Picture Libraries and Agencies.)

Markets -2
GREETINGS CARDS & CALENDARS

Greetings cards and calendars present a potentially lucrative market to the freelance photographer who can produce work of the required quality and on the right formats. Although the majority of publishers in this field prefer to work from 5″ x 4″ colour transparencies, most are prepared to accept 2¼″ square, and a few will even consider 35mm material if it is of the highest quality. Indeed, whatever the size of the transparency, this is the first thing which buyers in this field look for – really first class technical quality. They need pin-sharp transparencies with excellent colour saturation.

Fees are open to negotiation. If you are new to this field, the best plan is to submit your transparencies (after making an initial enquiry to ensure that the company is currently in the market for material), and let the firm make you an offer. But, in any event, you shouldn't accept less than about £25 for Greetings Card or Calendar Rights. Remember, too, that you are not selling your copyright for this fee. You are free to submit the same transparency to any non-competitive market (for example, a magazine), at a later date. But you should not attempt to sell a transparency to another greetings card publisher once you have sold Greetings Card Rights to a competing firm.

Readers will find further useful advice on supplying material to the greetings card market under the Wilson Brothers' listing. Although the information is principally concerned with Wilson's requirements, the listing – which incorporates a lengthy extract from a letter from their Creative Manager – contains a number of useful pointers which apply generally to the greetings card market.

E.T.W. DENNIS & SONS LTD
Printing House Square, Melrose Street, Scarborough, Yorks.
Telephone: Scarborough (0723) 361317.
Interested in transparencies for postcard and calendar productions. Views of seaside and inland towns, countryside showing well known places of interest, floral, animal studies, steam locomotives, diesel locomotives, interesting cars, traction engines, etc. Prefers 35mm or 2¼″ x 3¼″, although any size acceptable provided that it will mask to postcard proportion.

J. ARTHUR DIXON (DRG UK) LTD
Forest Side, Newport, Isle of Wight, P030 5QW.
Telephone: Newport (0983) 523381.
Publishers of greetings cards and postcards. Prefers to work from 5″ x 4″ Ektachromes. Will always consider interesting work from freelances.

KARDONIA LTD
Farrier Street, Worcester.
Telephone: 0905 611294.
Wants British landscapes; cottages; and floral subjects (mainly single and multiple rose themes). Prefers 5″ x 4″ but will consider 2¼″ square if the quality is high. Fees negotiable. Will consider material at any time of the year, but the critical periods are March/April and October/November.

LOWE ASTON CALENDARS LTD
Saltash, Cornwall, PL12 4HL.
Telephone: 075-55 2233.
5″ x 4″ only of scenes, animals, children and pin-ups. Fees negotiable.

THE MEDICI SOCIETY LTD
34-42 Pentonville Road, London N1 9HG.
Telephone: 01-837 7099.
This Company will consider transparencies of professional quality for possible publication in their range of greetings cards. Particular interests are flowers, animals and birds in their natural surroundings, snowscenes and woodland scenes, but not views of the picture postcard type. 35mm transparencies can be accepted, but larger sizes are preferred. Fees from £80.

J. SALMON LTD
100 London Road, Sevenoaks, Kent.
Telephone: 0732 452381.
Requires flower arrangement studies, cat and dog studies, horse studies, rose studies, countryside and farmyard scenes, natural history and garden subjects. 5″ x 4″ preferred; occasionally buys 2¼″ square, and will consider 35mm in the natural history field (only).
Fees 'depend upon the type of material offered, and would be quoted on sight of the transparencies'.

ANDREW VALENTINE LTD
Wester Gourdie Industrial Estate, Arrol Road, Kingsway, Dundee.
Telephone: 0382 622111.
Requires floral, animals, wedding subjects, juvenile designs suitable for children's birthday cards, and pictorial scenes. Prefers 5″ x 4″ but will consider top quality 2¼″ square transparencies of subjects not readily available on the larger format.
Fees: negotiable.

VALENTINES OF DUNDEE LTD
P.O. Box 74, Kinnoull Road, Dundee, DD1 9NQ.
Requires floral, animal and scenic subjects. Prefers to work from 5″ x 4″ and 10″ x 8″ but will consider 2¼″ square 'if the resolution is 100 per cent'.

WHITETHORN PRESS LTD
P.O. Box 237, Thomson House, Withy Grove, Manchester.
Telephone: 061-834 1234.
This firm publishes scenic calendars covering Cheshire, Lancashire, Yorkshire, Warwickshire and Worcestershire, Gloucestershire and Avon. Interested in good 2¼″ square transparencies of these counties. Vertical format preferred and there must be adequate 'free space' above the main feature to allow for possible title overprinting. Pictures must be identifiable – a woodland scene which could have been taken anywhere in Britain, for instance, would not be acceptable.
Whitethorn also publish county magazines covering the areas mentioned above.

WILSON BROS. GREETINGS CARDS LTD
Academy House, 45 Uxbridge Road, Hayes, Mddx.
Telephone: 01-573 3877.
Publishers of the 'Academy' series of greetings cards. The Creative Manager writes: 'We find that it is technically better to use transparencies either 5″ x 4″ or 10″ x 8″ in size, but good 2¼″ squares are acceptable. 35mm can present a reproduction problem and, therefore, would need to be of excellent quality and format to enable them to be considered for purchase. A vertical format is preferred, although some landscape shapes could be considered.
'The floral market is the largest and most competitive. To succeed in this is to make the conventional (in the main, rose subjects) different by means of clever lighting effects, background treatment and presentation. You will not sell a straight floral subject with plain background and flat lighting however perfect the flowers or technical aspect may be. Unusual props also help give a hackneyed subject a sales lift.
'Exposure must be accurate and good colour saturation essential. All greetings cards are sold to a very large extent on colour appeal. Under-exposed or sombre pictures are out.
'Roses are still the most popular flowers, but in recent times the odd different bloom is included in a range. On a roughly one in three basis, chrysanths, daisies and anemones are used, but it is still the rose that leads the field.
'Landscapes are mostly used in the male bracket and so should obviously be taken with this in mind. Unfortunately for the photographer, these again have to be vertical in format. Subjects range from boats – sea and river, cars in country settings, veteran cars, fishing – sea and river, cottages and general rustic views. Only a limited number of views are used for the female section and these usually take the form of flower gardens and cottages.
'Again, colour saturation is vital: subjects must be taken in bright sunshine at small aperture for large depth of field. Skies should be bright blue with preferably the odd white cloud or two. It is extremely unlikely that a shot taken on a day without sunshine would ever sell to a greetings card company.
'There is not such a large demand for animal studies; they are, of course, used, but in far less quantity than florals or landscapes. There are, in fact, certain areas in the North where an animal design is difficult to sell. However, those that are used require all the colour aspects already mentioned and again fall into two categories: For male designs: Alsatians, Great Danes, Boxers, etc., and for female designs: Poodles, puppies and almost any fluffy appealing cat or dog. Horses are not widely used these days but a small percentage do find their way into the male bracket.
'Child shots are always in short supply, although not used in vast quantities. These need to feature children aged between three and fourteen engaged in some form of activity; definitely not posed portraits. Action shots, although not widely used, are also difficult to obtain.
'In the majority of cases, space at the top for a greeting is required. However, more and more companies are dropping photographic designs into panels or creating subsidiary art to go with

these to produce different overall effects. Because of this, a good picture, even one excluding the space for a greeting, is purchasable.

'We purchase transparencies at any time of the year – it is not restricted to a specific time.'

Fees: negotiable.

Markets-3
GLAMOUR PUBLICATIONS

Glamour publications present a highly lucrative outlet for the freelance photographer who understands the market, and who can produce top quality work. But one point should be made clear at the outset: this is by no means an easy market to conquer. Competition in the glamour field is intense – which is hardly surprising when you consider the sort of fees on offer. A first-rate glamour set sold to one of the 'quality' men's magazines can fetch as much as £1,000 – or even more.

If you're tempted to try your hand at the glamour market – and those fees certainly make it an attractive prospect – you must adopt a thoroughly professional approach. First and foremost, you must study the market. Read the listings that follow carefully – then study at least two issues of the magazine to which you aim to contribute.

All magazines in the glamour field accept 35mm colour transparencies; indeed, some actually insist on this format and will not even look at larger sizes.

Approaching the market

Glamour magazines tend to be bombarded with material from hopeful freelances – but probably as much as 80 per cent of it is totally unsuitable. In fact, most editors seem to have similar complaints about those who submit material: 'They don't seem to understand our requirements . . . they think all they have to do is get a girl to take her clothes off, shoot a few pictures and sit back and wait for the cheque! They haven't studied the market . . . they don't put enough thought into their pictures . . . We get a lot of pictures that aren't even sharp.'

Of course, even a technically and photographically perfect set of pictures won't sell if the model is unsuitable. Editors are constantly looking for attractive new faces. Remember that it is often impossible to sell pictures of very well-known professional models – simply because their faces have already appeared many times in one or more of the glamour magazines. However, so long as the girl is attractive, can pose naturally, and feels at ease without her clothes, she could make a successful glamour feature.

In this highly competitive field, the importance of market study cannot be too strongly emphasised. No market analysis can fully replace a careful study of the publication. If you hope to sell to the 'quality' men's magazines, you must remember that you'll have plenty of competition from established glamour photographers. You must be able to produce top quality work. But don't be put off by those who tell you that the glamour market is a closed shop: it isn't. As with any specialised market, all it takes is the ability to produce precisely what the market requires.

See also 'Shooting Saleable Glamour,' Chapter 8

CLUB INTERNATIONAL
Editorial address: Paul Raymond Publications Ltd., 2 Archer Street, London W1V 7HE.
Club International is a sophisticated 'quality' men's magazine, in the *Playboy* tradition, and similar to Paul Raymond's other glamour magazine, *Men Only*. Only top quality colour material is required, and 35mm Kodachrome is the preferred format. *Club International* follows the usual quality men's magazine format, publishing a series of pictures of each girl, together with a story about her. However, the editor says that freelances stand the best chance of success with truly original work: 'don't just duplicate what you see in the magazine – the chances are you won't do it as well as we can. Go for something original and spectacular!' Anything from £500 - £1,000 is paid for a glamour set, depending upon the type of material offered, and the number of pages to which it runs.

FIESTA
Editorial address: Galaxy Publications Ltd., Hermit Place, 252 Belsize Road, London NW6 4BT.
Described as a 'down to earth men's magazine' with a high female readership. Required are excellent colour sets of exceptionally pretty girls, 'preferably those who look "real" rather than "modelly" and who have not been seen in other publications'.
Payment varies according to what is offered and how it is used, but a glamour set could fetch in the region of £500. All material submitted should preferably be shot on 35mm Kodachrome, although $2\frac{1}{4}''$ square is acceptable.

HEALTH & EFFICIENCY
Editorial address: 23–24 Smithfield Street, London EC1.
Although not strictly a men's interest or glamour magazine, *Health & Efficiency* does have similar picture requirements to the other publications in this section.
Required are outdoor pictures of people in the nude. No indoor pictures. The editor says: ' We prefer pretty young women, but men, and groups are all welcome. We prefer healthy, outdoor action pictures, and are not really interested in pure "glamour" work. We pay best for a series of pictures on one girl or group, both black and white and colour, shown in varying situations – but all nude, and preferably outdoors. The emphasis is on healthy outdoor activity. People enjoying the outdoors. We are not in competition with the "girlie" magazines. But at the same time we use a lot of singles both black and white and colour.'
Pictures for cover use are also required. A typical cover would be of a beautiful girl in an outdoor setting with plenty of colour in the background (for instance, a field of flowers). There must be room on the left hand side of the transparency for the magazine's title and summary of contents. If other than facing out, the figure should look towards the title edge. Any transparency size, from 35mm up, is acceptable. Fees – £8 per black and white picture published; £12–£15 for colour shots.
A leaflet, 'Notes for the Guidance of Authors', is available on receipt of a 9'' x 4'' or larger s.a.e.

KNAVE

Editorial address: Galaxy Publications Ltd., Hermit Place, 252 Belsize Road, London NW6 4BT.
Knave is aimed at a more sophisticated market than its 'down-to-earth' stable-mate, *Fiesta*. Only top quality colour sets of very attractive models are required. However, over 50 per cent of the glamour material published is bought from freelance contributors who submit their work on a speculative basis.

Glamour series normally run from 7 to 11 pages. The series should show the model in a variety of varying 'strengths'. It is important to include a mixture of vertical and horizontal shots. In general, the first four pages of the set will consist of a variety of poses of the model semi-dressed usually as vertical shots. She should fill as much of the picture area as possible and be seen from front, back, three quarters and sides. The latter pages of the features are normally horizontal (reclined and nude) shots.

35mm Kodachrome preferred. Submit about 80–100 transparencies to produce a set.

As far as cover shots are concerned, *Knave* say: 'The pose should be erotic, but the model should be partially covered so that the magazine can safely be displayed in newsagents. However, a smiling girl in a bikini is not suitable. The pose and dress needs to be more suggestive and erotic.'

Fees: £600 is paid for a centre set, and £500 for a supporting set. This is for U.K. and U.S.A. Publishing Rights. Cover pictures fetch £100 for U.K. Rights only.

MAYFAIR

Editorial address: Fisk Publishing Co. Ltd., 95a Chancery Lane, London WC2A 1DZ.
Mayfair is another quality men's magazine using a high percentage of freelance material. In fact, according to the editor, 'almost all the photographs and major features are the work of freelance contributors'.

Required are colour glamour sets taken in natural surroundings. The editor says: 'Much care and thought must go into the production of a glamour set, particularly the semi-nude photographs and the erotic use of clothing'. The magazine is also interested in seeing pictures for possible cover use. The cover girl must not be totally nude and, in general, nipples should not clearly be shown. She should be sexy, provocative, natural and head-turning. An occasional touch of humour in a cover subject is allowable. The subject should be shot as a square composition, but allowing a further quarter depth above the composition for the magazine logo. The background should be reasonably plain and not variable, so that a logo can either be projected on top or reversed out. A lot of thought should be given to the erotic use of clothing and suggestion of sex appeal or sexual situation, together with a fairly simple colour scheme.

The editor adds this advice for aspiring glamour photographers: 'Get your focus and flesh tones right before thinking of submitting. If these two factors are not right, nothing will work'.

35mm transparencies are preferred.

Fees for girl sets range from £200–£600.

MEN ONLY

Editorial address: Paul Raymond Publications Ltd., 2 Archer Street, London W1V 7HE.
Men Only, which has undergone some considerable changes in recent years, was first established in 1935 by City Magazines Ltd., a subsidiary of the News of the World Organisation. Several years ago, it was taken over by millionaire strip club and theatre owner Paul Raymond.

This is not a market for 'singles'; like the other quality men's magazines, each glamour feature revolves around a series of shots together with a short story about the girl pictured.

Required are good sets of nudes in colour only, including full frontal studies. 'Only beautiful girls in quality locations'.

Also required are 'situation' pictures to illustrate articles and stories in the magazine. These need not necessarily show a nude female; a well-photographed picture of a girl dressed erotically is more likely to be used.

For girl sets, *Men Only* pays 'anything up to £1,000 and sometimes more'.

Preferred format is 35mm Kodachrome.

PENTHOUSE
Editorial address: P.O. Box 381, Mill Harbour, London E14.
Penthouse uses top flight glamour material in colour only. Only series of pictures of 'very beautiful girls are required'.
The editor advises freelances to submit a few sample shots in the first instance to see whether he would be interested in a full-scale series of the particular girl.
Minimum basic rate averages around £75 per published page; girl sets normally run to between 6 and 10 pages.
Preferred format is 35mm Kodachrome, although 2¼ square transparencies are acceptable.

Markets-4
THE PHOTOGRAPHIC PRESS

As John Wade points out in *Selling to the Photo Press* (Chapter 9), photographic magazines have a ferocious appetite for freelance material. In this section, we give details of the requirements of the main photographic publications available in Britain.

As always, it is advisable that you make a careful study of the particular magazine to which you hope to contribute.

AMATEUR PHOTOGRAPHER
Published Weekly. Editorial address: Specialist & Professional Press Ltd., Surrey House, 1 Throwley Way, Sutton, Surrey, SM1 4QQ.
Aimed at the beginner as well as the more advanced amateur, *AP* is always looking for illustrated articles on all aspects of photography. Also, single pictures in colour and black and white for files and possible cover use (colour only).
Fees: by arrangement.

THE BRITISH JOURNAL OF PHOTOGRAPHY
Published Weekly. Editorial address: Henry Greenwood & Co. Ltd., 28 Great James Street, London WC1N 3EZ.
Aimed at the professional photographer. Interested in anything related to professional photography, particularly the more unusual aspects. Doesn't use amateur how-to-do-it type articles. Interested in creative portfolios (b&w only); also, striking colour pictures 'which show an awareness of design' for cover use. These must suit the magazine's A4 upright format. 35mm acceptable.
Fees: by negotiation.

CAMERA WEEKLY
Weekly. Editorial address: Haymarket Publishing Ltd., 38-42 Hampton Road, Teddington, Middlesex TW11 0JE.
Requires features on technique and anything photographic. These should run to 1,000 words and be accompanied by about 7 pictures.
Fees: 'negotiable'.

CREATIVE CAMERA
Monthly. Editorial address: Coo Press Ltd., 19 Doughty Street, London WC1N 2PT.
Aimed at 'those interested in fine photography'. Specialises in creative avant-garde photography.
No 'how-to' technique articles. B&W only.
Fees: £10 per published page.

CREATIVE PHOTOGRAPHY
Monthly. Editorial address: EMAP National Publications Ltd., Bushfield House, Orton
Centre, Peterborough PE2 0UW.
Described as 'a quality publication showing the best in contemporary amateur photography in
addition to comprehensive equipment news and authoritative test-reporting'. Wants well-
researched, well-illustrated articles on all aspects of photographic technique. Also, portfolios in
black and white and/or colour; submit with full information on equipment and techniques used.
Fees: about £20 per published page.

MOVIE MAKER
Monthly. Editorial address: Argus Specialist Press Ltd., 1 Golden Square, London W1.
All aspects of amateur film making. Will consider 'anything related to technical aspects of movie
making; general interest pieces about some film or personality might also be acceptable'.
Length: 1,800–2,200 words.
Fees: by arrangement.

PRACTICAL PHOTOGRAPHY
Monthly. Editorial address: EMAP National Publications Ltd., Bushfield House, Orton
Centre, Peterborough PE2 0UW.
News, views and how-to-do-it features for amateur photographers. Single b&w pictures
considered for the magazine's picture files. Portfolios required in colour and b&w: not less than 10
pictures with common style or theme. Submit with captions and background information about
the photographer. Also wants illustrated articles covering practical, how-to-do-it aspects of
photography. No travel features.
Fees: Minimum £10 per picture (b&w or colour); £45 per portfolio; £20 per 1,000 words published.

PROFESSIONAL PHOTOGRAPHER
Monthly. Editorial address: Maclaren Publishers Ltd., P.O. Box 109, Maclaren House,
Scarbrook Road, Croydon, CR9 1QH.
Aimed at the professional – whatever his field of operation. Will consider informative stories
about creative professional photographers: the type of jobs they undertake, unusual assignments,
etc. Will also consider portfolios from established professional photographers.
Fees: by arrangement.

SLR CAMERA
Monthly. Editorial address: Haymarket Publishing Ltd., 38-42 Hampton Road, Teddington,
Middlesex, TW11 0JE.
Wants 'high quality photographs for retention in our picture files for use in illustrating features'.
Also, portfolios with a common theme. Illustrated articles on aspects of SLR photography.
Fees: by negotiation.

35mm PHOTOGRAPHY

Monthly. Editorial address: Argus Specialist Press Ltd., 1 Golden Square, London W1.

A 'how-to-do-it' monthly aimed at the photographer 'who has reasonable photographic knowledge and who wants to learn more about pictures and equipment'. Requires illustrated articles which are informative and follow a do-it-yourself theme. A preference for features which show new ideas that the average amateur can turn his hand to.

Fees: 'negotiable'.

USEFUL ADDRESSES

ARTS COUNCIL OF GREAT BRITAIN
105 Piccadilly, London W1V 0AU.

ASSOCIATION OF FASHION, ADVERTISING AND EDITORIAL PHOTOGRAPHERS
9/10 Domingo Street, London EC1.
Telephone: 01-608 0877.

ASSOCIATION OF PHOTOGRAPHIC LABORATORIES
9 Warwick Court, Grays Inn, London WC1R 5DJ.
Telephone: 01-405 2762.

BRITISH ASSOCIATION OF PICTURE LIBRARIES AND AGENCIES
P.O. Box 4, Andoversford, nr. Cheltenham, Gloucester, GL54 4JS.
Telephone: 024 289 373.

BRITISH INSTITUTE OF PROFESSIONAL PHOTOGRAPHY
Amwell End, Ware, Herts.
Telephone: 0920 4011-2.

BUREAU OF FREELANCE PHOTOGRAPHERS
Focus House, 497 Green Lanes, London N13 4BP.
Telephone: 01-882 3315-6.

INSTITUTE OF JOURNALISTS
Bedford Chambers, Covent Garden, London WC2E 8HA
Telephone: 01-836 6541

INSTITUTE OF PHOTOGRAPHIC APPARATUS REPAIR TECHNICIANS
233 High Street, Brentford, Middlesex, TW8 0JQ.

MASTER PHOTOGRAPHERS ASSOCIATION
1 West Ruislip Station, Ruislip, Middlesex HA4 7DW.
Telephone: 08956 30876.

NATIONAL UNION OF JOURNALISTS
Acorn House, 314 Gray's Inn Road, London WC1.
Telephone: 01-278 7916.

PHOTOGRAPHERS' GALLERY
8 Great Newport Street, London WC2.

PROFESSIONAL PHOTOGRAPHERS OF AMERICA INC
1090 Executive Way, Oak Leaf Commons, Des Plaines, Illinois 60018.

ROYAL PHOTOGRAPHIC SOCIETY
The Octagon, Milsom Street, Bath BA1 1DN.
Telephone: 0225 62841.

SOCIETY OF PHOTOGRAPHIC PRINTERS
67 Albert Road, London E18.

INDEX